D0540417

MOTTY'S YEAR

John Motson's Footballing Year –
from Portsmouth to Portugal and Euro 2004

BOOKS

Published by BBC Books, BBC Worldwide Ltd,
Woodlands, 80 Wood Lane, London W12 0TT

First published 2004 © BBC Worldwide Ltd
Copyright © John Motson 2004
The moral right of the author has been asserted.

ISBN 0 563 52174 0

All rights reserved. No part of this book may be
reproduced in any form or by any means without
permission in writing from the publisher, except by
a reviewer who may quote brief passages in a review.

Commissioning editor: Ben Dunn
Project editor: Barnaby Harsent
Designer: Annette Peppis
Production controller: Kenneth McKay

Set in Requiem and Princetown
Colour separations by Radstock Reproductions, Midsomer Norton
Printed and bound in Great Britain by CPI Bath

If you require further information about any BBC
Worldwide product call +44 (0)8700 777 001 or visit
our website on www.bbcshop.com

TO ANNE AND FREDERICK
WHO HAVE HAD TO PUT UP WITH MY LONG ABSENCES.

2003

CONTENTS

2003

FRIDAY, AUGUST 1ST

When you have been following football as long as I have, you become conditioned to the season starting in August. Time was when that meant the third week in the month, just as they were playing the fifth and final Test at The Oval. How things change. For some clubs the season is already a month old by the time the league programme opens. In the old days the players trained behind closed doors, played the occasional practice match between the first team and reserves, and were only seen in their team colours for the first time when they ran out on the opening day. Now we have a proliferation of pre-season tournaments, countless friendlies starting in the middle of July, not to mention the complex preliminary rounds of all the major European competitions.

The financial implications of all these are an obvious explanation, but when clubs are losing players to injury before a meaningful ball has been kicked (Gary Neville, Wayne Rooney, Dietmar Hamann and Darren Anderton are this year's prime examples) it makes me wonder whether it's all worthwhile. My own medium, if not my own channel, must take a large slice of responsibility. If television thinks it can attract an audience for football in what used to be the cricket season, then it will pay for the privilege. Show the match, never mind the significance or the overkill.

Conscious that this season won't officially end until July 4th 2004, the date of the European Championship final in Portugal, this commentator stubbornly refused to spoil July this year and enjoyed an extended holiday. Two weeks were spent with the family in South Africa, so it was appropriate, as well as symbolic, that I spent today at the Test match at Lord's. Let's hope Eriksson's England fare rather better than Michael Vaughan's team did in taking only one wicket all day!

SATURDAY, AUGUST 2ND

The reason I am starting my season at Northampton Town's Sixfields Stadium is, at first sight, somewhat obscure. I have never commentated on a Northampton match, and barring coincidence in the FA Cup, neither am I likely to. Their opponents in today's friendly, Scottish Cup finalists Dundee, aren't likely to figure on my schedule either.

However, The Cobblers are one of many clubs to have moved out of their old ground into a modern stadium in recent years, and a quick calculation as to how many of the 92 grounds in the Premier and Nationwide Leagues I have never visited left me more than a trifle embarrassed. Leaving aside for a moment the Commonwealth Stadium, which will be the home of Manchester City, there are ten new grounds I have yet to experience. Northampton Sixfields, which to my chagrin is but 42 miles from where I live, is on the list along with the homes of Stoke City, Huddersfield Town, Brighton and Hove Albion, Wigan Athletic, Bristol Rovers, Scunthorpe United, Oxford United (all of whose original grounds I have worked at), Hull City and Darlington.

Then there are those to which I have never been. Comparative newcomers to the Nationwide League such as Macclesfield and Cheltenham offer some feeble excuse, but to have never visited the likes of Hartlepool, Bury and Doncaster leaves a gap in any football lover's education.

To become a fully qualified member of the '92 Club' means fulfilling the criteria of seeing a match on every league ground. I am not sure I will manage that, but I certainly intend to give it a go. So while David Beckham was making his high-profile debut for Real Madrid in Beijing, I made a decidedly low-profile bow at Sixfields, discovering to my shame that the ground has been open for nine years without my realising how accessible it is from the M1 motorway.

Most people remember Northampton Town for their meteoric rise from the fourth division to the first under the late Dave Bowen, and their equally rapid return – it all happened within a decade in the sixties. Since then the Cobblers have twice been in Wembley play-offs – taking 45,000 fans there on one occasion – but have just been relegated back to the Nationwide Third Division and are starting this season under new ownership. With the Bosman ruling now biting back at players in the lower divisions, Northampton have released ten players – only two of whom have found new clubs so far – and signed twelve new ones, mostly on free transfers. Josh Low, who cost £165,000 from cash-strapped Oldham, looks lively on the right-hand side, but with a virtually untried team it is clear Northampton will need time to knit together – even though the bookmakers made them second favourites to Hull City in the third division betting.

One of the other big changes I have noticed in my time as a commentator has been the quality of programmes. At £2.50 you would expect something better than average, and for their pre-season friendly fixtures Northampton supporters get 68 glossy pages with plenty of colour photographs. Lee Power, who I first met as a young player at Norwich, told me in the boardroom that his company Cre8 is now designing and producing programmes, brochures and corporate literature for a number of clubs in the Premiership as well as in the Nationwide League.

In this era of instant communication, the television screen behind him flickered constantly as the Sky Sports News service rolled into action with the latest team news. And they are still only playing friendlies!

SUNDAY, AUGUST 3RD

Brendan Foster, a great friend and colleague for more than 25 years, phoned today to invite me to start the Great North Run in September. In the context of North East sport, this is a great honour, accorded in the past to a number of celebrity sporting heroes like Jack Charlton, Alan Shearer, Sir Bobby Robson, Matthew Pinsent and Kevin Keegan.

Quite apart from being a listed event for elite athletes, the GNR always attracts a maximum entry of 50,000 running enthusiasts, be they decent club performers, fun runners, charity fund-raisers in fancy dress, or moderate joggers like myself. You can find yourself alongside Jimmy Savile one minute and Alastair Campbell the next. It is exactly 20 years since I first took part and, fitness permitting, I had intended to run this year for the thirteenth time. Brendan obviously feels I am safer on the starter's rostrum, with a gun in my hand, than I would be on the road. However, his call came just after I had completed seven miles on one of my regular courses near home. A nagging back complaint that has troubled me on and off for the best part of three years has subsided, for the time being at least, so we discussed the possibility of my firing the gun, then jumping off the platform and joining the race.

Brendan's call reminded me that the run is just seven weeks away, so I need to step up my Sunday morning outing by at least a mile a week between now and then.

Talking of half-marathons, a few readers may feel suitably exhausted when they have ploughed through the new *BBC Football Yearbook*, which I have endorsed on behalf of the author Terry Pratt. Terry has used designer-style drawings and diagrams, liberally sprinkled with colour illustrations, to supplement the season's facts and figures. He has replaced a lot of traditional history with detailed analysis of the top leagues in Europe, encouraging younger readers to measure the achievements of clubs and players against their counterparts at home and abroad. Being something of a technophobe, I still find some of the charts hard to absorb, but having tried in vain to shake off my reputation for being a football anorak, the least I could do was give the book my full support – it is a bold and imaginative attempt to do something modern and different.

MONDAY, AUGUST 4TH

I feel 'tagged' by the Foster family just now. A day after Brendan's phone call, his son Paul, one of the talented young producers in BBC Sport, picked me up to drive us north for a *Football Focus* film shoot based on 'Motty's Mission' to see these new stadia.

We headed first to Humberside, where Hull City have been in their 25,000 capacity Kingston Communications Arena since last December. Just for a moment, I thought somebody had taken one of those classy continental grounds set in parkland, and dumped it near to the Humber Bridge.

Internally and externally this has to be the most ambitious project yet attempted by a club outside the Premiership. With its wide corridors, spiral staircases and first-floor concourse, Hull City's new headquarters will be matched by huge expectation – and for former England coach Peter Taylor that means promotion in his first full season.

Taylor has already worked the trick at Gillingham and Brighton, but told me he hates Hull being made the bookmakers' favourites to win division three: 'What about all the money Northampton have spent?' he asked me. I daren't tell him I saw them play on Saturday and saw nothing special, but then my money isn't on Hull either – not at that price anyway.

The shadow squad that Newcastle sent for tonight's friendly was that in name only. Several internationals were included, Jermaine Jenas among them, and they ran out easy 4–0 winners.

Hull's chairman, Adam Pearson, set out his vision for the club at a financial seminar I chaired at Elland Road last year. After what happened at Leeds United, he has a good idea of what not to do.

TUESDAY, AUGUST 5TH

This morning, Paul and I drove down the road and quickly realised why Hull had to move. Curiously, I had never been sent to Boothferry Park in my reporting career, but when we got to the old ground it was far removed from the stadium it must have once been.

Barry Lowe, born and bred in Hull, was charged with acting as security chief and told us it was like being in a ghost town. 'Gates start clanging in the night sometimes,' he muttered. For a moment I had visions of Raich Carter returning at the dead of night to weave his sublime skills across the pitch he graced between 1948 and 1952. Crowds then reached 40,000 and the Hull City directors talked of doubling the size of the ground. Sadly, The Tigers never even made it to the old first division.

The legacy of City's better days is there to behold. A railway line behind one stand where supporters used to enter the ground from a special platform; a massive gymnasium which in its time must have been the envy of every other club; even a training pitch almost hidden at one end of the site. At the other end there is a supermarket, destined to be part of a massive rebuilding plan before the club crashed into receivership in 1982.

The last 20 years have been painful ones, one way or another, for Hull supporters. Barry Lowe expects the owners of Boothferry Park to put it to some other use within a year. In the meantime, Peter Taylor still uses the pitch to work on set pieces on Friday mornings.

Up in the old boardroom, somebody had left a half empty glass on a table. Perhaps Raich Carter was in a hurry to run down and take a corner.

It might sound cruel to compare what we saw at Boothferry Park with what we found a few miles away at Belle Vue, Doncaster, but it came as no surprise to learn that Rovers themselves have identified a site for a new stadium which could be as little as two years away.

In the same way that Hull City have to live alongside two rugby league neighbours, Doncaster Rovers tell people how to find the ground by directing them to the racecourse – literally across the road. We arrived in the middle of the Doncaster Sales, and before going about our football business, rubbed shoulders with breeders and prospective owners in a local hotel. When the bidding started outside, prices were anything up to £40,000. Rather more than our modest partnership paid for any of the three jumpers we have stabled with Nigel Twiston-Davies down near Cheltenham.

Talking of Cheltenham, their football team has taken a route that Doncaster are now following – out of the Conference into the third division – although Rovers had only been out of the League for five years.

Belle Vue looks like a prototype of so many lower division grounds in days gone by – standing room on the terraces behind both goals, with one grandstand which has remained since Rovers moved there in 1922 – a year before Wembley opened its doors. Pictures of former star players adorn the walls of the boardroom. Rovers had the equivalent of Raich Carter in the great Peter Doherty, and there is a fading photograph of the pair shaking hands before a second division match in the early fifties.

Rovers chairman John Ryan, who persuaded his manager Dave Penney to send him on as substitute after promotion had been assured, has revived the club with his personal input. I could sense that the new ground is not far away.

Not far down the road from Doncaster is Millmoor, the home of Rotherham United, where we were greeted by their chairman, 82-year-old Ken Booth, and the manager with a magic touch, Ronnie Moore. Having won two promotions and established Rotherham in the first division with players on wages of less than £3,000 a week, Ronnie would settle for a new signing, or at best a new stand, never mind the dream of a new stadium.

We walked in minutes after the club had signed a new sponsorship deal, and I bent the rules slightly by suggesting to Ronnie he put one of the new shirts on before we did a short interview on camera. All this was good therapy for somebody who spends most of his professional life covering international, European or Premiership football. I am starting to feel that the roots of the English game are still sprouting.

They certainly are at Scunthorpe, our last port of call on this two-day stint off the M18. I had never been to Glanford Park before, the first of the modern, purpose-built stadiums when United left the Old Show Ground in 1988. Scunthorpe were ahead of their time. The Taylor Report, and support from the Football Trust, were still over a year away when they moved home.

WEDNESDAY, AUGUST 6TH

Bearing in mind my room number at the hotel was 101, I suppose I was fortunate to come away unscathed from Humberside. In fact, it was a pleasant, gentle trip with which to start the season.

Two days away filming always means a pile of post and telephone calls to deal with when I get home. Although viewers' correspondence goes straight to the BBC, many of my personal contacts communicate with me direct, and the reasons vary enormously.

Today I received a letter from Stuart Clarke, the photographer whose *Homes of Football* exhibition at Ambleside and recent coffee-table tome evoke so many genuine feelings about the game. It was Stuart whose picture of me in the snow at Wycombe, some 13 years ago, helped to make my sheepskin coat something of a trademark. 'Where's the sheepie, Motty?' is a question I get asked by many stewards on arrival at some of our grounds.

Now a company wants to use an imprint of the picture on a range of T-shirts. Proposals like this have to go straight to my agent, Jane Morgan, primarily because any commercial exposure has to be approved by the BBC, who operate careful guidelines for contracted contributors like myself.

There is no need however, to refer a letter from an educationalist on Merseyside, Peter Lupson, who, as a labour of love, is writing a book about the Christian heritage of football. His latest chapter is a brilliantly researched profile of William McGregor, one of the Football League's founding fathers. I know myself what a few words of encouragement can do for an author, and Peter is determined to press on with his *magnum opus* before he looks for a publisher. 'Otherwise I'll be under pressure with deadlines,' he said when I rang him.

THURSDAY, AUGUST 7TH

Talking of books, one of my priorities in the week before the start of the season is to update my library with all the relevant annuals and handbooks. Rather than worry anybody at the BBC or waste time by ringing all the different publishers, I find it easier to buy in bulk from John Robinson, the Grimsby dealer whose catalogue you will see in all the leading football magazines. When it comes to handbooks or media guides issued by individual clubs, a call to their press office serves a dual purpose — it also re-establishes contact at the outset of another busy campaign.

There is a lot of reading to do at this time of year. Show me a newspaper or magazine that isn't trumpeting its 'exclusive' pre-season supplement. Whether your taste is the *Daily Telegraph*, the *Racing Post* or *Shoot Monthly*, you don't have to look very far to find a list of summer signings and a host of widely differing predictions.

I wouldn't call myself a big gambler by any stretch of the imagination, but a little flutter this time of year sustains your interest in all the divisions over the season. Two of my personal contacts at the big bookmakers, Colin Miles of Ladbrokes and Dave Brown of William Hill, are used to me haggling over the published prices.

I placed combination bets of one sort or another with both today. Going partly with the 'value' at certain prices, I put my money on Newcastle and Liverpool to finish in the top three in the Premiership; Sheffield United, Ipswich and West Brom to do well in division one; a fancy for Bristol City, Sheffield Wednesday and Queens Park Rangers in the second; and each-way bets on Huddersfield, Oxford and Scunthorpe in the third.

In nine months' time I'll know how wrong you can be.

FRIDAY, AUGUST 8TH

This was to be quite a momentous day in the history of BBC Sport, but for me it started painfully. I had long considered the idea of a personal trainer, partly to improve my fitness for running, and partly because I feel so self-conscious about going to heavily populated gyms where everybody looks so toned up compared to me.

Providence intervened when our local newspaper carried an advertisement from Dean Austin, who played with distinction at right-back for Tottenham and Crystal Palace. Dean, whose father plays at our local golf club, has set up a personal fitness centre in his garage. He has taken all the relevant qualifications and offers a free assessment to anybody considering signing up for a regular one-to-one session.

He was quite impressed with my heart rate on the running machine, but totally unimpressed with my failure to manage even one press-up. But now, in my fourth session, he had me lifting weights (very modest ones of course) and doing stretching exercises my 58-year-old body had never seen fit to attempt in the past. Creaking badly, I then drove into the BBC, ostensibly to put some words on the item Paul Foster and I had filmed earlier in the week.

The corridor on the fifth floor of BBC Television Centre, is now a *Who's Who* of television sport, the walls packed with pictures of presenters and commentators and the floor marked out like a football or rugby pitch.

The output from Five Live is relayed on loudspeakers as you make your way to the relevant office, and on my way to the football unit I could tell there was plenty of speculation about the announcement to be made that afternoon regarding television coverage of the Premiership from the start of next season.

A good hour before the press conference, the word was passed around the department that the BBC had regained the Premiership highlights. A great cheer went up from the *Match of the Day* team, who had had to swallow hard three years earlier when ITV had secured those same rights.

What the viewing public may or may not have appreciated, is that access to Premier League action also services programmes like *Football Focus* and *Final Score*, which have had to survive without being allowed to show any Premiership footage for the three seasons when the contract lay elsewhere.

Bearing in mind that Greg Dyke and his team had secured a new, exclusive deal for England matches and the FA Cup only a few weeks ago, the champagne that flowed at the BBC this afternoon signified that our football portfolio will be stronger from next season than at any other time in my 33 years with the programme.

You can always rely on instant reaction to miss the point. The interviewer who grabbed the BBC Director of Sport, Peter Salmon, at the end of the press briefing at Premier League headquarters, couldn't wait to ask whether this meant a return to the BBC for Desmond Lynam. If only he, and many of the newspapers which went down the same road, had known that Des had already rung Alan Hansen to say: 'Enjoy your Saturday nights, I will be in a restaurant.'

Which is where I finished up this evening. Not because of the announcement, but to celebrate my 27th wedding anniversary. My wife Anne and I had already booked a table at the St James's in Bushey with ex-professional footballer Gordon Riddick and his wife Josie. The Italian owner Alfie already had the champagne on ice, but just in case I was feeling smug, Josie pointed out that she and Gordon have been married 37 years. Will Anne put up with me for another ten?

SATURDAY, AUGUST 9TH

The new season has started in sombre mood. I drove to Portsmouth to see them play a friendly with Feyenoord, with a view to putting in some homework in preparation for my radio commentary a week later. No sooner had I sat down to lunch with Pompey chairman Milan Mandaric, than manager Harry Redknapp came into the boardroom with two pieces of tragic news. Ray Harford, one of the best coaches in English football and a friend to many of us for 30 years, had died after a long battle against cancer. And Jimmy Davis, a young Manchester United player on loan to Watford, had been killed in a car crash on his way to play against Coventry.

Football takes a back seat at times like this. Television and radio coverage of the opening day of the Nationwide League programme was tinged with sadness. Presenters and reporters alike dropped their voices out of respect.

Watford cancelled the fixture and we were left to dwell on the fragility of life. The euphoria of yesterday has been replaced by an emptiness that only time can heal.

SUNDAY, AUGUST 10TH

As tributes pour in for Ray Harford, the game he left behind continues to attract and amaze in equal measure. Chelsea's Russian owner Roman Abramovich has taken his summer spending to a staggering £72 million by paying £14 million for Parma's Romanian star Adrian Mutu. Much of the speculation in the Sunday football supplements concentrated on the chances of Chelsea, or Newcastle and Liverpool for that matter, disturbing the monopoly Arsenal and Manchester United have enjoyed for the last few seasons.

Today, those two clubs had the opportunity to put a marker down in the Community Shield at Cardiff. When I last wrote a diary like this eight years ago, I remember saying that Sunday had become a working day for commentators. That is an understatement now. Rather than making the long, hot trek to Cardiff, however, I decided to watch the match live on Sky (keeping an ear on the Five Live commentary) and then stay on to see the highlights on our own channel with Gary, Alan and Steve Wilson. If you haven't watched the game in the afternoon, you are definitely out of the conversation in the pub in the evening.

I broke my summer ban on lager and allowed myself a pint after losing several pounds in weight in the morning. It has been the hottest day ever in England – the thermometer reached 100 degrees fahrenheit – but I still managed to add my weekly mile and complete an eight-mile course.

Annie and our dog Cleo faithfully followed me round with water. I hope it's cooler than this in Newcastle come September.

MONDAY, AUGUST 11TH

Motorway driving, and all its frustrations, has been part of my life since I started with *Match of the Day* 32 years ago this month. So I pointed the car north today, heading eventually for Wigan and a look at their four-year-old JJB Stadium. It was only when I chose the A50 from Derby, rather than the M6 through Birmingham, that I realised I would be passing Stoke City's Britannia Stadium, opened six years ago by the late Sir Stanley Matthews but not on my itinerary up to now.

A quick call to the club put me in touch with Terry Conroy, the genial Irishman who was such a clever forward in the early seventies and who is now the club's commercial executive. There was quite a buzz about the place as Terry showed me around. Stoke had won 3–0 at Derby in their opening game and Tony Pulis, a manager well versed in operating on limited resources, filled me in on his revamped squad. He wasn't exactly spoilt for choice when it came to numbers.

Statues of the finest and famous are now a modern, welcome feature at many of the bigger clubs, and the three-dimensional sculpture honouring Matthews was something I admired before leaving.

Back in the car, Mark Lawrenson phoned to say he had fixed up my visit to the National Football Stadium at Preston the following morning. He added that the curator wanted to put my sheepskin coat on display as part of their broadcasting section. Knowing Mark's caustic sense of humour, I took it with a large pinch of salt, but I am looking forward to seeing the museum, which Ray Stubbs has described as 'fantastic'.

TUESDAY, AUGUST 12TH

I t wasn't a joke! No sooner had I walked in the front door of the museum, than I was approached by BBC North West, the *Lancashire Evening Post*, and BBC Radio Lancashire. Would I be donating my coat to the museum?

Well, no, not at the moment. Having auctioned off my 'old' coat at Gillingham Football Club last season, I am now down to my last one and need it in the wardrobe for the coming winter. I explained to Mark Bushell, the museum's curator, that buying a new coat is not as easy as it sounds. Half-length suede jackets are on sale in good retail stores, but the full-length job that covers the knees doesn't come off the peg. Years ago, an Essex furrier used to make the coats to measure from skins in his garage. When he disappeared, a firm in Borehamwood responded to an appeal by Giles Smith in the *Daily Telegraph*, and donated a coat that was bound for export to Russia. That is the one I am still wearing.

Mark Bushell took the point. While he patiently guided me round the museum – more of an experience than a tour – he undertook to find me a new coat on the understanding that he could have the old one.

Some of the exhibits on display are priceless. Hundreds more lie in a storeroom, including some recently purchased from a private collector, which include the ball used in the first World Cup final in 1930. The whole display is beautifully presented and any fan who has not been is missing a treat. The museum runs underneath half of the Tom Finney Stand which dominates Preston North End's Deepdale ground, so when I surfaced I had a look round a stadium I had not seen for many years. Three new stands have been built and dedicated to three former Preston heroes: Bill Shankly, Alan Kelly and Finney himself. The seats are patterned to display their faces.

The old stand on the far side has stood since before the war, so I had a peep in the home dressing room to see where Finney used to get changed. Matthews one day, Finney the next. The old FA Cup finals that I saw on our small black and white set in my primary school days are still vivid in the memory. Matthews in 1953, with his winner's medal at last; Finney in 1954, on the losing side in his only final; and a few years on, and a few hours later today my first meeting with, Dave Whelan, who was carried off with a broken leg when Blackburn lost to Wolves in 1960.

Everybody knows how Whelan built up his gigantic JJB Sports empire, and you only have to approach the stadium carrying that name in Wigan to appreciate what he has done for sport in the town. Rather like the Britannia Stadium at Stoke, what struck me was the amount of space for hospitality, corporate entertainment and conferences. Compared to the pokey restaurants that clubs launched for the first time in the seventies, the wining and dining facilities in these new grounds are positively five-star.

WEDNESDAY, AUGUST 13TH

The new Premiership season is almost upon us, and anticipation is building. My colleague Barry Davies has gone to Slovakia to cover Chelsea's Champions League qualifier – the first glimpse for television viewers of Mr Abramovich's hand-picked collection of super talent.

When I started at the BBC, two years behind Barry, it used to take weeks to set up a broadcast from overseas. This one was secured at little more than 48 hours' notice, travel arrangements put in place, and hey presto, we have live football on the BBC again tonight!

My thoughts are already turning to my first commentary of the season – Portsmouth against Aston Villa for Five Live on Saturday lunchtime. No matter how many years you have put in, there is still an edge of nervousness as the adrenaline begins to flow. Will I recognise all the new players? Have I got enough information? In the case of a promoted club like Portsmouth, do I know exactly how to get there and the lay-out of the ground?

In my dual radio/TV role, I have fixed up a *Football Focus* interview with Harry Redknapp an hour before the lunchtime kick-off on Saturday. That means I need to be on the south coast on Friday night. How convenient – Anne and I have just fulfilled a long-held ambition and bought a flat overlooking the sea in Bournemouth.

THURSDAY, AUGUST 14TH

Dean Austin was quite demanding of me this morning, but as he put me through my paces on the running machine and stepped up the weights, I hardly noticed. My only son, Frederick, was on his way to his St Albans college to collect his 'A' Level results, and I was anxious to get home to find out how he had fared.

I need not have worried. Fred gets all his brains from his mother, and has taken two subjects a year early. He got an 'A' in English Literature and in Politics, and an 'A' in his 'AS' level History, averaging 94 per cent over the three papers.

We went down to our local, The Hollybush at Redbourn, to celebrate with a lunchtime glass of champagne. Next year he hopes to take his 'A' level collection to three and go on to university. Not bad for a boy whose father never got beyond 'O' Level, and who spent the afternoon cobbling together information about Aston Villa and Portsmouth ready for Saturday.

The squad numbers for all the teams come across from the Premier League – always a relief – together with handbooks from Manchester United, Arsenal, the Nationwide League and the Conference. John Robertson sends me the *News of the World Football Annual*, and slowly but surely my shelf is filling up. Sadly Middlesbrough, whose media guide last year was a hard-back book the like of which I have never seen, are not producing one this season. However, Sarah Brookes, the vivacious press officer at Fulham, has got hold of the publishers and quite properly pinched the idea. So have Tottenham Hotspur. Is it just me, or is the season warming up behind the scenes as well?

FRIDAY, AUGUST 15TH

I took a quick three-mile run round our estate before driving Anne down to Bournemouth. While she supervised curtains and other items of soft furnishings for our flat, which is starting to look habitable at last, I got down to some more telephone calls and pinned down what I believe will be the starting line-ups at Fratton Park tomorrow.

When Anne returned to London by train, I moved to the Yenton Hotel in Gervis Road, where for years my Sunday football team, Roving Reporters, have stayed on their spring tour. I don't fancy staying in the flat by myself, and certainly don't want to be cooking my own breakfast on the first day of the season!

SATURDAY, AUGUST 16TH

The journey from Bournemouth to Portsmouth was not without incident. Sarah, our *Football Focus* producer, phoned me in the car to say that the interview with Harry Redknapp had to be done and dusted by eleven o'clock because Sky Television, who own the rights to the match, wanted us out of the way. Quite apart from the fact that I was on an eleven-thirty schedule, her concern made me miss a junction off the M27 and I charged back to Portsmouth to find an enormous traffic jam within a mile of the ground. Racing up the outside of two lanes of traffic, I was aware that cameras will have picked me up, and with six points on my licence already, disqualification looms. Sol Campbell has got nothing on me.

But I have never been late for an interview, let alone for a match, and I roared into Fratton Park at ten to eleven, grabbed Harry out of his office, and thankfully remembered the questions I had sketched out the night before.

My next assignment, set up by Harry's assistant Jim Smith, was an informal meeting with Boris Zivkovic, Portsmouth's summer signing from Bayer Leverkusen. Zivkovic is in the Croatian squad to face England at Ipswich next Wednesday, a friendly I will be covering for BBC1. Portsmouth's kit man kindly let us use his office, and within five minutes Boris had used his perfect English to put me in the picture regarding pronunciation, positions and the likely line-up. He even volunteered to point the players out to me when I go to Croatia's training on Monday.

The thought occurred as to whether our English players would treat an overseas commentator as courteously as that, but within minutes I was whisked up to the Five Live commentary position by producer Charlotte Nicol to deliver two preview pieces live on the air. I had prepared neither of these, but when you have been down to the dressing room corridor and rubbed shoulders with a few people you know, it is a mixture of journalistic instinct and spontaneity that gets you through.

Fortunately, Jonathan Pearce was in the box seat for the first period of the commentary, so I was able to watch the match for 20 minutes before picking up the microphone. Teddy Sheringham obliged just before half-time with the first goal of the game, and my season was off and running along with Pompey's. They ran out winners by two goals to one and in the boardroom afterwards the chairman, Milan Mandaric, made a fitting presentation to secretary Paul Weld, who has served the club for more than 30 years.

John Jenkins has been at Fratton Park even longer. He attended his first game in 1928 and now, at 84, supervises the guest list in the chairman's suite. Before I leave he gave me some old memorabilia for my collection and told me how to get on the M27 the proper way.

Now I am heading for Lymington, in the New Forest, to visit a lady who played a very important part in my professional life. Back in 1968, when I read the racing results in my first-ever broadcast for radio sport, Julia Brooke was the studio manager on the other side of the glass panel who calmed my nerves. We have been family friends ever since. Last April I ran a 10k in Lymington for Julia's son Jamie's Lifeboat charity, so I was alarmed when he phoned me a fortnight ago to say that Julia had collapsed and been taken to hospital. Now well on the way to a full recovery, she made me a cup of tea and told me the quick way back to the M3, because if this day hadn't been busy enough already, I was due to meet Anne at a dinner party in Epsom this evening.

This is another family connection; Jennifer Plowman, who was once the commentators' secretary at the BBC, has also remained a good friend. She and her husband Philip had invited Ricky George and his wife to dinner as well. Anybody who knows me also knows that Ricky needs no introduction – a lifelong companion after his winning goal for Hereford against Newcastle in my first FA Cup tie in 1972 – but quite why he came to Epsom via Accrington took a bit of explaining.

Rick writes a regular non-league column for the *Daily Telegraph* and had spent nine hours on the road covering Accrington and Shrewsbury's arrival in the Nationwide Conference – they, like him, had come from a different direction.

Not that it mattered very much. Jenny put the roast lamb back to 10.30 and I ate, wine on my knee, watching *The Premiership* on ITV. A year from now, there will have to be no Saturday dinner parties. The return of *Match of the Day* will take up all my time.

SUNDAY, AUGUST 17TH

Not getting home until the early hours of the morning was hardly the best preparation for my early morning run. This week, a couple who are also entered for the Great North Run, Jack and Elaine Darvell, accompany me over a nine-mile course which I manage to complete in 72 minutes – averaging the eight-minute mile I am aiming for at present. The

South East has been in the middle of a freak heatwave for more than two weeks and, what with the humidity and the early sunrise, running has been as uncomfortable as I can remember. There is always a consolation. The couple who ran our local for many years, Alan and Jenny Sanders, organised a farewell party in their back garden today and it was the first time I had sat down and relaxed for well over 48 hours.

Chelsea's victory at Anfield this afternoon – only their second there in the League in more than half a century – showed the Premiership that Mr Abramovich means business. It has been a first weekend of red cards, penalties, contentious goal celebrations and the usual managerial spat with referees. But with all of that has come some gripping football and no little drama.

In days gone by, newspapers did not publish league tables until three games had been played. Now they appear after just one match. Pointless? Well, not if you are Blackburn Rovers. Their 5–1 victory over Wolves means they are the first leaders of the Premiership this season.

MONDAY, AUGUST 18TH

Having mentioned our flat in Bournemouth, it will sound dreadfully boastful to admit that we also have a cottage in Suffolk. Let me say right away that I bought it 20 years ago for the princely sum of £23,000, so don't run away with the idea that the Motson family has a range of luxury homes.

We have not used this little bolt hole as often as we would have liked. The departure of both Ipswich and Norwich from the Premiership in recent years means that my professional visits to East Anglia have become few and far between, so it was nice of the FA to organise an international at Portman Road while summer was still with us.

Anne and I travelled up in separate cars, partly because she likes to take the dog and can easily fill two vehicles with all the bits and pieces she has been storing up since we last went. As Fred and I drove up together in the morning, England got the day off to a good start by winning the Test match at Nottingham. The series against South Africa is now nicely poised at one each, although the match would have been over by the time most *Daily Telegraph* readers had pored over the four separate articles delivered by their bevy of cricket writers.

It is not because I work in an instant medium like television that I sometimes find it hard to work my way through the sporting press. It is just that the proliferation of newsprint, rather like televised football, sometimes exceeds the time available to absorb it. No sooner is one event analysed to the last detail, than the previews of the next one are fighting for space. At least the start of the Premiership has meant that England's friendly against Croatia is condensed into a mere three days' coverage.

The media circus that descended on the England camp today did not need to look far for their copy. David Beckham reported from Spain with a slight back injury after playing for Real Madrid against Valencia. He appeared at a press conference at roughly the same time as Croatia held their only public training session at Ipswich Town's training centre. On the basis that I can recognise the England players rather better than their opponents, I joined a couple of photographers and a handful of onlookers to try to make some sense of Croatia's 19-man squad.

What you need on occasions like this is a bit of help from somewhere, otherwise everybody in identical tracksuits looks the same from the side of the training pitch. The FA's liaison officer with the Croatian team, Danielle Every, pointed me in the direction of their security chief, a gigantic, friendly character called Zoran, who spoke perfect English. It took the best part of 90 minutes, but by the time the Croatian coach called a halt, I had familiarised myself with the majority of the party. Zoran made an educated guess as to how they would line up on Wednesday, but I made an arrangement to see him again tomorrow when they go to inspect the pitch at Portman Road.

This sort of research often baffles people who say they would never know if I incorrectly identified one of England's opponents. That may be so, but in this business you take nothing for granted. A year ago, in the World Cup in Japan, I managed to mix up Paul Scholes with Nicky Butt. Sometimes I wonder how I have kept this job so long.

TUESDAY, AUGUST 19TH

Preparing for an international match is rather like doing a jigsaw from a commentator's point of view. You know the picture you want to finish up with – both line-ups neatly listed side-by-side with relevant information – but the pieces don't always fall into place as and when you please. The morning papers added nothing to what I had learnt the previous day – as I said, this was a friendly and does not carry the same weight as a qualifier. Indeed, it was a nice change to see England's cricketers dominating the front page of the sports sections.

After a run through Tunstall Forest, I started to assemble in some order what I had gathered from the Croatians last night. Their training gave me a good clue as to their starting line-up, confirmed when Danielle phoned to say that Igor Tudor had been withdrawn with an injury and a fresh player, Jasmin Agic, was being flown in from Croatia.

Almost simultaneously, Sven Goran Eriksson announced that Sol Campbell and Jonathan Woodgate had joined Gary Neville, Owen Hargreaves and Wayne Rooney on the England sick list.

The best yarn up to now is that Chris Kirkland's father, Eddie, put on a £100 bet at 100 to 1 when the Liverpool goalkeeper was still at school, that his son would keep goal for England one day. Chris has just recovered from a serious knee injury, was on the bench on Saturday, and will be again tomorrow night. Nice story if it happens.

I popped down to Portman Road to run the eye over Mr Agic, who turned out to have very distinctive long, blond hair – a commentator's dream. I was rescued from the tedious business of another training session by Ipswich manager Joe Royle and his coach Willie Donachie. Both were curious to see the Croats, but only after organising a cup of tea in the police security box overlooking the pitch. I have met them both on football travels at home and abroad in the past and they are great company. Joe said Ipswich were out of administration but 'still skint', however his optimism convinced me that 10 to 1 was a good price against them for Division One.

WEDNESDAY, AUGUST 20TH

Match day brought with it the Wembley debate all over again. When I drove through Ipswich and saw the flags, the replica shirts and the souvenir sellers, it made me wonder whether it would have been better to have kept the England team 'on the road' and had £750 million to spend on something other than a new national stadium.

Portman Road is the 13th club ground to be chosen to stage an England international in the three years since the old Wembley was consigned to history. The response in every town and city has been overwhelming, tickets sold within hours of going on sale, and the welcome for the team wide-eyed and wonderful.

Mark Palios, the FA's new chief executive, whom I met for the first time at the game today, made the point in the match programme that part of the 'new Wembley' agreement means England's senior internationals will all be played at the glittering new headquarters from 2006. That is cast in stone, and it is his job to say so. But many of us will remember forever the affection with which the England team has been treated across the country. Just ask the hoteliers of Ipswich, who have had no rooms to spare, even for regulars, these last couple of days.

There was a sad aspect to the day. Ray Harford's funeral took place in Surrey, attended by a host of football luminaries who loved him and his coaching. A minute's silence was held for Ray and Jimmy Davis before today's kick-off, and the England team wore black armbands in respect.

David Beckham, whose wife and sons were present, received a massive ovation as he led England out. Still to make his league debut for Real Madrid, he scored from a penalty and made the second goal for Michael Owen with a sumptuous cross, before both were substituted on the hour. In all, Eriksson made ten changes – par for the course in England friendlies.

England's 3–1 victory was their sixth in succession, one behind the post-war record. But it didn't entirely convince me. The defence wobbled horribly on crosses and there was still no sign of the left-sided player to give balance to the midfield.

After the match, I joined three former Ipswich stalwarts – Brian Talbot, Mick Mills and Terry Butcher – in the FA Club to debate the performance. Quite appropriate really from their point of view, because Sir Bobby Robson was the guest of honour at the match and they were part of his team that put Ipswich on the map in the seventies. Now, despite their lower status, they have staged a full international for the first time. As I said, England on tour in England has been an unqualified success. It has always worked for the Germans and the Italians, and I can't imagine them spending so much on a national stadium.

Unless we can't find anywhere else to play the FA Cup final, other than in Wales, why do we need it?

THURSDAY, AUGUST 21ST

Rusty after ten weeks without a television commentary? You bet. Having listened back to the tape today, which I do less often these days, I realised how quickly you can lose your edge. Not that I would change my schedule for anything. A proper break in the summer is the only chance to recharge the batteries, and then it takes a little time to get back up to speed.

Nobody needs to tell me when I slip below the standards I have set myself over the last 30 years. Working for the BBC, it's always better to criticise yourself before it comes from elsewhere. The scrutiny is intense, but that's why BBC Sport has been admired across the world for almost half a century.

Trevor Brooking must have wondered last night whether he was working alongside the same guy as last season. My observation was fitful, my statistics were all over the place, and trying to cope with 17 substitutions in the course of the game made me feel grateful that the BBC highlights were transmitted just before midnight and I was not at the mercy of a live audience.

The only consolation was that my two days with Croatia paid off to the point where I identified their players better than ours. Which made me wonder how, last year in Japan, I ever managed to commentate on Mexico v Ecuador without seeing either team play or train previously.

Many years ago, when I was just starting in television, David Coleman told me the first rule of commentary was survival. Don't I just know it.

FRIDAY, AUGUST 22ND

Eight years ago I walked into a sound studio in Soho and shouted a few phrases like, 'What a goal!' and, 'Didn't he do well there?' into a microphone, making them up as I went along. Then a Canadian producer gave me one page of club and player names to record. Little did I know that I was in at the birth of what is generally accepted in the computer industry as the most successful football game ever made. Within a couple of years, Vancouver-based Electronic Arts had extended the FIFA licence to brand the game for the next decade. I was lucky enough to be retained as the commentator, despite remaining pretty oblivious to the technical achievement and complications that went into the making of FIFA 2000 or whatever year we were in.

A visit to the EA factory in Canada in 1999 enabled me to appreciate the dedication and attention to detail of the 60-strong team who work permanently on the game. They involved me in a number of 'think tanks', where my role was to enlighten those who did not see top class football at first hand, as to some of the game's culture and credibility. The aim, quite simply, was to replicate as closely as possible what happens on the pitch, on to the computer screen.

As the gameplay and the graphics improved year by year, so my own role in the London studio developed as well. At first I spent six hours a day dutifully recording long lists of names and phrases (with different intonations), scripted by a producer. It was exacting to the point of sometimes being tedious, but it worked as far as the team in Canada were concerned.

Not that I was the only commentator. For a game that sells millions of copies worldwide, I have opposite numbers in several European countries and in Asia. The Motson voice goes only to the English-speaking world.

This year we attempted a major breakthrough. Co-commentator Ally McCoist and myself sat in front of a video screen and broadcast to pictures of a real match, being careful not to refer too specifically to individual players. Although the team in Vancouver found the editing much harder, we are hoping the product in *FIFA 2004* will be that much more authentic.

Today I was on my own, recording 'tutorials', which explain how the game play can be improved by using various devices during the match. I had to take the scripts home tonight and ask my son Fred what it all meant. He has played the game since my first involvement in 1995, and from time to time people from the *FIFA* production team have asked him for his views on certain aspects of it.

He is certainly not on his own when it comes to enjoying it. When I started in television, and for some years afterwards, fans at the ground used to say, 'Heard you on the box the other night.' Now many of them have become parents, they moan with a smile, 'We have to put up with your voice every day, and sometimes most of the night.'

We have made special editions of the game to coincide with World Cups and European Championships, and from a starting position of just selecting which team they wanted to be, *FIFA* enthusiasts can now nominate their own players, tactics, substitutions and formations. They can choose which competition they want to play in, take control as player or manager and create their own league tables. And just to think, this commentator is still using a portable typewriter.

SATURDAY, AUGUST 23RD

So what did I do in my spare time before *FIFA* came along? Well, before the computer age truly kicked in, prior to the internet and e-mail, one of the innovations of the mid-eighties was the football club telephone line. The idea was for fans to dial a number and listen to news, views and interviews from their favourite club. Tottenham Hotspur were first out of the blocks with Spursline, launched in 1986 by their commercial manager Mike Rollo. When other clubs got together to form the joint Clubcall service, Mike kept the Spurs version independent. And in 1987 he asked me to take on the role of interviewer and presenter.

Before the knowing looks, let me say straight away I was not brought up as a Tottenham supporter, but there is no question that my commentaries on successive FA Cup finals in 1981 and 1982, coupled with the Spursline involvement, have convinced a great many people that my loyalties lie at White Hart Lane.

Steve Perryman, the former Spurs captain, blames the transfers of Ricky Villa and Ossie Ardiles in 1978. He always reminds me that when I got back from the World Cup in Argentina that year, the then Tottenham manager Keith Burkinshaw rang me for some information about both players before he flew out and eventually signed them. Keith, Steve and a number of their Tottenham contemporaries became friends, and I hosted Spursline from 1988, when the BBC lost League football for the first time, thereby removing any accusation of bias on my part.

When Tottenham reached the FA Cup final again in 1991, I told Mike Rollo that, as the commentator on the final, I could not risk the conflict of interest. Spursline continued quite happily without me, until Rollo – who temporarily left Tottenham and has now returned as commercial director – decided this season that it had come to the end of its natural life.

He kindly invited me to lunch today before the match against Leeds, but it was far from a sad occasion. Mike was responsible for other innovations that are now commonplace at most big clubs – sponsors' lounges, player appearances, celebrity speakers among them – and now has a team of former Tottenham stars hosting the various corporate outlets on match days.

When I arrived today, Martin Peters, Martin Chivers, Cliff Jones, Ralph Coates, Phil Beal and John Pratt were all suited and booted, ready to entertain the paying customers before the match, at half-time and after the game. It was also good to see the club looking after President Bill Nicholson, architect of the great double-winning side of 1961. Bill is 84 now, but brought by a driver to every home game and still an instantly recognisable figure in the directors' box.

I remember how terrified I was when I first had to interview him in my first season on *Match of the Day*. He was coming to the end of his time then as Tottenham manager, but what an imposing figure he cut. Honesty was his middle name, and I'm not sure they make them like Bill any more. He and his contemporaries, like Bill Shankly and Don Revie, certainly weren't put under the voracious demands their successors have to endure today. With just one game of the season gone, the current Spurs boss Glenn Hoddle was popularly described as 'under pressure'. I have known Glenn since he was a teenager in the Tottenham team of the late seventies, and when I phoned him on his mobile all he wanted to say was, 'Can't they wait until I get my best team on the pitch before they judge me?'

Injuries have haunted Tottenham more than most for several seasons, but despite being without five key players, they beat Leeds with a bit to spare, Taricco and Kanoute scoring spectacular goals.

SUNDAY, AUGUST 24TH

With more and more Premiership fixtures being moved for a variety of reasons, we have reached the stage where up to five games on any given weekend could be played on what used to be the Sabbath.

Having been brought up as a strict Methodist, with my father preaching three times on a Sunday, I can recall the days when shops didn't open, the television was rarely turned on and professional entertainment was not licensed. What a total contrast with today, when there is so much sport for the television consumer that you find yourself watching one gripping event, only to miss something of significance on another channel.

The BBC majored on the World Athletics Championships. The second day brought a thrilling finish to the 10,000 metres, and sheer chaos on the track when John Drummond was disqualified in the 100-metre heats. Over on Channel 4, England could be seen conceding the initiative to South Africa in the fourth Test at Headingley, while satellite television offered two Premiership matches: a goalless draw between Aston Villa and Liverpool, and a cakewalk for Arsenal at Middlesbrough.

For all that, the biggest news story of the day was West Ham's dismissal of Glenn Roeder. The timing seemed strange, but it would have looked callous to have taken the decision in the summer when Glenn was recovering from a serious brain operation and clearly determined to return to work. So my co-commentator Mr Brooking steps in again as caretaker manager, and my former next-door neighbour Iain Dowie is one tip to take the job permanently.

MONDAY, AUGUST 25TH

B ack to my ground-hopping mission today. No Premiership matches this afternoon, so it's off to Oxford United's Kassam Stadium, now in its third season after their move from the higgledy-piggledy Manor Ground, held in such affection for so many years by Oxford fans.

The contrast could not be sharper. The Manor was right on the main road, just north of the Headington roundabout, while the Kassam is on an old waste site four miles round the ring road. Oxford have not extended themselves in capacity. At present, there are stands on only three sides and the ground holds 12,500, quite enough for their present requirements in division three.

Ian Atkins, the manager, is a true football man with a wide CV and a firm opinion. In his programme today he calls for a better standard of coaching, claiming that at some of our football club academies, coaches are getting jobs because of who they know, rather than what they know. When you see how many players are predominantly one-footed, you feel he has a point.

A point was all he looked like getting against top-of-the-table Swansea with the scores level at 0–0 after 85 minutes. Then two of Atkins' substitutes changed the game: one won a penalty, the other scored with his first touch, and Oxford ran out 3–0 winners, replacing their stunned opponents at the top.

My 14–1 shot looked a decent bet for Oxford to win the third division. Although it was, in theory, a day off, I managed to grab hold of a Five Live microphone for a two-way chat with Ray Stubbs on *Final Score*.

The more I see of football at Nationwide level, the more I enjoy it. Sometimes I think the Premiership is losing the common touch.

TUESDAY, AUGUST 26TH

They say Sven Goran Eriksson is unemotional, but I can categorically deny it. I found myself sitting next to the England coach in the front row of the directors' box at The Valley when Charlton played Everton tonight. For 72 minutes it was a routine match, although Charlton were leading 2–1 courtesy of two contested penalty decisions. At which point, 17-year-old Wayne Rooney took a hand.

Rooney's performance up to this point had been indifferent. Certainly not up to the mind-boggling impact he made last season, when Eriksson selected him as the youngest footballer ever to play for England. But if form is temporary, class is permanent. Collecting a pass from Gary Naysmith inside the Charlton penalty area with his back to goal, Rooney killed the ball with his first touch, turned with his second and sent a stunning drive past Dean Kiely in the Charlton goal.

Eriksson got out of his seat to applaud, and it would have been churlish not to. It was reassuring to hear him use the commentator's cliché, 'What a goal!' – raising his eyebrows in appreciation. At that moment it was apparent that Rooney would be back in the England squad for the qualifying matches ahead against Macedonia and Liechtenstein.

Before the match, I asked Eriksson how many times he had seen Rooney play 90 minutes. 'Never,' was his reply, and that had nothing to do with the fact that Sven usually slips out before the final whistle. It was the first time I had seen Wayne start and complete a game too. Mindful, no doubt, of the hype that followed Paul Gascoigne around at 17, Everton's manager David Moyes is keeping Rooney on the back burner from time to time. That way, he could play for 20 years. After all, Teddy Sheringham scored a hat-trick for Portsmouth tonight, still going strong up front in the Premiership at 37.

WEDNESDAY, AUGUST 27TH

We're not even into September, but I venture to suggest that today is the busiest we shall experience in the whole of this football season.

Just think about what's on. The likes of Newcastle, Chelsea, Rangers and Celtic are playing the final qualifying round of the Champions League, hoping to figure in tomorrow's draw for the group stage. Then there is the continuation of the midweek Premiership programme, with Arsenal, Manchester United and Liverpool all in action. Lower down the scale, the UEFA Cup is slowly grinding into action. Some overseas clubs are playing the final of the Inter-Toto Cup, which English clubs have swerved this year, while many more are involved in the qualifying round of UEFA, in which Manchester City and Dundee play tomorrow.

After another punishing workout with Dean Austin, I settled down to watch three video tapes of Macedonia – England's next opponents in ten days' time. An easy way to spend five hours.

Sky chose to show Manchester United's game with Wolves, perfect preparation for my Radio Five Live commentary at Molineux on Saturday. Then, well beyond cocoa time at 11.45pm, there was an ITV highlights show which finished shortly before 1am. Fred and I decided a couple of pints wouldn't go amiss, so we staggered our visit to the pub over two shifts, one before the football and one in between. Nice excuse.

The transfer market is still bubbling towards Sunday's deadline. Chelsea signed Hernan Crespo from Inter Milan and the Russian Alexei Smertin from Bordeaux, promptly loaning him out to Portsmouth for the rest of the season!

THURSDAY, AUGUST 28TH

A social day, and not one which is going to help control my weight. Lunch and dinner in London, with an afternoon drinks appointment in between, is a severe test of stamina.

Sorry to harp on yet again about the sheepskin coat, but I am still hoping that a certain Leslie Azoulay down in Cannes will eventually end up making one for me. He was in the fur trade when he lived in England. A business friend of his, Nina Ziemie Rowska, who I met in his Station Tavern bar, is passing through town on a modelling engagement and Leslie has asked her to show me some material. It seems bizarre having to get this coat made in France, especially when Nina declined the offer of measuring me up and said that was Leslie's responsibility!

We went easy on the wine because Nina was driving and I had to meet Jane Morgan at the Café Royal to run over the extension to my BBC contract, which has just been agreed. She witnessed my signature over an appropriate glass of champagne.

Next up was my regular Italian in South Kensington, Il Falcionere, where Ricky George and I are already planning our Christmas lunch. Jenny Plowman, who does the donkey work, and Lisa Faye, who will be singing for us that day, have come along so that Lisa can get an idea of the acoustics. My proposed list of 38 guests is more than Jenny was expecting, and Lisa certainly got a shock when she saw the list of songs I was asking her to sing. She normally does showtime stuff, so *Saturday Night* by Wigfield and *99 Red Balloons* by Nena is something she'll have to learn – along with loads of Debbie Harry and Kirsty MacColl.

FRIDAY, AUGUST 29TH

Whatever the rights and wrongs of the Hutton Inquiry into the 'sexed up' dossier over Iraq, I have always been a committed fan of BBC News. Not because I work for the Corporation – what I do pales into insignificance alongside the correspondents and reporters who deal with world affairs – but because I admire their dedication and professionalism.

Some shining examples of this are Caroline Hawley and Orla Guerin, whose reports from the trouble spots of the Middle East are calm, controlled and nothing short of a class act, and Andrew Marr, who has made politics make sense to me. The resignation today of Alastair Campbell, the Prime Minister's 'spin doctor', brought out the best in Marr. He described Westminster as a 'Serengeti' and Campbell as the 'supreme carnivore'. Watching people in your own business doing things better than you is not a chastening experience, more an uplifting one. You just feel proud to be part of the same organisation.

As for Mr Campbell, he also has two claims to fame I could never match: he has run a marathon and he supports Burnley. We met at a midweek match at Millwall last season, when he seemed surprised that I had never met Tony Blair. This was something he promised to fix, and no doubt would have done before today's events.

Never mind. All this was a pleasant distraction as I prepared my Five Live commentary for tomorrow. Good practice for a year ahead, when I shall be back in my exacting Friday routine for *Match of the Day*.

SATURDAY, AUGUST 30TH

Sir Jack Hayward, owner of Wolverhampton Wanderers and English football's biggest single benefactor since Jack Walker at Blackburn, is a man I had never met until today. I wasn't disappointed. Nicknamed 'Union Jack' because he strives to preserve virtually the last outpost of the old British Empire from his Bahamas base, he loves his country with all the courtesy and charm of an old imperialist. There were many besides the devoted fans of Wolverhampton Wanderers who were pleased to see his dream realised when Wolves returned to the top flight after an absence of 19 years.

One of Sir Jack's former managers who briefly tried to restore the club to former glories was Graham Taylor, who had an 18-month stay at Molineux after giving up the England job. Graham was my co-commentator today as Wolves, still looking for their first point in the Premiership, took on promoted companions Portsmouth, who had started well. The goalless draw they shared was hardly a gripping broadcast for listeners, but the fun of Saturdays on Five Live lies in cueing over to reporters at all the other grounds, so that the commentator at the main game also plays the part of presenter in the second half.

The programme moves at a heck of a pace, and after penning a one-minute summary for Sports Report I was quite ready for the roast beef and Yorkshire pudding that Sir Jack put on offer in his boardroom.

Jack Harris, an old friend of mine and long-time director, was also there. Wolves have named their four stands after him and three Molineux heroes, Billy Wright, Stan Cullis and Steve Bull. A nice touch.

As for Sir Jack Hayward, he played the part of the true Englishman to the letter. 'I won't even have French wine in the boardroom,' he said with a twinkle in his eye.

SUNDAY, AUGUST 31ST

Eriksson picked Rooney of course, but the announcement of the England squad for the qualifiers against Macedonia and Liechtenstein had a familiar ring to it. Sadly, I mean in terms of fitness doubts.

I first covered England for the BBC in 1971, when I was in the old Radio Two sports department and Alf Ramsey was still manager. By my calculations, there have been ten England managers since then, but very rarely has one of them ever picked a squad without at least one player either being unavailable, or dropping out, through injury. Maybe once in 32 years!

Today it's Paul Scholes who is ruled out completely with a hernia problem. There will be late fitness tests for Rio Ferdinand, Nicky Butt and Owen Hargreaves. I will be pleasantly surprised if they are all on the plane on Thursday. And then people wonder why England have won only one major trophy in their history. The club game and its demands will always dictate the international agenda in this country, at least until somebody finds a way of reducing the number of games the players are expected to fulfil.

Eriksson told the press that Lampard, Dyer or Joe Cole all had a shout when it came to replacing Scholes. My money is on Lampard, who scored his first England goal against Croatia 11 days ago. Scholes is a lovely footballer, but he hasn't scored for England for well over two years.

SEPTEMBER

MONDAY, SEPTEMBER 1ST

The start of a ten-day international period, and already my thoughts are focused on Macedonia and Liechtenstein, the two countries England play before their showdown with Turkey in October.

Two live matches like this, with the BBC audience likely to reach a combined 20 million, don't give the commentator much spare time, but this morning I popped in to Ladbrokes' headquarters in Harrow to record a European Championship preview which goes out in their betting shops. On the way out of the building I bumped into Mike Dillon, whose contacts in racing are the stuff of legend, and he told me that Christa Murphy, widow of our late mutual friend Michael, had given birth that morning to a baby girl. Mike's untimely death earlier in the year was much lamented by his host of friends in the media, and I had the privilege of speaking at his memorial service.

It was a cheerful piece of news to send me on my way to the Hurlingham Clinic and Spa, in Chelsea, where they have been giving me some laser treatment for a couple of veins that have coloured my complexion. Imagine being scratched by a needle in short, sharp bursts and you'll realise it isn't that comfortable, but the results have been striking!

On the way back I called into the football office at Television Centre to collect my air tickets and travel details for Macedonia. Our sports assistants had prepared some detailed notes on the opposition, so together with Albert Sewell's well documented research on the England team, I have plenty of paperwork to keep me busy before I leave on Thursday.

TUESDAY, SEPTEMBER 2ND

Slavishly tied to my office desk at home, I ploughed through the Macedonia notes as meticulously as I can, having established that I can attend their only public training session soon after we arrive in Skopje on Thursday.

The problem with 'double headers', as far as commentators are concerned, is that there is precious little time to get the first match out of your system before you are into the second. I won't get back from Macedonia until late on Sunday night, and early Tuesday I will be on my way to Manchester for the Liechtenstein game. So although it sounds back to front, I spent some time today watching England's away game in Vaduz on the video, confirming when and where the Liechtenstein team will be training next week, and familiarising myself with some of *their* names.

As for England, they are based in Manchester for the entire period, so to save a trip north I will wait and attend a training session when we get to Macedonia. Rio Ferdinand, with kidney trouble, is the latest withdrawal, but having covered the friendly against Croatia I feel pretty much up to speed with Eriksson's selection.

My 'bible' as far as England statistics are concerned is the *FA Yearbook*, of which I have every edition since it started in 1948. These days it is lovingly put together by the FA librarian David Barber, who lists the line-ups for every international since the war, along with goalscorers and much more.

From this it is easy to confirm that England's best run of consecutive victories in that period stands at seven, achieved under Walter Winterbottom and Alf Ramsey. Eriksson needs to win the next two matches to set a new record.

WEDNESDAY, SEPTEMBER 3RD

Arrangements are moving fast for the Great North Run, which is now only two and a half weeks away. Brendan Foster rings to say Mark Knopfler, the Dire Straits guitarist who is a hero in the North East, will be playing on the platform as I start the run.

Firing the pistol is something I am apprehensive about, never having done it before. What happens if the gun doesn't go off and 50,000 runners are left in limbo? That apart, jumping off and joining in the race is another issue. My training is having to be put on hold while I go to Macedonia and Manchester, so Dean Austin put me through a fierce hour this morning.

When England play, the whole nation sits up and takes notice. In our local pub tonight, a group of regulars are constructing a wager on how many goals England will score and concede over the two games ahead. I go for a bold 7–1, on the basis that I can see Sven's team squeezing a 2–1 win in Skopje, and then overpowering Liechtenstein at Old Trafford by five clear goals. Frederick Motson is not so sure; he goes for a cautious 4–2. We all put £10 in the kitty so there is an £80 pay out for the winner.

One of our producers has told me luggage sometimes gets lost in the short stop-over in Frankfurt en route to Macedonia, so I decide to get three days' clothes and notes into one hold-all and call it hand baggage. Overseas trips still make me nervous. You never quite know what to expect.

THURSDAY, SEPTEMBER 4TH

What I wasn't expecting was to have my pocket picked and my money stolen. Having arrived in Skopje bang on time, in the company of Garth Crooks, I thought things were going well when I went straight to the stadium and caught Macedonia at the start of their training session. My opposite number from the local television service, Goran, proved more than helpful when it came to identifying their 19-man squad. We walked round the pitch unchallenged for about 20 minutes – the normal time alloted for the media these days – and by the time we left I had a good idea of what Macedonia looked like and how they might play.

Our production team was now arriving in force – it had been decided to bring the full BBC unit to cover this one – and in the evening five of us went to a local brasserie for a simple and inexpensive meal. I had my euros in a small plastic packet given to me by the bank and, having paid my share, put the remainder back into the inside pocket of my jacket.

As we walked through the square on our way back to the hotel, we were surrounded by four or five young children – somewhere between ten and thirteen – begging for coins. I got a couple out and handed them over, but they still ran around our group shouting and pleading. They were obviously streetwise. When I got into the hotel bar and put my hand into my pocket, the packet of notes had gone.

FRIDAY, SEPTEMBER 5TH

What has surprised me is the fuss that people have made about the incident. Most of the English journalists were staying in the same hotel and by lunchtime today I must have been asked about the story on a dozen occasions. Two news reporters from Sunday papers came to take photographs and seemed disappointed when I told them that there was no physical attack or mugging, no credit cards or passport involved and the amount of money did not exceed £50.

Even at the England training session we attended, when we inspected our commentary position for tomorrow's match, the word had got round. I got hold of Charles Sale, the *Daily Mail* sports gossip man, and asked him to use the truthful version in a simple paragraph to get people off my back. Charlie did me a real favour. He took the sting out of the story by saying that Motson, the statistics sleuth, had worked in 49 countries for the BBC and never had his pocket picked before.

I hate borrowing money, and what nagged at me more than the theft was having to be 'subbed' by my colleagues. It came as a welcome relief when two travel ladies working in conjunction with BAC Sports – the company who organise media travel – said they were hosting a meal in an Italian restaurant this evening and asked if I would be a guest.

That wasn't the only good thing that happened today. While Garth Crooks was interviewing Eriksson at the England hotel, David Beckham walked through the foyer and kindly signed my commentary card for a charity auction I am conducting next week. Beckham is all over every paper every day at the moment, but he seems to revel in his celebrity status rather than resent the intrusions. He brushed aside doubts about his fitness and seemed keener to talk about his Spanish lessons.

SATURDAY, SEPTEMBER 6TH

Match day dawned bright and clear. I had slept well and decided to get down to some final preparation. Ricky George phoned from home to wish me good luck. 'You wouldn't have lost that money if I had been there,' he said, reminding me of the time we spent together in Japan during the World Cup.

Trevor Brooking and I were interviewed by Ray Stubbs for *Football*

Focus, and I went off the England topic to ask Trevor whether he was still the acting manager of West Ham. It appears he is, since their preferred choice Alan Pardew is having contractual problems with his employers at Reading.

When we returned to the stadium for the match I went through my usual routine of getting as close to the dressing rooms as I could. Sitting in the commentary position waiting for the teamsheet has never satisfied me – not when players can sometimes swap numbers, substitutes get altered at the last minute and incidents happen like the classic case of Ronaldo at the 1998 World Cup final.

My plan was to check the teams with the coaches or referee where possible, but on this occasion Macedonia were being deliberately evasive. They wouldn't even submit their teamsheet to the referee at the appointed time, so Sven Goran Eriksson and his coach Brian Kidd were standing in the corridor looking anxious.

It was Georgi Hristov, once of Barnsley, who saved the situation for me. He pointed to a small room where a lady was tapping the team out on a computer, and refusing to be rushed. I looked over her shoulder and made a note of the numbers. Having checked the formation with Goran, I thrust a copy into Eriksson's hand and rushed back to the broadcasting position, where the other commentators were wondering how long they would have to wait before they got the team.

I didn't have any problem sorting out the first goalscorer. Hristov looked as confident in the penalty area as he had in the corridor, putting Macedonia ahead after 27 minutes. It reminded me of the match in Bratislava a year earlier, when Nemeth of Middlesbrough had put Slovakia ahead, only for England to come back and win 2–1.

The equaliser this time was a landmark moment in England's football history. Wayne Rooney, still seven weeks short of his 18th birthday, caught the goalkeeper unawares as he latched on to Heskey's lay-off. He became our youngest scorer in 130 years.

When Beckham put England ahead from a penalty, Trevor and I were trying to keep abreast of the racist chanting that again spoilt the occasion, and also trying to spot any crowd disturbances. When England play abroad, these issues occupy the commentator as much as the match. Sad, but a sign of the times.

The other subject on which I had to weigh my words carefully was the presence of 500 England supporters who had travelled and bought tickets mostly on the black market, against the advice of the English FA. When England scored, the players went over to that section to celebrate. Without taking anything away from the impact of the goal for viewers at home, it was necessary to make the point that it sent out a bad signal. So did England's time wasting in the closing minutes, but mercifully there was no significant crowd trouble, nor did things go off in the city afterwards.

The three points mean England only need to beat Liechtenstein, and a draw in Turkey will ensure direct qualification for the finals.

SUNDAY, SEPTEMBER 7TH

Travelling is part of the commentator's lifestyle, and it can be tedious. When you have been away for three days and finished work, you ideally want to get home as soon as possible, but our flights out of Skopje did not leave until early afternoon. Trevor, Garth and I couldn't even find an English newspaper to pass the time but, landing at Zurich to change planes, we struck lucky when we reached the lounge expecting a two-hour wait for our connection.

Just as Trevor sipped his first diet Coke (I have never seen him touch alcohol), I heard the announcement for a British Airways flight leaving in ten minutes. A quick dash to the desk, exchange of tickets, and we were on our way home much sooner than expected... with the English papers on our knees.

I never expect the match reports to tally completely with my commentary. For a start, football remains a game of polarised opinion, but when you are spotting the players and looking to cover every incident as it happens, you are not the best judge of the wider picture. For instance, I felt Gary Neville had a poor game by his standards at right-back, but some of the journalists rated him one of England's better players.

When I got to the pub in the evening, two of the regulars brought in a hat full of 2p pieces. It was their amusing response to the Sunday newspaper stories about my street urchin experience three days earlier. I hate to think what would happen if I got into real trouble.

MONDAY, SEPTEMBER 8TH

The diet went to pieces in Macedonia and I wish now I had taken my sports gear and got into a gym. Instead, I rushed over to Dean Austin's and he got me on the running machine in three short, sharp bursts at seven-minute-mile pace. I was sweating so much he wondered what I had been eating and drinking.

The BBC sent me a tape of the other match in the group on Saturday. Liechtenstein had lost 3–0 at home to Turkey so I was able to get a last-minute update on their team and practise my player recognition. Usually I watch back the tape of my own match, trying to be self-critical, but there just wasn't time today. No sooner had I unpacked from Macedonia than I was re-packing the same bag for Manchester, where Eriksson was likely to make a few changes.

The audience figures came through and more than nine million had watched on Saturday – a great return bearing in mind the kick-off was 5.30pm in England. We had had the Macedonia match to ourselves; Liechtenstein would be shared with Sky; while there was already speculation about what would happen over the match in Turkey in October.

Sky paid a lot of money for exclusive rights to the match – gambling when the group was drawn that this would be the decider – and as yet not even highlights are available to terrestrial broadcasters. But with the FA again pleading with England fans not to travel, that situation may change.

TUESDAY, SEPTEMBER 9TH

Conscience forced me to take a hurried four-mile run before going to the airport at the start of what proved a very busy day. Both countries had opened their training to the media for a period, so I went to Manchester United's old training ground at the Cliff to see what England were up to. Rio Ferdinand had not reported fit, Nicky Butt trained but was not match fit, otherwise it was much the same.

I heard a whisper that Eriksson was thinking of playing Bridge and Beattie from the start, and leaving out Campbell who was on a yellow card. So were Beckham and Gerrard, although both wanted to play.

Liechtenstein trained on the pitch at Old Trafford. As befits a nation for whom this was a once-in-a-lifetime experience, they were courteous and helpful and, luckily, all of them were fairly easy to identify. Training sessions become boring in time. The '20 minute' rule is almost a godsend, otherwise you would be standing there for an hour and a half and would start to confuse yourself.

Carling were throwing a dinner for the media to mark their return to major sponsorship through the League Cup, and two or three senior writers had the England team verbatim. It was a convivial evening, as they always are when Keith Pinner's Arena company are the organisers, but the week had its sad side with the absence of Joe Melling, the *Mail on Sunday*'s popular football editor, who is suffering from a serious illness. These guys are competitive, but there is a sense of camaraderie about them too. After all, they have been round the world together following England, and the time spent at hotels and airports lends itself to a spirit of togetherness.

WEDNESDAY, SEPTEMBER 10TH

Match days can drag a bit if you've done most of your homework in advance, but not this time. Gary James, Manchester City's historian, picked me up at the Victoria and Albert Hotel where the BBC party are staying, and took me to Eastlands, the new home of Manchester City. It was my first visit to the former Commonwealth Games arena, now expensively converted into the 47,000 successor to Maine Road, where the capacity was about 12,000 less.

At first sight, with its grey exterior, wide approaches and stilts holding up its curving roof, Eastlands reminded me of the Olympic Stadium in Munich. Not aesthetically pleasing at first, but given that City supporters rate among the best I have known, a perfect backcloth for their loyalty and enthusiasm.

I have always had a special affection for City. They were one of the first clubs to make me feel at home when I started more than 30 years ago, mainly thanks to secretary Bernard Halford, who became a lifelong friend. Today I was able to repay him in a small way. City have followed the example of other big clubs and started to open a museum. They asked me to put my voice on a couple of videos – one about City's achievements in the FA Cup and the other a personal tribute to their famous German goalkeeper Bert Trautmann.

The other little bonus was that I could now tick off another new stadium I had visited. Hopefully I will be working there next season with *Match of the Day*.

When I got back to the hotel, Alan Hansen and Gary Lineker had arrived and both went to their rooms for a couple of hours' sleep. I wish I could learn the footballer's trick of sleeping during the day! Both were on top form, along with Peter Reid and Peter Schmeichel, when the BBC programme started half an hour before kick-off. I'm biased, of course, but the present BBC panel is the most entertaining in my experience, a nice blend of football expertise and humour.

Hopefully, they bring out the best in us, although I nearly put the mockers on England by reminding everybody that San Marino once scored against them in nine seconds. Liechtenstein's Mario Frick came close to embarrassing Eriksson's team in the first minute.

There has been a strange symmetry to this qualifying campaign. England have been notoriously unbalanced in the first half of their games, yet capable of turning matches round after the break. After this 2–0 win they have also scored two goals in every one of their seven matches so far. Let's hope they can manage that in Turkey next month, although a 0–0 draw would suffice.

One thing we were all sure about after tonight – Wayne Rooney is the real deal. I have never seen a 17-year-old with such a mature appreciation of the game. He left the field after 70 minutes to a huge ovation and later received the 'Man of the Match' award.

Thinking back to George Best and Paul Gascoigne, you just hope nothing goes wrong for Rooney. He could be the focal point of the England team – but not until David Beckham retires, of course!

THURSDAY, SEPTEMBER 11TH

Due to the fact that I had a hospital appointment today, the BBC arranged for me to share a car back to London after the match, and I got home about two o' clock in the morning. It's a long trek at that time of night, but the motorway was clear and sleep is only fitful when the adrenalin from the broadcast is still flowing.

My first appointment when I woke up was with Dr Andy Platts at the Wellington Hospital, next to Lord's cricket ground. Every three months or so I need a booster steroid injection in my lower back to reduce inflammation in the facet joint – probably the result of wear and tear from 30 years of regular running.

As it is ten days before the Great North Run, my visit to the CT Scanning X-ray department was well timed. Three days for the injection to settle, then I can do my last long preparatory run on Sunday. The main event will then be just a week away.

In the afternoon I skimmed through the recordings of the two England matches. You never give yourself full marks, but it was a relief to know that Trevor and I had not committed any howlers. Not that he does that very often.

This evening I attended a golf dinner in Harpenden. Former Arsenal and England full-back Lee Dixon has combined with two local business-men, Robert Murphy and Brian Luckhurst, to raise funds for St Albans City Youth football club, who run no fewer than 20 teams. They have raised over £50,000 towards draining a huge area for new pitches to be laid.

My job was to conduct the auction, with the welcome assistance of comedian and rabid Arsenal fan Bradley Walsh. My Beckham-signed commentary card, now framed, raised £1,200, the auction in all delivered £8,000, and the golf day itself a grand total of £15,000. It was a nice way to wind down after an exhausting week with England.

FRIDAY, SEPTEMBER 12TH

It's only when you get back from an international week and start to relax, that you realise it can be quite draining mentally. Today I did very little, apart from catch up on all the post and telephone calls that were waiting for me when I got home.

Jim Lawton, the highly respected sports columnist of the *Independent*, and one of my favourite writers, had sent me a copy of Nobby Stiles' autobiography *After the Ball*, which he had penned for the former World Cup winner and which he had promised me over a large whisky (he paid, I had lost my money) in Macedonia.

I decided to put the book in my bag for next week's trip to Newcastle. Reading at home is something I do when I can, but too often interrup-tions, sometimes self-inflicted, mean I have to start again when I go back to the book in question. Lawton's book is a welcome exception in an era when a proliferation of football books have exceeded quality with quantity by some distance. Since the game became fashionable again at the turn of the nineties, would-be authors seem to have sprung up like weeds in a garden. Rather like football on television, an unregulated diet just means indigestion and, in the end, boredom.

Now that the internationals are out of the way, our two television competitors are turning their attention to the Champions League. Sky is promoting the fact that 14 of the 16 matches can be seen across their digital channels. I can't believe anybody is going to watch them all, but then choice is the modern panacea, whether it is mobile phones, motor cars or foreign food.

The best news of the day came when the BBC's Head of Football Niall Sloane phoned to say that more than ten million people had chosen to watch our coverage on Wednesday night. How many would watch if Eriksson got us to the final of Euro 2004? There's no harm in dreaming.

SATURDAY, SEPTEMBER 13TH

It was a good three weeks ago that I looked at today's fixture list and decided to go to Upton Park. Despite a tempting trio of London matches in the Premiership, including Chelsea v Spurs and Charlton v Manchester United, it looked a good opportunity to examine two promotion candidates, West Ham and Reading.

In the time that has elapsed since I booked my ticket, the game has taken on an unexpectedly newsworthy significance. The Hammers have been refused permission to speak to Reading's Alan Pardew about their vacant manager's job; he has resigned in protest; a face-off has resulted.

So both teams are under temporary management. My BBC colleague Trevor Brooking is still unbeaten as caretaker, standing in for Glenn Roeder at the end of last season and again when Roeder was dismissed three weeks ago, while Kevin Dillon is in charge of Reading, who feel the approach to Pardew was in breach of his contract.

The atmosphere between the two acting managers is polite, that between the directors decidedly restrained. West Ham win narrowly, remaining in third place, and Trevor remains in charge for Tuesday's trip to Crewe.

'Five of our next eight games are against teams in the bottom half,' West Ham's managing director Paul Aldridge tells me excitedly.

'If I was up there in the boardroom that's what I would be saying,' says Brooking in the manager's room after the game. 'Down here it's a bit different.'

The fans ringing 606 on Five Live are pleading with Trevor to take the job permanently. His family were sitting in front of me in the stand, and I get the feeling they might have a say in that.

SUNDAY, SEPTEMBER 14TH

My last long run before the Great North in seven days, and my first for a fortnight. After nine miles I've had enough – the hot weather is freakish for this time of year and I don't want to risk injury or jeopardising the effects of Andy Platt's injection. I'll do the other four separately later in the week – not quite the same as a full 13 but at my time of life I'm not exactly tilting at records.

Thanks to our trainer Nigel Twiston-Davies, I got back the money I lost in Macedonia. His horse Barney's Lyric won the first race at Bangor yesterday at 10 to 1, and I backed it on the recommendation of my fellow owners.

Just for fun, I tried to take a personal interest in the two televised games today by putting a small wager on Manchester City and Birmingham to win their home games. Keegan's team obliged with a 4–1 victory over Aston Villa, but Birmingham were held to a draw by the surprise team of the season so far, Fulham.

Having been brought up as a strict Methodist, I am a very modest punter when it comes to gambling. My biggest success so far was predicting the winners of the three Nationwide divisions last season – Portsmouth, Wigan and Rushden – which brought a handsome return. On the last day of the season, only a Hartlepool victory at Rushden could spoil the bet. As a 'saver', I had to back Hartlepool quite heavily – the bookmaker said he had never taken such a hefty wager on that team before!

MONDAY, SEPTEMBER 15TH

Thanks to Garth Crooks and his friendship with Tony Banks MP, Fred and I went to the Houses of Parliament so that he could see a debate in the Commons. He wants to study politics at university from next year, and this was a priceless opportunity to see government at work.

While Fred was occupied in the House, Tony took Garth and me out on the Members' Terrace for a glass of wine. As a keen Chelsea fan of 50 years' standing, Tony had expressed reservations when Abramovich took over at Stamford Bridge, but that wasn't what was bothering him today. He had laid down a motion to the house stating that the upcoming Turkey v England European qualifying decider should be available on terrestrial television, and not restricted to satellite subscribers. It didn't take a lot to get Garth and me involved in that little debate, and while we were reminding Tony that Sky Sports had paid £3 million for the exclusive rights to the match nearly two years ago, the Home Secretary David Blunkett walked past and was persuaded by Banks to stop and listen to the argument.

Blunkett said time was running out – the match is less than a month away – and promised to raise the matter with the relevant Minister, Tessa Jowell. Tony asked my advice on how to get some press coverage of his point of view. I suggested he spoke to Mihir Bose on the *Daily Telegraph*, who usually gets to grips with this sort of issue.

As I drove Fred home, I said Sky would hardly be expected to release their grip on the live coverage, but that nearer the time recorded highlights might be made available to a terrestrial broadcaster. Just in case, I had already watched two or three tapes of recent Turkish games and made some notes. I didn't want to get caught out a week before the game.

Of more pressing concern was tonight's Premiership match between Leicester City and Leeds United. I was scheduled to join Ian Brown for the Five Live commentary at the Walkers Stadium, with Glenn Roeder making his debut as summariser. Normally I make it a rule to get to the ground three hours before the kick-off when I am working, but getting out of London meant I was still sweating on the outskirts of Leicester less than an hour before kick-off. Fortunately, their streamlined media arrangements under the aegis of Paul Mace made life easy when I got there. It was pretty comfortable for Leicester too on the night, their 4–0 victory their first in the Premiership since promotion.

As for Leeds, their motley collection of loan players only confirmed my view that they would struggle against relegation this season. With the players they have sold and the debt they are still facing, I can't quite see how Peter Reid can pull this particular rabbit out of a hat. What he has done is signed the World Cup-winning centre-back Roque Junior on loan from AC Milan. But the pace of the Premiership clearly caught the Brazilian by surprise on his debut.

Leicester are just getting their act together off the field after coming out of administration. Before leaving I was talked into speaking at their second sportsmen's lunch in November. It's not a role I take on very often, but when they said Alan Birchenall was the MC there was no way I could refuse. You would have to go a long way to meet two bigger characters than 'Birch' and Tony Banks in one day.

TUESDAY, SEPTEMBER 16TH

Only five days to go now, and the Great North Run is starting to feel like a millstone round my neck. Brendan Foster's company organised a London press launch at Langan's Brasserie, and although the papers were only interested in Paula Radcliffe, they pulled me in to represent the fun runners.

The journalists met in a huddle outside, and when they came to the table they were all drinking Perrier water. How come I was having a glass of wine when I was the one supposedly in training? I was able to confirm that the BBC Sport team for the run would include Ray Stubbs, Mark Lawrenson and Mark Bright. Ray is a staunch supporter of the event, Lawro has never run more than four miles in his life, and Brighty has been training secretly after smarting over the fact that I overtook him after 11 miles last year. It won't happen again.

Brendan took a fair bit of ribbing about his own training and potential performance. John Caine, the chief organiser, whispered quietly to me that he thought Foster's time would be around one hour 42 minutes – a target I had managed to meet myself on three occasions in years gone by.

I left Foster in the capable hands of the *Daily Telegraph*, and went home to watch ITV launch their Champions League coverage for the season. Manchester United thumped Panathinaikos, but at the end of the evening you were left with that empty feeling that the real stuff just hasn't started yet.

WEDNESDAY, SEPTEMBER 17TH

One of the advantages of the BBC not having the Champions League contract means I get some time off in a week like this. Tonight Sky launches its new interactive coverage, offering any one of up to eight matches live – although most viewers would surely stick with Arsenal v

Inter Milan, the best fixture of the night. Nevertheless, it is still a new breakthrough in football broadcasting.

The venue of my choice today is Sandown Park. I fulfilled a long-standing promise to five ladies from our local pub who had never been racing before. Not in a stretch limousine, anyway. Come to that, I had never been in one either, but when they popped the first bottle of champagne before we left the car park at 11am it didn't seem such a bad idea.

Friends of mine at Ladbrokes had arranged a window table in the restaurant overlooking the course, and although flat racing never appeals to me as much as National Hunt, we enjoyed a splendid day including lunch and afternoon tea.

One or two of the girls made a bit of money, and as usual I came out about even. What I had not bargained for was being sidetracked to one of their favourite hostelries on the way home.

Days like this never run entirely smoothly. One of the girls left her handbag in the pub, but fortunately our driver was able to get it back later in the evening.

Watching the football on ITV later, I felt as dazed as Arsenal look. They were beaten 3–0 by Inter Milan and with Newcastle already out, I am not optimistic about the English clubs' prospects.

THURSDAY, SEPTEMBER 18TH

Dean Austin presided over what was positively my last training session this morning. One hour in the gym, and then I was away to catch the flight to Newcastle. Something tells me this is not the sort of preparation a good athlete would consider. Three nights out in the North East prior to the run is hardly going to help somebody of my vintage.

One of my horse-racing partners, Ian Robinson, and his friend Brian Phillips, a vice-president of Newcastle United, kindly agreed to take me out to dinner. The venue they chose is in quite a prosperous part of the city – apparently our first drink was in Alan Shearer's local – well away from the temptations of the quayside. But this is not just a pleasure trip. Tomorrow I am carded for the latest *Football Focus* episode of 'Motty's Mission', visiting the homes of Darlington and Hartlepool.

It is new territory for me, but fortunately Ian knows where both grounds are and agrees to pick me up at the hotel in the morning.

FRIDAY, SEPTEMBER 19TH

Little did I know last night that I was about to meet one of the most candid and colourful characters I have ever encountered on my football travels. George Reynolds is a man you do not mess with. Any man who builds a new stadium for more than 25,000 people at a club where the average attendance is less than 5,000 obviously has a plan, and he wasn't in the mood for wasting time. However, having harangued me about television crews always taking too long to get set up, George embarked on a long statement about how he was being targeted by a small section of critical supporters, and what he was prepared to do with them.

As a former safe breaker as well as a self-made millionaire, he didn't seem a man to trifle with. At one point he asked me to read aloud a chapter of the autobiography of Michael Knighton, the erstwhile chairman of Carlisle, who George maintained had suffered similar lack of appreciation from supporters. Fortunately the camera wasn't running when I was cast in the role of errant schoolboy, but it certainly was when Reynolds took us on a tour of the arena – including the men's toilet, where he insisted on waiting for the automatic flush.

I was too nervous to tell him that the *Football Focus* item the following day would only last about three minutes, but I mumbled something about sending him a tape of all we had recorded, and would certainly not challenge his plans to approach Paul Gascoigne, not when he had come close to signing Tino Asprilla!

Hartlepool's Victoria Park was a much quieter experience. The team had left for Brentford and the ground that had seen football in three centuries – and where Brian Clough cut his managerial teeth – was strangely silent. I did a short link to camera and the producer rushed the tape back to London.

I wondered what the editor would make of George Reynolds.

SATURDAY, SEPTEMBER 20TH

Ever since I have been doing the Great North Run – and people are now tired of hearing that this marks my 20th anniversary – Newcastle United have always played at home on the day before. Today their opponents are Bolton Wanderers, and the natives are restless. Robson's team are out of the Champions League and still looking for their first Premiership victory. A stuttering 0–0 draw does nothing to quieten rumours of cliques in the dressing room and unrest behind the scenes. The mood in the boardroom is sombre, except for the Bolton directors who are delighted with a hard-won point.

For the third year running, a Newcastle director seeks my opinion on which manager should bridge the gap between Sir Bobby Robson and, ultimately say, Alan Shearer. This was not a slight on Sir Bobby. He is approaching 71 and has the job for as long as he wants it, but nobody wants to see his health suffer and there are stories of players' behaviour that he just doesn't need. My shortlist of three, when the time comes, would be Martin O'Neill, Graeme Souness and Gary Megson. But then, what do I know?

Talking of kingmakers, Alastair Campbell was at the next table when I attended the Great North Run celebrity dinner tonight. An avid Burnley fan, I had, as I said, met him at Millwall last season, and he reiterated his invitation to Chequers before he left Downing Street. What with the Hutton Inquiry and so on, I was surprised he remembered that conversation. But he looked lean and ready for the following day, and shamed me into ignoring the champagne that was on offer.

SUNDAY, SEPTEMBER 21ST

I ran so badly that the champagne wouldn't have mattered. In ten or more attempts, I have never before resorted to having to walk, never had a calf strain, never struggled to finish. Today my body was telling me something.

My feeble excuses included having to fire the gun at the start and then jump off the platform before I was mowed down in the rush; running the first mile far too fast; the freak heat wave that hit us when we reached Gateshead Stadium; and the shock of being stopped for an interview by none other than Sally Gunnell.

Don't believe a word of it. Steve Cram and Paul Dickenson – holding the fort in the BBC commentary box while Brendan recorded a respectable 1 hour 33 minutes – found words of sympathy hard to come by when I shuffled disconsolately over the finishing line.

Now it was Sue Barker with the questions, and I realised why I had spent the last 30 years on her side of the microphone. It was no fun announcing your retirement when most people wondered why you bothered in the first place. The only consolation was the helicopter that stood waiting in a nearby field. Brendan and John Caine had kept their promise to propel Stubbs, Lawrenson and me back to our hotel in ten minutes, rather than three hours later as in years gone by.

Stephen Deakin, the manager of the Copthorne, kindly sent a bottle of champagne up to my room in sympathy. This time, I had no hesitation in drinking it.

MONDAY, SEPTEMBER 22ND

My luck was still out when we got to the airport. The walk to the gate was one of the longest in my experience, and it was just the same at Heathrow. Ray Stubbs looked a lot fresher than I did, and we had to endure a few ribald comments from fellow passengers who had watched the coverage the previous day.

What you need at a time like this is something to take your mind off things, and I certainly had that. I was privileged to be speaking at a small party tonight to mark the 60th birthday of my former BBC colleague and flatmate Bill Hamilton. Bill and I first met in the early seventies, when we worked together in the radio sports department that has now grown into Five Live. Quite apart from being a first-class reporter, who later had a distinguished career with BBC Television News, Bill is a wonderful companion and at times delightfully eccentric.

When we shared a flat in Finchley we lived in the next road to a man called John Webster, who for years read the football results on *Sports Report* in the era before James Alexander Gordon. Every time we passed his house, Bill would maintain his last ambition in radio sport was to read the results at five o'clock on a Saturday. And he did, in his last week before he moved, first to Carlisle, then to Glasgow, before returning to London.

Bill made a more serious impression in broadcasting with his campaigning work in Albania, on one occasion taking the Duchess of York to witness the plight of under-nourished children there.

His party was typically understated. There were friends from the world of local refereeing – Bill still officiates every weekend – from the Salvation Army, of which he was always a great supporter, and neighbours past and present. A fitting tribute to a great professional and a lifelong friend.

TUESDAY, SEPTEMBER 23RD

When I was a little boy at Sunday School in the fifties, we used to support a Methodist-based charity called the National Children's Home. It provided accommodation and support for homeless and orphaned children, whose photographs we used to buy for a shilling to support the organisation. They used to call the pictures Sunny Smiles.

Nowadays, the charity is known as NCH – The Children's Charity. There are no longer any residential homes, instead there are any number of day centres, the upkeep and furnishing of which still depend largely on public and private donation. The money raising ideas these days are also very different – and more imaginative – than in the past. The latest is to persuade those of us in sport, media and the entertainment industry to 'give up' something they like or use for a month in the New Year. Viv Fowle, the organiser with whom I have worked closely, persuaded me to leave off my sheepskin coat for a month – and that's the reason I took it with me on a hot afternoon into London.

The famous society photographer Terry O'Neill agreed to take photographs of the celebrities concerned, and these will then be sold to support NCH – The Children's Charity. O'Neill had set up his equipment in a suite at the Savoy Hotel, and his subject before me was Chris Eubank. What with his cane and my coat, Terry wasn't short of props as he clicked away.

Rarely is a photographer a bigger celebrity than his subjects, but O'Neill's career goes back nearly 50 years to Sir Winston Churchill – who he memorably captured being carried in a huge chair – and includes a marriage to Faye Dunaway. I first met Terry when he linked up with the journalist Peter Lorenzo – a kind BBC colleague when I first joined – to take some offbeat photographs of footballers in the seventies. It was an honour to be on the other end of his lens, especially for such a good cause.

WEDNESDAY, SEPTEMBER 24TH

Paid speaking engagements aside, there are plenty of requests to talk at schools and societies. Although it is often hard to commit to a date well in advance, I have always believed those of us lucky enough to have a media career should be prepared to put something back by sharing our experience with those who would like to go down the same path.

The students at Nottingham University had invited me to speak a year ago, when my diary was full, but when they persevered with a second letter this season, I was happy to put aside an afternoon in Fresher's week and deliver a short talk followed by a question and answer session.

Fred came with me to run his eye over the university. Any time now, he has to select his shortlist of those where he intends to apply, and Nottingham is one of them. Two students were detailed to show him round while I addressed an audience of about a hundred. However hard I try to turn my talk into a responsible careers lecture, I always finish up answering questions about my favourite team, match and goal. Whatever, informal football chat has never been anything other than food and drink to me, and the Nottingham crowd were lively, attentive and seemed pleased I had come.

I rescued Fred before he got too distracted in the students' bar and we had a pint at our local on the way home instead.

THURSDAY, SEPTEMBER 25TH

Steven Nicholas is a London lawyer who I met by chance when we were at adjacent tables in an Italian restaurant five years ago. We struck up an immediate friendship, partly because I know nothing about the law and he isn't bothered about talking football. Every so often, when we've both been busy, we return to the scene of our first meeting and chew the fat for an afternoon. The owners of Isolabella in Red Lion Street, Vicenzo and his wife Lena, have become firm friends and we usually finish up sitting with them when all the other customers have gone.

The first time I was ever taken to their restaurant was back in 1996, when another television company was kind enough to offer me a job. I always remember Lena making sure I was at a corner table where nobody would spot me. There used to be a little Portuguese waiter who would try to steer the conversation away from Italian football. Sadly he has now moved on, because he would have been a useful reference point with Euro 2004 now looming large.

Without the lunches, I would certainly be a stone lighter and would probably be able to go on doing half marathons. But convivial days like this are a comfortable part of my lifestyle now, and long may that continue.

FRIDAY, SEPTEMBER 26TH

In those far off days when Bill Hamilton and I shared the apartment in Finchley, our third flatmate was a close friend of mine called Jim Currie. I played Sunday football with Jim when we were teenagers, and although he, like Bill, has moved all over the country in his time, we have remained firm friends.

Jim also spoke at Bill's party last Monday, and reminded us that on the day my career took off with the Hereford v Newcastle cup tie in February 1972, he was best man at Bill's wedding. So there has always been a strong bond between the three of us, and today Bill and I are driving down to Bristol to mark the opening of new premises for Jim's relocating careers company DBM. They specialise in advising executives and the like how to go about looking for new employment when they are made redundant. It is not something Bill and I have ever had to face, but it was an enlightening experience meeting those who have.

Jim had invited me to stay the night and that suits me fine, because tomorrow Bristol Rovers are at home to Cheltenham Town and the Memorial Ground, where Rovers now play, is one of the 'new' venues on my list to visit for the first time.

SATURDAY, SEPTEMBER 27TH

It was a better stadium than I had expected. Rovers are now the landlords and the rugby club the tenants, rather than the other way round as was the case when the football club moved back to Bristol after a ten-year sojourn at nearby Bath.

There is a nice traditional air about Rovers, dating back to their old ground at Eastville, from which they were evicted when greyhound racing ceased. They still wear blue and white quartered shirts, and when they are playing well the crowd still sing *Goodnight Irene*.

It was goodnight Cheltenham today. They were well beaten, but it was nice to meet up again with Bobby Gould, who was an Arsenal player when I started in the business and who helped me enormously in his itinerant career both as player and manager. In my early days, when he was playing and living in Bristol, I went to his house to do a television interview and his wife Marge made me a quite delicious cake. Quite why that seemed so memorable at the time I have no idea, except that Bobby mentions it every time I see him. He managed at Rovers too, of course, so this local derby held a special interest for him and his family.

Rovers' chairman Geoff Dunford, and his father Denis who preceded him, were both in buoyant mood. They have done well to keep Rovers going through troubled times, although the thought persists that in a city like Bristol, should the two football clubs not be sharing a purpose-built stadium? Local rivalry is fierce down here, so it may well be a few more years before they get that off the ground.

SUNDAY, SEPTEMBER 28TH

Back to real work today. Charlton v Liverpool for Radio Five Live is an assignment I have been looking forward to because The Valley was the ground where I saw my first league match with my late father in 1952. Those memories came flooding back when I got there today and opened the programme. An article by Sue Townsend, a supporters' representative on the board of directors, concerned an early hero of mine, the legendary Charlton goalkeeper Sam Bartram.

Sam played in the first two FA Cup finals after the war, when Charlton lost to Derby and then returned a year later to beat Burnley. With his mop of red hair, he was an unmistakable character in those sepia days of the forties and fifties. Sue Townsend wants to raise money to build a statue to Bartram, as well as some memorial gates, honouring him in a similar way to that adopted by Liverpool (with the Shankly Gates), Leeds (Billy Bremner's statue), Stoke City (Stanley Matthews), Wolves (Billy Wright) and so on. Already her proposal has attracted interest from Charlton fans on websites all over the world. She has chosen a good day to launch the scheme, because Charlton beat Liverpool 3–2 and Kevin Lisbie scored a hat-trick.

When he ran more than half the length of the field to score his third goal, I was grateful to the Barclaycard press bulletin for pointing out that the last hat-trick in this fixture was scored by Ronny Rosenthal when Charlton were playing at Selhurst Park in 1990. The only way I had envisaged mentioning that was if Michael Owen struck gold for Liverpool. He was relatively anonymous, and Lisbie stole the headlines to become the unlikely hero.

Sam would have been proud of him.

MONDAY, SEPTEMBER 29TH

Spending my early days on the *Barnet Press* has meant I that have retained an interest in local football. I am president of the Barnet Sunday League, of which my club Roving Reporters were founder members, and never cease to admire the amount of voluntary effort that goes into organising the game at grass roots level.

World Class Homes, who specialise in apartments in Portugal, sponsor one of our local Hertfordshire leagues and have this year extended that to cover a reserve league and a cup competition. Ted Colley, one of those uncomplaining diehards who keep the game going for the benefit of hundreds of players, has invited me to launch the new sponsorship, which brings the relevant clubs together for a morning function at Broadhall Way, the home of Stevenage Borough. This is the ground where Kenny Dalglish and Newcastle nearly came a cropper at the hands of the Conference team in the FA Cup a few years ago.

The playing and entertainment facilities at grounds like this are the equal, if not better, of those at most third-division clubs, proving again that the two-up two-down policy adopted with the Conference last season was well overdue.

We have the usual photo shoot for which Ted produces a football, and World Class Homes supremo Bob Brewster seems very happy, as a former local player himself, with his side of the deal. Mind you, nothing is for ever. He will review it at the end of the season.

TUESDAY, SEPTEMBER 30TH

Tony Banks sort of got his way, when Sky Sports announced today that they were prepared to sell the rights to a delayed recording of the Turkey v England match to a terrestrial bidder. However, the match cannot be shown until Sky's live coverage is finished, and that would mean BBC1 or ITV reshuffling their carefully guarded Saturday night schedules.

The controllers are reluctant to play around with slots for *The National Lottery*, *Silent Witness*, *Casualty* or *Pop Idol*, especially when viewers may not watch highlights if they know the result. So it came as no surprise to hear that ITV had won the rights to the deferred recording, but would not be showing it until 9.35pm.

I must admit to having mixed feelings about not going to Istanbul. The security issues have matched the importance of the match, and I am not sure how easy it will be to concentrate on the football.

That wasn't difficult tonight at Moss Rose. In the company of two thousand others, two BBC colleagues and myself were in the crowd to see Macclesfield play Rochdale. Paul Armstrong and Lance Hardy were kind enough to share the driving and I was glad they did. Macclesfield is not the easiest place to get to from London, but the welcome was warm enough to forget the journey and I was able to tick off another of my hitherto unvisited grounds.

I now only have six to go, and one of them is Rochdale. Their directors are ribbing me about leaving them until nearly last, but as I said, somebody had to be. I'll get there soon, I promise.

A year after I joined BBC Television Sport, Tony Gubba came down from the North to join the team. Anne and I were made godparents to his second daughter Libby. Tony and I went to our first World Cup together in 1974 and we have been to all seven since, up to and including Japan last year.

To mark Tony's 30 years with the department, a few of his colleagues have arranged a lunch in his honour. Not to be outdone by anything mischievous we had planned (we hadn't), Tony produced documentary evidence of where we all were on the day he joined. One or two round the table were still at school or university, but he produced an old BBC stock library picture of yours truly, when my hair was jet black and my tie worn a lot wider than it is now.

There was a fair bit of reminiscing, not least my recollection of Gubba walking along the Berlin Wall in 1974, prior to East and West Germany meeting in the World Cup.

My next stop was Savile Row, where I was measured up for a new sheepskin coat, and then I dashed out to The Greyhound at Chalfont St Peter to join Mark Lawrenson for a small corporate dinner organised by the manager Will Oakley. We knew him when we used to stay at The Halcyon Hotel in Holland Park after late nights at the studio.

I was tired when Russell, the friendly chauffeur, picked me up at midnight, but I got off lightly – Mark told me the following day he was still talking football at 3am.

THURSDAY, OCTOBER 2ND

Another double bill today, and my first engagement is quite scary. I left Culford School, my Methodist boarding establishment outside Bury St Edmunds in Suffolk, at Christmas 1961, armed with a modest eight 'O' levels. In the 42 years since, I have only been back a couple of times.

There were reasons for that. Culford was a committed rugby school that, in my day, frowned on soccer. My career seemed a bit of an embarrassment to the staff and successive headmasters, although one of my contemporaries, Gary Newbon of ITV, was in the same year and also made his mark in sports television.

The main difference was that Gary was First XV rugby captain and stayed a bit longer than I did, so when the current headmaster John Richardson decided to offer the olive branch and invite me to lunch, I insisted Gary came as well.

We had a charming meal in the head's study, and some of the Methodist traditions held firm. The only alcohol was a small sherry before we sat down, but Gary had them eating out of his hand with stories of his school days, and the lady archivist never stopped writing.

We excused ourselves early in the afternoon, and the irrepressible Bill Hamilton was back at his busy best in the evening. The local branch of the Salvation Army had organised a football quiz in the British Legion headquarters in Harpenden, where we live, and Bill held the fort until I arrived to present the prizes. I had to adjudicate on one disputed answer, but otherwise the event ran very smoothly. Luckily there was no need for a tie-break question, because I had completely forgotten to bring one.

FRIDAY, OCTOBER 3RD

The Barclaycard Premiership Manager and Player of the Month awards are voted by a panel drawn from all sections of the media. We are asked to cast our votes every month, usually by telephone, but two or three times a year our sponsors kindly invite us to lunch.

Today, after we had solemnly raised hands in favour of Claudio Ranieri and Frank Lampard, they had a bigger announcement to make. Barclays, the parent company, are taking over the Premiership sponsorship from Barclaycard, and committing £57 million over three years.

What a far cry from when I started in television. There were no sponsors to speak of then, no names on shirts, no corporate entertainment, hardly any advertising boards round the grounds. Whether the change has been altogether for the better is arguable, but certainly the game is better served now in the way of facilities and presentation.

The main debate during lunch today concerned the fall-out from the recent fracas at Old Trafford between Manchester United and Arsenal. Several players have been charged by the FA and are awaiting the hearing. The sight of six Arsenal players surrounding Ruud Van Nistelrooy was ugly and demeaning, but as a concerted reaction on the final whistle it was most unusual. It left me wondering whether perhaps the Dutchman should have been charged, along with, or even instead of, two of his Manchester United colleagues.

Nobody can defend Arsenal's disciplinary record of 52 red cards under Arsene Wenger, but on this occasion Van Nistelrooy's part in the incident, which led to Patrick Vieira being dismissed, could have been said to be unsportsmanlike, at the very least.

SATURDAY, OCTOBER 4TH

Mark Lawrenson is in Glasgow for the first Old Firm meeting of the season, so I am brought on as substitute to join Ray Stubbs and Garth Crooks on *Final Score*. The studio at Television Centre is a five minute walk from Loftus Road, so I can see the first half of Fulham v Leicester before slipping round the corner, getting made up and going on air.

Confession time here, because Fulham were on my list for relegation, along with Wolves and Leeds. At this early stage of the season they are proving a lot of us wrong. Chris Coleman, the youngest manager in the Premiership, has got his crop of overseas players nicely integrated with the rest of the team. Nobody is playing better than Luis Boa Morte, whose two goals here dispense with Leicester, who are struggling already.

Final Score moves fast with the lead in several matches changing while we are on air. Your opinion can be rendered irrelevant by the next score flash.

The Turkey v England match is now just a week away and the omens are not good. Premiership players have been linked to an alleged gang rape in a London hotel, and in Leeds a senior player* has been linked to a sexual assault.

*Later to be identified as Jody Morris. All charges against the player were dropped.

SUNDAY, OCTOBER 5TH

The Reverend William Motson was the superintendent minister at the Deptford Methodist Mission from 1950 to 1957. During that time, the church celebrated its Golden Jubilee in 1953. Now, 50 years on, the mission is marking its Centenary and felt it appropriate to invite his son to speak at a special service and lunch to mark the occasion.

If going back to Culford after 40 years had seemed surreal, returning to a church I had last seen when I left for boarding school in 1956 was a decidedly unnerving experience. To meet up again with a lady called Elsie Green, now 97 years of age, who had patiently taken me to Sunday School on the bus every Sunday afternoon from the age of five; to see my father's old vestry, where on a Saturday evening I would rush in with the football results at the church social; to be reminded how we played football on a bomb site that later became the new church; to see the social centre which had once been the classroom where we bought Sunny Smiles; to be introduced before I read the lesson by the lady minister, who in a previous life would have been called a deaconess, was all very strange and yet in its way deeply spiritual. The work of the mission among the poor and needy was a constant factor. The selfless service of the workers there was humbling to say the least.

On the car radio on the way home, I scarcely paid attention to the announcement that Sven Goran Eriksson had delayed naming his squad for Turkey by a further 24 hours.

MONDAY, OCTOBER 6TH

Then they delayed it by another day. Something was going on; not just the injury to Michael Owen, sustained against Arsenal on Saturday and making him doubtful for Turkey; nor the ongoing tabloid disclosures about the rape allegations – none of Sven's players had been directly linked with that. While the nation scratched its head in puzzlement, I nearly had my car scratched in a road rage episode in West London. Parking carefully (and legally) outside the Hurlingham Clinic for my final thread vein removal appointment, I was assailed by a lady who urged me to move on the grounds that she was a resident. When I pointed out my rights, she took her angst out on the local postman who happened to be passing.

The day, as the Cheshire cat said to Alice, got curiouser and curiouser. At a veterans' get together of my old Sunday football team this evening, one of our number who works on the sports desk of a national newspaper alerted me to the following day's drama. Another England player was at the heart of serious allegations, but he knew not who.

TUESDAY, OCTOBER 7TH

It was less than 24 hours before we found out. When Eriksson finally released the squad, Rio Ferdinand's name was not there. Suddenly football scandal stories were the first item on the news, and the second, and the third. It became apparent that Ferdinand had failed to report for a drugs test at the Manchester United training ground. Despite being reminded twice that the testers were waiting for him, he said it slipped his mind because he was moving house.

Three other United players dutifully took their tests, and Ferdinand claimed the testers had left by the time he remembered his. He reported for one 36 hours later, and it was negative. In the eyes of the anti-doping lobby however, missing a test is as much an offence as a positive one. Speculation is rife as to the penalty Ferdinand could receive. As it is, his first punishment has been exclusion from the Turkey game. Eriksson, steering well away from criticising the player, expressed regret that in the circumstances he is not allowed to select him.

Ferdinand's England colleagues held a meeting at their Sopwell House Hotel headquarters and felt he had been victimised – found guilty without trial so to speak. One player, who had a column in a national daily, told the newspaper that a vote had been taken. The squad had unanimously decided that if Ferdinand was not reinstated, they would consider refusing to travel to Turkey.

It made a good headline, but it was a threat nobody should have taken seriously. Their international careers would effectively have been over if England had failed to fulfil the fixture, or even if the beleaguered FA had been forced to send an under-21 team. For once, you couldn't blame their agents – they would have been the biggest losers of all.

WEDNESDAY, OCTOBER 8TH

Three things kept me out of the debate, despite several calls from national newspapers asking me to comment on the furore that was now leading every bulletin. 'How Dare They?' screamed one national newspaper.

I had spent the previous day with a dear friend of mine, Roger Ball, a rabid football fan whose son Kester died in the Hillsborough disaster. The Taylor Report that emanated from that tragedy, allied to the start of the Premier League and the influx of Rupert Murdoch's money, had made the England rebels millionaires before their time.

Secondly, the BBC's absence from the Turkey coverage meant I was not on the trip and, therefore, had no professional reason yet to get involved.

And thirdly, today was the re-opening of Towcester racecourse. Tony McCoy, whose only militant involvement was to support his fellow jockeys over the ludicrous banning of mobile phones on racecourses, responded with a treble. Back to proper sport. I can't remember him threatening not to ride.

Hurried consultations and press conferences eroded the strike threat, but did not diffuse the growing tension between the Football Association, Manchester United and the Professional Footballers' Association. The last two were stubbornly behind Ferdinand, who was now at the heart of a *cause célèbre*.

Nobody was in a position to be judge and jury, but I felt the events of the week, including the lurid rape allegations and headlines, were part of a wider issue that had needed for some time to be addressed. As a responsible football reporter, I was obliged to have a view.

THURSDAY, OCTOBER 9TH

So it was no surprise when Andrew Clement, the editor of *Football Focus*, rang me this morning and asked me to join the panel on Saturday. Anybody who thinks television reporting is bland should have been in the meeting when it was decided that Saturday's original guests, Dion Dublin and Gary Pallister, should be stood down and replaced by Trevor Brooking and me, alongside resident pundit Mark Lawrenson.

By now, the England team were on their way to Turkey, and so were the press party. How ironic that the threat of England fans breaking the boycott and trying to get to the match had now become a side issue. Keeping the supporters away had given way to making sure the players turned up.

Nobody was entitled to prejudge the Ferdinand case, but what the whole episode confirmed to me was something I have felt for a very long time. The FA's role as guardians of the game has long since been eroded. Certain clubs in the Premier League, fuelled by player power, agents, the PFA and sections of the media, are becoming too powerful. The ruling body is no longer seen to be running the show.

I am not sure how valid an opinion is that of a commentator. But I am wrestling with how to express it on Saturday. I need a tried and trusted old friend as a sounding board.

FRIDAY, OCTOBER 10TH

'Don't you think the game has lost any sense of morality?' I asked Ricky George over a beef sandwich at lunch time today.

'I tell you what it's lost,' he replied, 'it's lost its dignity.'

And that just about summed it up. The Ferdinand issue was a catalyst, almost a sideshow in the wider picture. Over the last few years we have had stories about bungs, bribes, a court case with allegations of match-fixing, under-the-counter payments and drunken escapades by the number. It may be a minority at fault, but they have disgraced the game that the public love and support with their hard-earned cash.

I was alerted again to the book by Tom Bower, *Broken Dreams – Vanity and Greed in Professional Football*. Bower went as far as he could in identifying a modern Babylon, but as usual, nothing could be conclusively proved and no action was taken. Bower's first chapter was a reminder that, not so long ago, a couple of concerned MPs suggested that the game was out of control, incapable of monitoring itself and in need of an independent regulator. I don't think they were far wrong.

SATURDAY, OCTOBER 11TH

The one man who can lay that theory to rest in the present climate is Mark Palios. The recently appointed chief executive of the FA is now in the eye of the storm, possibly torn between confrontation and compromise, certainly needing to rebuild bridges between his organisation, the PFA and Manchester United.

The *Football Focus* discussion, I have to admit in hindsight, was rather one-sided, but there was no collusion between Lawrenson, Brooking and myself before we went on air. We all felt the players had been out of order with their empty threat about boycotting the game, and that Ferdinand's case should be subject to the normal process of anti-doping regulations.

Over in Istanbul, David Beckham had diffused some of the anger directed towards the players, with a sensible and skilful performance at the last press conference before the game. They owed the public a performance, was his message in a nutshell.

Alongside Beckham, Sven Goran Eriksson was not as forthright. He still sounded unconvincing when asked to confirm his commitment to his England contract, and Garth Crooks reported that one body of opinion in Turkey thought he might resign after the game.

Oh yes, we nearly forgot the match. With Ferdinand and Owen missing, the England team more or less picked itself. I forecast a draw, although I felt Turkey were capable of scoring, so I predicted 1–1.

I was determined not to waste an afternoon without football, so they let me out of the studio early to go to Brighton. The Withdean Stadium, another ground I was seeing for the first time, was certainly an eye-opener. Dick Knight, Brighton's effusive chairman, who first watched them play in 1946, was perfectly frank about the temporary stands, the running track and the profusion of trees around this converted athletics stadium. 'It's like coming to see a pre-season friendly in Norway,' he joked.

It hasn't been a great week for Dick: his manager Steve Coppell left for Reading (and a ready-made 25,000 seater stadium) after compensation had been agreed; and the public inquiry ordered by John Prescott is about to start – Brighton have already received planning permission for a new £40-million stadium at Fulmer, on the outskirts of the seaside town.

It was Dick's namesake Leon who lit up his and my afternoon. Formerly with Chelsea, Leon Knight had loan spells with Huddersfield, Sheffield Wednesday and Albion themselves before Brighton signed him permanently.

He inspired a second-half performance which brought a 3–0 victory over Grimsby and kept Albion top of the table.

I was home in time to see the England game, and after 20 minutes my impression was that Turkey were not the team they had been built up to be. Terry Butcher, the Five Live summariser, made the point that the absence of England fans in the stadium had made the Turkish supporters raise their expectations of their own team. As a viewer, I thought it was a bit of an anti-climax, but Beckham was right – England were focused on the job in hand and did it to the letter. We can now pack our bags for Portugal.

SUNDAY, OCTOBER 12TH

The repercussions from England's visit to Turkey were fuelled by Alpay's confrontation with David Beckham, and new TV pictures of a bust-up in the tunnel at half-time. What with the Ferdinand case still pending, and Arsenal's players now pleading guilty to the charges from Old Trafford, there will be no shortage of off-the-field headlines this coming week.

On the field, the most dramatic event in yesterday's final qualifiers went virtually unnoticed in this country, and was only seen on television if you checked in to the three-hour Eurosport round-up last night. The minnows of Latvia have qualified for the play-offs for the first time, courtesy of a 1–0 win in Sweden, who had already won the group. With five minutes to go, Latvia conceded a penalty, and had Marcus Allback scored from the spot, the play-off place would have gone to Poland, who won 2–1 in Hungary. But Allback (or should it be quarterback?) skied his penalty even higher than Beckham did in Turkey, breaking millions of hearts in Poland but damaging his own country's credentials not one bit.

Latvia join Wales and Scotland in tomorrow's draw, and after so many fallow years the Scots seem to have discovered a couple of lively young forwards. James McFadden made the winning goal against Lithuania for Darren Fletcher, in front of a capacity crowd at Hampden. Meanwhile, 72,000 in the Millennium Stadium in Cardiff saw Wales go down 3–2 to Serbia and Montenegro.

The Eurosport programme also featured scenes of fanatical crowds in Croatia, who booked their place in the play-offs by beating Bulgaria and Bosnia, who were edged out by Norway. These countries are so proud of their recently found independence that big sporting occasions are still a cause for national celebration. What a pity that innocence has been lost elsewhere.

MONDAY, OCTOBER 13TH

Scotland and Wales were brought down to earth by the play-off draw this morning. The Scots got the one nobody wanted – Holland, with the first leg at home – while the Welsh at least have the second leg against Russia in Cardiff.

Memories were stirred of the World Cup meeting between Scotland and the Netherlands in Argentina in 1978, when Archie Gemmill's goal was voted the best of the tournament, even though it came too late to rescue Scotland's chaotic campaign under Ally MacLeod. That was one of four World Cups in which Lawrie McMenemy served on the BBC panel of pundits. I caught up with him today along with three other former colleagues of ours – Alan Hart, who as controller of BBC1 first brought *EastEnders* to the channel; Bob Abrahams, a brilliant film editor who taught me how to write to pictures; and John Rowlinson, who worked in the sports department for my first 30 years and now heads media affairs at the All England Club, Wimbledon.

Reunions like this make you realise how quickly the years have flown by, and in my case how lucky I am still to be surviving at the sharp end. Retirement is something I rarely contemplate, but it will be forced on me sooner or later, and when you've enjoyed your job as much as I have you hope there will still be bits and pieces you can turn your hand to. In the meantime, the work for Euro 2004 is about to start in earnest.

TUESDAY, OCTOBER 14TH

Ally McCoist arrived in Wardour Street on the back of a motorcycle this morning. Not that the inhabitants of Soho turned a hair, such is the variety that spices up their lives every day. It was the quickest way for Scotland's last natural goalscorer to get from the airport to Aquarium Studios, where we were booked for a day's recording for the Euro 2004 game now being rushed out by Electronic Arts.

The two guys from Canada had come armed with goal highlights from at least ten recent Premiership matches. Ally and I delivered our usual two-handed commentary, trying not to mention the teams or the individual players.

Although we work for different channels, and that doesn't look like changing in the near future, our natural enthusiasm for the game seems to gel on the few days a year when we get together. Ally is easy on the ear, never lost for words, and the quickest to the bar when we break for lunch!

The commentators in the other countries who record the annual *FIFA* game must be a bit different to us, because the Canadians are always pleasantly surprised how quickly we get through the script. I guess it saves studio costs, now I come to think of it, but then again, soccer is not their number one sport at home, and they are always receptive to the way we do things. They're off to see Birmingham v Chelsea tonight, so when they see the real thing they might wonder what on earth Ally and I are talking about!

WEDNESDAY, OCTOBER 15TH

News reached me today about the death of Johnny Angus. His name will mean nothing to the reader, nor to anybody else outside the coterie of friends who knew him as the licensee of the Potters Bar Hotel back in the sixties when I started work on the *Barnet Press*.

When my old chief reporter Bill Field gave me a little notebook and told me to make a few local contacts, I got directed fairly swiftly to Johnny's establishment. He had jet-black hair, swept back like one of those pop stars of the time, a lovely engaging manner and a publican's nose for news and an ear for gossip. People told Johnny all sorts of things, and quite a few of them appeared in the paper in unattributed form.

If I was short of copy for the front page of our Potters Bar edition, I took a 50-yard walk down the main shopping street, visiting the local cinema manager Frank Seymour, a young Cypriot hairdresser called Nico Sallas, and finally dropping anchor at Johnny's. Years later he took over a pub in Harrow and I tracked him and his wife Nesta down there. Since then, I've lost track of him. But the impression he made on a young trainee reporter was there for ever. I always remember one of our female colleagues leaving her husband and having nowhere to go. Johnny gave her the best room he had and never asked her for a penny.

THURSDAY, OCTOBER 16TH

In little more than a week's time Wayne Rooney will be 18 years old, and just to show that David Beckham doesn't get all the headlines, Rooney's name has been plastered across the front page of Britain's biggest selling daily newspaper on two mornings this week. First, the *Sun* had him throwing a punch in the mayhem of the players' tunnel at half-time last Saturday, then this morning he was apparently on his way to Chelsea for £35 million.

In the days when I was trying to find front-page news for the *Barnet Press*, it was 17-year-old George Best who made the football headlines – but nobody put them on the front page at that stage of his career. His celebrity lifestyle they latched on to a bit later. And he's still in the papers now.

In between Best and Rooney, it was Paul Gascoigne who was thrust too early into the limelight, and suffered as a result. Now 36, Gazza has crept back into the papers today – he is training with Wolves. These three players are arguably the most gifted produced by the British game in the last 40 years. How much responsibility do the media and its readers take for building them up too quickly and leaving them to face the consequences?

One hopes Rooney's advisers will learn from what has gone before. But when you read today that Roman Abramovich is selling his entire Russian business empire for five and a half *billion* pounds, the £112 million he has already invested in Chelsea may soon be a drop in the ocean. So would £35 million for Wayne Rooney.

FRIDAY, OCTOBER 17TH

While I was labouring on the exercise bike today – going down to the shed at the bottom of the garden is less stressful than taking to the streets – Bob Wilson and Billy Bragg were together on the Simon Mayo Show on Five Live. Bob has brought out his autobiography, which covers a career in football and then two in television. We worked together when he fronted *Football Focus* for 20 years, before moving to ITV after the 1994 World Cup and presenting there until his retirement last year.

By coincidence a letter arrived from Bob this morning, inviting me to the London Football Coaches' Association Dinner, which is always held at Highbury in December. Coaches from all levels of the game get together for what is normally a boisterous occasion with Bob in the chair.

I have never had the pleasure of meeting Billy Bragg, but I have a huge respect for him as a songwriter and he figures on one of my most precious videos – a tribute to the life and work of Kirsty MacColl, one of my favourite artists, who was so tragically killed in a speedboat accident in Mexico. Kirsty's best songs and those of Debbie Harry are the most played cassettes in my car. Most of the other stuff is older still. My record collection runs out with The Who and Simon and Garfunkel.

Enough of all this. I am going to Highbury tomorrow to see the meeting of the top two teams in the Premiership, Arsenal and Chelsea. I haven't looked forward to a match so much for ages.

SATURDAY, OCTOBER 18TH

I got to Highbury early because today's *Football Focus* has been extended to an hour and a half – it is up against ITV's World Cup rugby match between England and South Africa – and I don't want to miss it.

Paddy Galligan has been the dressing room attendant at Arsenal for 27 years, and I have known him almost as long. He used to look after us when a group of young broadcasters, including Jim Rosenthal, Alan Parry and myself, enjoyed the privilege of a Thursday night training session at Highbury under the former Arsenal youth coach Roger Thompson. Today, Paddy took me into the little staff room opposite the Arsenal dressing room, put me in front of a television and made me a cup of tea and a sandwich while I watched *Football Focus*.

Upstairs in the boardroom, the focus was on Sven Goran Eriksson, who was talking to two directors' ladies as I walked past. 'No centre-backs for Chelsea,' he smiled as he tapped me on the shoulder. The team sheet had just revealed that Desailly, Gallas and Terry were all missing injured. On the other side of the room, Sven's agent Athole Still was lambasting the press for persisting with the rumour that Eriksson was soon bound for Chelsea. 'I am his sole representative and I promise you I have had no contact with Chelsea. Sven is staying at least until after Euro 2004 – the only change in those circumstances might have been if England had failed to qualify.'

I put it to Athole that Sven could have made his position clear if he had given the press more positive answers. 'He says nothing has changed since last week, and nothing has. He wasn't going to leave then, and he certainly isn't now.'

The mood was lightened by a joint deputation from Arsenal vice-chairman David Dein and his friend Irving Scholar, formerly chairman of Tottenham. Anybody who thinks directors are not football nuts should get a load of these two when there are quiz questions around. Can you name six pairs of players with the same surname, one white and one black, who both played for England? They had only managed five.

I came up with Geoff and Michael Thomas; Mark and Ian Wright; Peter and John Barnes; Ian and Des Walker; the obvious one I missed was Joe and Ashley or Andy Cole, and we all struggled on the last one.

Appropriately, with the Kick Racism Out of Football campaign on show, there were 11 white and 11 black players on the pitch today, and I sat next to a lady who is Ken Livingstone's representative in the campaign. As for the match, David Pleat sat behind me and seemed to agree with my assessment. A ready-made team (Arsenal) against a team in the making (Chelsea). Roman Abramovich, with his wife and friends, sat two rows in front; they celebrated heartily when Hernan Crespo equalised for Chelsea, but sat in glum silence when Carlo Cudicini's unforced error gave a goal to Thierry Henry and the points to Arsenal.

'You'll be working on games like this next season,' said Arsenal director Danny Fiszman as he put a glass of white wine in my hand. He touched a nerve.

Two of the key incidents in the match were missed by most people watching. Ray Parlour had deflected Edu's free-kick for Arsenal's first goal; and Crespo had come back on the pitch after adjusting his boots, without waiting for permission from the referee, before joining the play and scoring Chelsea's goal.

Those are the sort of observations that can sometimes mark out one commentator from another. 'Did he spot that?' is a common question among television people.

SUNDAY, OCTOBER 19TH

It is 40 years this month since a nervous 18-year-old in a green corduroy jacket walked up Barnet High Street and started a four-year apprenticeship as a trainee reporter on the local weekly newspaper. At that time each paper would employ two 'juniors' on an indentures scheme, sending them to college one day a week to study essential law for journalists, local government, shorthand, and an English course roughly equivalent to 'A' level.

My opposite number was a local lad by the name of Roger Jones, who was already six months into his apprenticeship and quickly took me under his wing. Even so, I was there nearly a week before I plucked up the courage to ask him where the toilet was.

Today, Roger organised a reunion of those among our contemporaries who are still around. Seven members of the editorial staff from 1963, together with the widows of two who have passed away in recent years, gathered at a steak house in Potters Bar to talk over old times and pore over some photographs and cuttings that took us back to our early days. It was a sharp reminder of how some of the principles instilled into us then – like the little contacts book I mentioned a few days ago – hold good today. I still try to base my commentaries and match reports on the old local paper adage: a good intro, an orderly explanation of what went on, and hopefully a decent 'end line'. That's why I advise so many of the young aspirants who write to me about getting into the media to consider starting on the local paper, or more often these days perhaps, in local radio.

MONDAY, OCTOBER 20TH

October is often called 'sacking time' in football, and managers are falling like the autumn leaves just now. My old friend Bobby Gould has left Cheltenham just three weeks after that defeat at Bristol Rovers – they lost again at home to Rochdale on Saturday and Bobby walked in afterwards and resigned.

Things weren't much better at Kidderminster – Ian Britton was dismissed after only four wins in 25 games – and all this followed the departures of Glenn Hoddle (Spurs), Mark McGhee (Millwall), Carlton Palmer (Stockport), Ray Matthias (Tranmere), Lawrie Sanchez (Wycombe), Roddy Collins (Carlisle) and Paul Brush (Leyton Orient). Furthermore, Glenn Roeder's earlier sacking at West Ham led to changes that brought Alan Pardew to Upton Park (Trevor has handed over after just one defeat in 14 games!) and took Steve Coppell to Reading from Brighton.

We are not even one third of the way into the season, but it happens to those at the very top – Inter Milan dismissed Hector Cuper just a month after he presided over a 3–0 win at Arsenal in the Champions League – and to those in more modest surroundings – Tommy Taylor (Farnborough) and Mark Patterson (Leigh RMI) have both left Nationwide Conference clubs in the last few days.

One thing is for sure, job applications will come piling in from those out of work, and even these men mentioned here won't be too scarred by the experience to try again. Football management is a painful bug when it bites, and it's one they cannot get out of their system.

TUESDAY, OCTOBER 21ST

There's never a dull moment when you go to football. As I walked towards Loftus Road Stadium for tonight's Premiership match between Fulham and Newcastle, a man in a yellow coat was sitting on a stool in South Africa Road, pleading to supporters through a megaphone not to buy tickets from unauthorised sources. Apparently a lot of Japanese visitors, keen to see Junichi Inamoto play for Fulham, had caught a cold on the black market.

A few minutes later, the police closed the road completely. Nothing to do with tickets, but a car had been found suspiciously parked near a Territorial Army building, and with the Northern Ireland peace talks having stalled two hours earlier, they were taking no chances. After two controlled explosions, they gave the game the go-ahead, although it kicked off half an hour late. Fulham made up for lost time by scoring twice in the first seven minutes, but a peerless performance by Alan Shearer inspired a Newcastle comeback – three wins in a row have taken them out of the bottom three into the top half of the table.

Their recovery tonight reminded me, not for the first time, of a comment made nearly 40 years ago by Dexter Adams, Barnet's manager when I was on the local paper: 'Two-nil is the most dangerous lead in football.' And every time a team has scored twice early in a game, the opposition have almost invariably replied.

Not that the theory escaped the dry humour of Ron Atkinson when I put it to him a few years ago. 'I'd rather be two-nil up than two-nil down,' he said.

WEDNESDAY, OCTOBER 22ND

The memory of my dismal performance in the Great North Run has not gone away. It was put firmly into perspective at Fulham last night when Freddy Shepherd, the Newcastle chairman, told me his 82-year-old father-in-law had completed the course in under two and a half hours. The run also brought back a nagging back strain – the injection had obviously worn off – so most of my home-based exercise is on the exercise bike now. I aim for nine miles in 45 minutes, moving the gradient up and then down again.

The tedium was relieved this morning by a call from Alan Birchenall, Leicester City's 'character in chief'. You have to go to the Walkers Stadium (and formerly to Filbert Street) to appreciate 'Birch' and his special brand of humour, delivered before the game and at half-time on the pitch microphone. Today he recorded a telephone interview, to be used in the club programme prior to my visit to Leicester for November's sportsmen's lunch.

Birch was playing in the Leicester forward line when I started my television career, and to remind him just how long ago that was, I point out that 13 managers have come and gone at the club in that period. The first one I came across, Jimmy Bloomfield, was in charge when Leicester played non-league Leatherhead in the fourth round of the FA Cup in 1975. Birch and his first-division boys found themselves two goals down – Chris Kelly, nicknamed 'the Leatherhead Lip' scored one of them – before recovering to win 3–2.

The smile Birch brought to my face this morning disappeared later in the day when my Harley Street doctor, John Newman, told me my blood pressure and cholesterol level were a bit too high.

John has looked after me for over 20 years – he was formerly a BBC staff doctor – and this was the first time he had had to give me what is now known as a 'wake up call'.

I had to starve for 24 hours before the test, and when I came out of his surgery I was so desperate I went straight into Burger King and ate a cheeseburger. Not what he had in mind.

Before going home to watch the Rangers v Manchester United match, I called in to see my agent, Jane Morgan, and bumped into Desmond Lynam. While I had been on the wrong end of the 'Newman needle', they had enjoyed a Variety Club lunch.

Des cheered me up with a glass of champagne, and said he was helping chairman Dick Knight to find the right man to manage Brighton. They had targeted Iain Dowie at Oldham and Des asked me what I thought.

Dowie used to be a near neighbour of mine but that wasn't why I said, 'If you can get him, look no further.'

THURSDAY, OCTOBER 23RD

Things have turned against Ray Graydon at Bristol Rovers since I was down there less than four weeks ago. A couple of bad home results have led Geoff Dunford, the chairman, to ask for Ray's resignation. But there is an argument over compensation and Dunford's quote was eye-catching: 'I won't support paying off a manager for being unsuccessful. The club can't afford it.'

The League Managers' Association work hard at implementing a criteria for compensation when managers are sacked, and at third-division level they are not on fortunes either. However, some of the pay-offs to the big boys can run into hundreds of thousands and it makes you wonder whether their huge salaries should be linked to performance. As the man who supplies my car says, 'It's the only job I know where you get paid for failing.'

Tonight it was back to school. My good friend Dave Carr, an ardent Huddersfield Town supporter, has installed a new ICT Suite at Broadfield Junior School in Hemel Hempstead and has asked me to cut the ribbon at the opening ceremony. Not that the parents and guests who helped to raise funds for the project need know, but I am probably the most inappropriate candidate for the job. I dare not tell them I have never got to grips with a word processor and am still hacking away on a portable typewriter. How else would this book get written?

FRIDAY, OCTOBER 24TH

Twenty-four hours is a long time in football, and the news today is that Ray Graydon is not leaving Bristol Rovers after all. 'Things are tough at the moment, but I never give in,' was his reaction to yesterday's reports. A lot may depend on how Rovers fare at high-flying Oxford tomorrow.

Curiously, it was when he was a coach at Oxford that Ray and I first met. Prior to that, he was flying down the right wing at Aston Villa when I started working for *Match of the Day* in the early seventies. At the same time, Peter Lorimer was playing in the same position for Don Revie's Leeds

United. Armed with the hardest shot in football, Peter became Leeds' all-time top scorer, and now hosts a Friday night football chat show on BBC Radio Leeds. He got me on the telephone at our local pub, The Hollybush, this evening, to chat about my visit to Huddersfield tomorrow. The Alfred McAlpine Stadium, just a few hundred yards from Town's old ground on Leeds Road, is another I have never visited.

'It's bitterly cold up here,' Peter told me. 'You had better bring your sheepskin coat.'

Normally it doesn't come out of the wardrobe until November, but that's only a week away and we put the clocks back this weekend, so in the back of the car it goes.

After the interview I returned to my Friday night ritual of reading the weekend football preview in the London *Evening Standard*. I am growing increasingly impressed by the pungent column written by the sometimes maligned David Mellor. He has a fearless way of facing up to the unacceptable side of the game and pushes as far as he can up to the frontiers of libel law, by taking on issues such as the Rio Ferdinand case and the need for an independent regulator in football. With all that's going on at present, hard opinion like this will do no harm.

SATURDAY, OCTOBER 25TH

You hear a lot about bust-ups in the tunnel and I was a few feet away from being involved in one today. As the players came off at half-time with Huddersfield leading Carlisle 2–0, Denis Law and I were waiting to go on to the pitch for half-time presentations. Carlisle's centre-forward Ritchie Foran had caught Huddersfield's Efe Sodje with his arm on the side of the head in the first half, and as the teams left the pitch words were exchanged between Foran and the Huddersfield manager, Peter Jackson. Foran then pushed Jackson, and other players joined in the mêlée. Brian Curson, the referee, was last off the pitch and some way behind the scuffle. One of the club staff grabbed the emergency telephone and within a few seconds two burly policemen arrived on the scene.

While Denis and I marched on to fulfil our duties – he was promoting his new book *The King* on the ground where his career started – Mr Curson showed a red card to Foran and Huddersfield's Steve Yates. Fred Robinson, a former Town player who now runs the hospitality suites, took me into the sponsors' lounge so that I could give them a first-hand account of what I had just seen. At least they knew only to expect ten-a-side in the second half!

That apart, it was a splendid day. Huddersfield seemed the best organised of all the clubs I had visited, quite a compliment to chief executive Andrew Watson and his staff, bearing in mind they had only come out of administration on the eve of the season. I was able to make a special presentation on behalf of Nationwide to Bill Exley, who had worked for the club as long as anybody could remember. And it was good to meet Bob Pepper, whose work for the survival trust had helped Huddersfield from going out of business.

Down in the boardroom, owner Ken Davy had just watched the draw for the first round of the FA Cup. Huddersfield have been drawn away to Accrington Stanley, and I told him this could mean live TV coverage and a fee of £50,000.

In Peter Jackson's office I had a beer with Terry Yorath, now Peter's assistant, who I knew in those early Leeds days with Peter Lorimer and company. Terry was often 12th man in that great company when I was just starting with the BBC. More often than not he would tip me the wink about team changes. 'Good job Revie never knew,' he joked as we said goodbye.

It will be an uphill task for Peter and Terry to steer Huddersfield to former glories. Crowds of 9,000 in that super 25,000-seater stadium are not going to pay the bills, but it is often the soul and spirit at a football club that dictates its fortunes, and I came away thinking the McAlpine had no fears on that score.

SUNDAY, OCTOBER 26TH

I stayed the night in Huddersfield with the family of a friend of mine, Rob Jepson, who had done the Great North Run with me two years ago. He was a bit late with his entry and I managed to get him a wild card. Rob's sister Helen was one of Huddersfield's sporting heroines, having swum for Great Britain and won a swimming scholarship to an American university.

His mother Margaret cooked us a lovely dinner last night and this morning we watched a recording of *The Premiership* and read the Sunday papers. When I got home, Angus Loughran's Champions League guide for the new season was awaiting me – more than 400 pages of statistics and pen pictures together with a complete history of the competition. Angus doesn't do things by halves.

Anything I say about the Champions League lays me open to accusations of bias, because BBC television has never had that contract, and I have never commentated on a single match in that competition. But I do find myself in sympathy with the view of Portsmouth manager Harry Redknapp, who in his newspaper column this weekend called the Champions League 'a disaster – overhyped and overcooked. With the top two teams going through and a seeding system, it's all very cosy for the top teams in Europe. Crowds of 12 to 15 thousand are turning up at clubs like Juventus for group games.'

I agree with Harry's views on the group system, but fortunately UEFA have already scrapped the second group stage and we shall have straight knockout from the round of the last sixteen. Then it will be more like the European Cup used to be – when it was for Champions only.

MONDAY, OCTOBER 27TH

It's half-term week, and the Motson family are going in different directions. Mrs Motson is visiting her mother and sister, Fred is spending time with his girlfriend and his mates, while yours truly is taking a break from football in order to attend the first National Hunt meeting of the season at Cheltenham.

A gentle, two-hour drive into the Cotswolds brings me to the Dormy House at Broadway, my favourite hotel since I was introduced there by Bob Sims, one of our racing syndicate and the central figure in the Earth Summit partnership which won the Grand National in 1998.

This evening I spent a convivial couple of hours over two pints (or was it three?) with Jon Champion, a former BBC colleague of mine who now works on *The Premiership* and Champions League as a commentator for ITV. Jon has moved to Gloucestershire recently and lives about ten minutes from the hotel. Despite now working for rival channels, we have always shared a common approach to the job and we cover a lot of ground on subjects connected to football and television. My satisfaction in telling him I now have only four grounds left to visit in 'Motty's Mission' is tempered by the sacking this weekend of David Moss, who I met at Macclesfield just a few weeks back. What did I say about managers and October?

TUESDAY, OCTOBER 28TH

M y parking spot at the racecourse was directly behind Tony McCoy's sponsored car, and moments later the man himself appeared. Once I got him off the subject of Arsenal's current form, he told me his best ride of the day was Puntal in the second race. I duly backed it, and he duly won.

More profitable was my wager on Un Jour à Vassy, which won at 5 to 1, and all told I came off the course in front, a decent day's work for a modest punter.

Our own trainer Nigel Twiston-Davies also saddled a winner, Ollie Magern in the first race, and invited me to join Bob Sims and him at The Hollow Bottom in Guiting Power, a well-known hostelry frequented by racing people. Ian Robinson, who I had last seen on the trip to Darlington and Hartlepool before the Great North Run, joined me at The Dormy House and we took a taxi to Nigel's haunt.

The stables were quietly satisfied by Ollie Magern's performance, but the real celebrations among trainers and their staff were reserved for the pouring rain, which rattled against the windows. For weeks the dry weather has slowed down the start of the jump season proper. Owners and trainers have been reluctant to risk their horses on the hard ground, but as soon as it gets softer the fields will increase and the better horses will come out of the yard and on to the track. Which means we shall probably see more competitive fields tomorrow, on the second day of the meeting, than we did today.

WEDNESDAY, OCTOBER 29TH

W e went down to Nigel's yard at Naunton first thing this morning, to see our horses work out on the gallops. I am part of three seven-handed syndicates, with different partners in each. Our newest acquisition is a tiny four-year-old called Henry The Great, whose sire was the famed Alderbrook. Actually, our syndicate organiser Nigel Payne, one of racing's leading public relations men, prefers to pronounce it 'Henri' The Great, because he insisted on naming the horse after Arsenal's French centre-forward. Nigel is a committed 'Gooner' and follows them home and away.

Anyway, the stable head lad Fergal tells me that Henry will be ready to make his racecourse debut in about three weeks, first in a bumper (a flat race) and then over hurdles.

Corroboree, our six-year-old in which some friends from the North have a share, won a conditional jockeys' race at Kempton Park last autumn, but a week later injured a tendon when three horses came down in front of him. He is now ready to go again, maybe having one race over hurdles before moving up and over fences.

Polar Summit, no relation to Earth Summit, but owned by nearly the same partnership plus this writer, has been out injured for nearly two years. Watching him work this morning reminded us all of what a big horse he is – more than 17 hands. At seven he is the oldest of our 'string' and hopefully he will be back over those big fences soon.

All three looked in good shape on Twiston-Davies's new gallop which was laid down in July. It is a faster surface than the old one, with a more gradual gradient, enabling the horses to go quicker. Ian Robinson, who drove me down, was pleased to see his horse Bobby Dazzler looking lively too. This is a time of keen anticipation and guarded optimism for jump owners – you look forward to the season but you don't know quite what's round the corner.

A bit like football, I suppose. But the racing people don't want to talk about that, which is why the horses are such a welcome release for me.

THURSDAY, OCTOBER 30TH

But I still couldn't keep away. Just when yesterday looked like winding down on the racecourse, I realised that Cheltenham Town were playing a low-key Gloucestershire County Cup tie against Bristol City at nearby Whaddon Road, one of the grounds I still had to visit.

There were only a handful of spectators, a referee in Clive Wilkes who had come out of retirement, and hardly anybody in the boardroom. But I was well looked after by Paul Godfrey, the club secretary, who put me to shame when he revealed he had only one ground to go before completing the 92.

Having parted company with Bobby Gould, Cheltenham are drawing up a shortlist of possible new managers. Bob Bloomer, a former player and now a coach at the club, is there in an acting capacity, but seemed to have all the enthusiasm you might need at this level.

There was also an unexpected reunion with Andy King, now manager at Swindon Town, and scorer of one of the most famous goals of the seventies, when Everton beat Liverpool for the first time in ages.

So the night dragged on a bit, and today I drove home from the Cotswolds after a slow early morning run. The weather was beautifully autumnal down there, and I am glad I am going back for a flying visit in two weeks' time.

FRIDAY, OCTOBER 31ST

My near-neighbour Robert Murphy, who is getting two of my commentary boards framed for auction, was in the hairdresser's when I rang his mobile early this morning. Apparently he goes to a young lady in nearby Redbourn for his haircut, and wanted to know where I go for my trim and shampoo. When I told him Finchley, he nearly dropped the phone. Admittedly, it is 40 minutes' drive from where we live, but he didn't appreciate that I have been going to the same old-fashioned barber for the last 30 years. Not that the present owner Steve, who bought the business from his predecessor Philip 12 years ago, would appreciate that description. 'Men's Salon' it says on the door, and he can cut and shape with the best of them.

Old habits die hard, and having got used to the place when I lived in Finchley in the early seventies, I still feel comfortable there. 'Not that the £9 Steve charges has anything to do with it,' said Robert wryly.

It's much the same story with Christine Palmer, the chartered physiotherapist I have got to know well as a semi-regular patient over the last few years. If it hadn't been for Christine, I probably wouldn't still be running – I have lost count of the number of minor knocks and strains she has treated.

Christine gave me a good half-hour of ultra-sound and laser treatment today, ironing out the referral pain still emanating from the facet joint in my back. But I don't need to drive to Finchley to find her. She practises from her house at the top of our road.

NOVEMBER

SATURDAY, NOVEMBER 1ST

Going to two football matches in one day is not something I would attempt as a general rule, but the opportunity fell quite conveniently today.

As part of 'Motty's Mission' to visit all 92 grounds in the league, I had been waiting for the opportunity to experience at first hand Wimbledon's new surroundings at Milton Keynes. Their home match with Bradford had been selected for Sky TV coverage with a 5.35pm kick-off, so rather than kick my heels all afternoon, I decided to take in the Watford v Rotherham fixture, in the same division, with a traditional three o' clock start.

Living just a few miles away, I have been going to Vicarage Road for some 25 years, witnessing at first hand the job Graham Taylor and Elton John did in putting Watford on the map in the late seventies and early eighties. Three sides of the ground have been impressively developed since then, but the quaint 'old' stand is a reminder that Watford's flirtation with Gianluca Vialli, after their relegation from the Premiership, proved so costly that Taylor's pledge not to mortgage the club's future, in his second spell there, has been consigned to history.

The financial crisis gripping Wimbledon is more acute still. Having negotiated ten roundabouts to locate the National Hockey Stadium, where the welcome from the car park attendants must be the warmest from any of their normally suspicious breed, I found most of the faces in the tea room unrecognisable from the jolly crew who used to live the dream at Plough Lane and later at Selhurst Park.

Rather like Watford, the Dons have had their unforgettable moment in the sun and are now feeling the cold draught of financial reality in the Nationwide League. The club is in administration and patently unsure of its future. Peter Winkelman, the music promoter trying to relocate the club to a new site on the other side of the town, struck me as genuinely enthusiastic, as were the crowd of just over three thousand. But whether Wimbledon can improve on that fan base, and quieten the critics who see this as an unacceptable form of football franchise, is another matter.

In the meantime, those who stayed behind in south-west London to form AFC Wimbledon, can point to attendances not much lower. Much of the club's genuine support has chosen not to travel 60 miles from home.

The romantic in me regrets the day Sam Hammam sold the club to Norwegian businessmen. They still haven't built a supermarket on the Plough Lane stadium he also sold, and sadly his premise that the London Borough of Merton did not want to encourage or support a then successful Premiership team appears to be the bottom line below which Wimbledon, in their original form, may not survive.

SUNDAY, NOVEMBER 2ND

Embarrassing to admit this, but I made the *News of the World* today. 'Ned' Kelly, formerly the head of security at Manchester United, is writing his memoirs, having enjoyed privileged access to the inner sanctums of Old Trafford over several years of Alex Ferguson's reign.

In addition to his memories of secret doings in the boardroom, Kelly recalls the dressing room banter about the size of Dion Dublin's manhood, and to my amazement suggests Dion and I had something in common. This was based on a story from the changing rooms in the days of the commentators' charity football team, which has since ceased to exist and where my punitive efforts on the field are a good ten years old.

Having taken some good-natured ribbing over the story today, I was reminded of another Kelly *News of the World* connection from three years ago. Ned was good enough to phone me one day and warn me that the Sunday paper had got its hands on a photograph of yours truly embracing a blonde girl in a night club. It transpired a photograph of me with Rick George and his wife Pat had been taken at the launch of a website at a trendy bar in London, which normally I would not have even heard of, never mind frequented.

It wasn't the first time in my life I had hugged Pat and it probably won't be the last, since Rick and I have known each other for 40 years.

Once the facts were established, the newspaper elected not to use the picture. Pat took the story in good part, and knowing Dion Dublin quite well, I would imagine he would react the same way to today's nonsense. We haven't got much choice.

MONDAY, NOVEMBER 3RD

It's still nine months away, but everybody at the BBC is looking forward to the return of *Match of the Day*, and from my travels around the country I get the impression that goes for a lot of viewers as well. This is not to detract from *The Premiership*, where I think ITV's editorial standards and match coverage have been fine, but there is something about football highlights and advertising breaks that somehow doesn't cut the mustard. Maybe it is to do with heritage and tradition. After all, *Match of the Day* started in 1964, so when it returns in its Saturday night format next season, the programme will be 40 years old.

Charged with conducting a table quiz at the football department lunch before Christmas, I have counted twelve different presenters of the programme between Kenneth Wolstenholme, who introduced the first show from the pitch at Anfield, and current host Gary Lineker. Over a glass of wine today, Head of Football Niall Sloane and I racked our brains to see if we could think of anybody else who had sat in the presenter's chair (no, I was never a studio host myself) before we tried it out on the rest of the team.

One man who certainly figures on the list is Bob Wilson, whose 20 years as the face of *Football Focus* meant he often occupied the *Match of the Day* chair as well. Bob's publishers today sent me a copy of his new autobiography *Behind the Network*, and a very good read it is too.

TUESDAY NOVEMBER 4TH

Mark Pougatch has made a name for himself as the vibrant presenter of *Sport on Five* on a Saturday afternoon, and has now started to make the breakthrough into television. Young, bright and modern are three adjectives that come to mind where Mark is concerned, and he certainly opened my eyes today when he took me to lunch with the Sporting Statz company, who publish the OPTA index which covers just about everything that happens in a football match.

These are the boffins who come up with who has the most shots at goal, who makes the most accurate passes, which side of the pitch most attacks develop and many more details which break a game down into computer-style analysis. Aidan Cooney, the Managing Director, wanted an honest opinion as to how useful this sort of analysis would be to commentators. I told him I thought that part of what they do is so technical that it becomes almost obscure, whereas the more simple, undiluted facts and figures would save people like me a lot of research.

Being older and set in my ways, and having been a disciple of Albert Sewell's match notes for many years, I should not speak on behalf of the younger commentators. Most of them work off computers while I am still carrying around a zip-up pencil case full of felt tip pens.

WEDNESDAY, NOVEMBER 5TH

After nearly a year off the course injured, Corroboree ran again today at Kempton Park – and won exactly the same race as he did last year. The main difference, from my point of view, was that this time I was there to see it. Twelve months ago, the rest of the syndicate had celebrated victory while I was speaking at a lunch for Derbyshire County Cricket Club. Collecting the money from a winning bet was no substitute for watching the race at first hand.

Today it was a big thrill to see Robert Biddlecombe hold on to win after leading nearly the whole two miles four furlongs. The horse jumped quite beautifully and Nigel Twiston-Davies is anxious to move him up from hurdles to fences.

Four members of our seven-strong partnership were in the winners' enclosure, and all of us had some pound coins to count as well as collecting a small trophy, a video of the race, and complimentary champagne.

Corroboree needed a couple of routine stitches in a small leg wound afterwards, but otherwise was fit and well and should be running again in two or three weeks. The firm ground means the fields are still quite small and trainers and owners are again praying for some rain. Hopefully it won't be long before Polar Summit and Henry the Great are entered for their first race of the season, but it may be too optimistic to expect another winner so soon.

THURSDAY, NOVEMBER 6TH

Events on the field have been overshadowed again by lurid headlines concerning the behaviour of certain footballers, and Rio Ferdinand's failure to report for a drugs test at Manchester United's training ground has developed into a seven-week saga.

After leaving Ferdinand out of the match in Turkey, the Football Association has charged him with 'wilfully' missing the test. His defence, supported by his club, is that he forgot, and left the scene before phoning in later and eventually taking a test two days afterwards.

The episode also represents a different sort of test for the FA's new chief executive Mark Palios, who has taken office on a mandate to enforce discipline and streamline the association's dreadfully drawn-out procedures when it comes to dealing with offenders. I can see a clash ahead between Palios and Gordon Taylor, the highly paid chief executive of the PFA, who wields a significant amount of power and influence in the game. Throw in a few lawyers, agents and managers with an agenda, and the landscape becomes very clouded. But the image and reputation of the game has to be protected, or else standards will slip even further.

I am not referring directly to Ferdinand or Manchester United, but certain people in football have got away with too much for too long. The FA must stand their ground and enforce their authority, however unpalatable some of the publicity may be.

FRIDAY, NOVEMBER 7TH

It was the jockey Carl Llewellyn who first introduced me to the Institute of Well Being, a health clinic in West London headed up by managing director Maitland Cook. I went there a couple of years ago for a food allergy test, which revealed I was susceptible to nuts and pineapple, neither of which appeals to me anyway.

After the cholesterol warning from John Newman and the continual irritation in my lower back when I run, I had two appointments in one morning. They think my pace of life and attendant stress may have led to the cholesterol problem, so I came away with four little bottles for a saliva test. For a moment, all this current talk of illegal substances makes me wonder what they might discover.

The pain in my rear remains a bit of a mystery, but a prescription for a powerful cream to apply before running is just another route to go down. One thing's for sure, I'm not likely to go back on my decision about the Great North Run. I received a complimentary video of this year's race today, with a note attached from Nova International thanking me for my support. I think Brendan has got the message. And I certainly have.

SATURDAY, NOVEMBER 8TH

Saturdays will soon be occupied by FA Cup business, so this will be the last chance I get to take Fred to Pride Park to watch Derby. He usually gets the train, so it makes a change for his journey to be that bit easier, even though we part company in the car park. He goes to his seat in the south-east corner, where as a season ticket holder he can shout and sing as much as he likes, while I find myself being introduced to the club's new owners.

John Sleightholme's consortium has taken over from original owner Lionel Pickering, and there is talk of Derby's debt of some £30 million having been halved by the new investors. Today's opponents are Ipswich who know all about a cash crisis. However, their directors have remained in place throughout a painful period in administration, which has cost the club several of their better players, and are trying to pave the way for a new share issue.

It's a far cry from the heady heights when they finished fifth in the Premiership less than three years ago, although the Ipswich debt and fall from grace is not as catastrophic as that of Leeds United, whose latest figures almost defy belief.

The Derby v Ipswich fixture was the last one I covered before *Match of the Day* lost the Premiership contract in 2001. Seeing the two teams again today, hardly any of the players were the same. Established stars have been replaced by scarcely tried youngsters and loan players, after both clubs were relegated the following season. They receive the 'parachute' payment to soften the financial blow for two seasons, but if they fail to win promotion this time round it will disappear and there will have to be more belt-tightening. For Derby, managed ironically enough by the former Ipswich boss George Burley, a return to the Premiership looks some way off. They led 2–0 today, but Ipswich forced a 2–2 draw.

SUNDAY NOVEMBER 9TH

However much preparation you put in as a commentator, events on the day and last-minute changes can make a mockery of some of the homework, and prompt a lot of eleventh-hour scribbling in the press room.

I arrived at Stamford Bridge today – my first visit since the 'Russian revolution' – with what I thought was a clear picture of the likely line-ups for Chelsea and Newcastle. Both had obtained good results in Europe – Ranieri's team whipped his old club Lazio 4–0 – and changes would be few and far between, even for 'the Tinkerman'.

As it turned out, it was Newcastle who sprang a surprise, not of their own making. Alan Shearer, with nine Premiership goals to his credit already this season, went down with a throat infection. It was lunchtime before Bobby Robson ruled him out and put Hugo Viana in the team to play behind Shola Ameobi. Any commentator will tell you that the numbers on Newcastle's striped shirts are a nightmare, so losing such a familiar figure as Shearer can make identification even more hazardous.

As for Chelsea, Ranieri came out of the dressing room to tell me the team was unchanged. The Tinkerman had decided to stop tinkering for once, and it was the meticulous Rob Hawthorne, working for Sky Sports, who quickly referred to his record book and confirmed it was the first time since March that Ranieri had left his line-up alone.

Simon Brotherton was my co-commentator, and as we made for the heady heights of the Chelsea gantry with summariser Graham Taylor, he volunteered to start the match and allow me to take the second period of each half. It wasn't the best decision Simon has ever made on his own account. The first 20 minutes passed uneventfully, Graham and Simon telling Five Live listeners that the match just hadn't caught fire. When I took over, things changed. Chelsea scored three times in 17 minutes and Newcastle had Andy O'Brien contentiously sent off. It goes like that sometimes, and it's only when you do radio, as opposed to being the sole television commentator, that you realise the two-man formula means you are effectively silent for half the game.

The producer assured me that Simon is not as worried as one or two others about who 'gets the goals'. Which is a good thing really, because the second half followed a familiar pattern. The score was still 3–0 when he handed back to me, whereupon Chelsea scored twice more.

Graham Taylor had a good natured chuckle at all this, not knowing that

Simon was once a near neighbour of mine and kindly allowed my son Fred to broadcast from his house into the *Wright and Bright* programme on a Saturday morning on Five Live.

Anyway, when *Match of the Day* comes back next season, Simon will be doing some television commentaries and then all the goals will be his to describe. He is a fine young broadcaster and is sure to get lots of opportunity in the future.

MONDAY, NOVEMBER 10TH

Sven Goran Eriksson told me when we talked at Fulham a few weeks ago that changes and additions to his England squad would now be few and far between. The 27 or so players he was currently naming were simply the best available. His squad for the friendly against Denmark was announced today, and with six or seven of the regulars unavailable for one reason or another, there was a recall for Charlton's Scott Parker – an unused substitute earlier in the year – and a call-up for Chelsea's young right-back Glen Johnson, who scored against Newcastle yesterday. Jermaine Jenas, who had been on the other end of that 5–0 scoreline, was also included after coming on three times as a substitute for Eriksson.

But the frustration of not being able to get his best team on the pitch continues to haunt the England coach. No Campbell, Ferdinand or Woodgate in defence, no Scholes in midfield, no Owen up front. To make matters worse, Steven Gerrard had to withdraw after the squad was named, so with Kieron Dyer and one or two others still injured as well, half of last year's World Cup team are missing.

Denmark will be desperate to lay to rest the memory of their miserable performance against England in Japan, and they have named a squad with all their front-line players. The early bookmakers' prices for next Sunday's friendly offer Denmark at a generous 9 to 2. Could be worth a bet, because we all know that Sven sees friendlies as an opportunity to change the team at half-time.

TUESDAY, NOVEMBER 11TH

Fifty years ago this month, as an eight-year-old attending Ennersdale Primary School in Hither Green, south-east London, I came home early one afternoon to watch the next door neighbour's television. My family did not get its own set until three years later, so when they showed a football match – not very often in those days of early black and white coverage – we had to find a friend with a nine-inch screen.

The news from Wembley that misty November afternoon was grim. England were 4–2 down at half-time against the Hungarian Olympic champions captained by Ferenc Puskas.

We watched the second half in awe as Hungary ran out winners by six goals to three, and today I flew to Newcastle to watch a re-run of the match with Sir Bobby Robson, who was in the crowd at Wembley in 1953 when he was a young professional playing for Fulham. Robson was typically eloquent and passionate as he recalled what an impact that defeat had on English football. The interview we recorded will be shown on *Football Focus* in two weeks' time, to mark the anniversary of the match.

I also recorded Robson's reaction to his forthcoming induction as a manager in the Hall of Fame at the National Football Museum in Preston. He is in good company; Herbert Chapman, Stan Cullis and Bill Nicholson are the three other giants being honoured this coming weekend.

It was stimulating as always to be in Robson's company. I first met him at Ipswich when he had just taken over in 1969, and I was a young radio reporter. He has been a joy to work with ever since.

WEDNESDAY, NOVEMBER 12TH

Matt Le Tissier rang from Southampton today. He and his former colleague, Francis Benali, have set up a website swapping football gossip, and he wanted to know if the *News of the World* story had any truth in it.

'You probably want to say no comment at all,' he laughed. 'Exactly,' I replied, and he merrily went on his way after promising to buy me a drink when I next go to St Mary's. Matt was always one of the most approachable players we dealt with, and now entertains corporate guests on a match day. A popular host for sure.

On a more serious note, there are now 214 days to go to the start of

Euro 2004 in Portugal. Ten stadiums, 16 teams, 352 nominated players when the time comes – most of whom I shall be expected to recognise with or without their shirt number. This is the background work commentators spend most of their time on, and which the viewer doesn't see or indeed need to know about. After all, I don't worry about how the milkman gets my morning pint to me, and I have no idea what is involved in delivering the post. As long as such things arrive on time and intact, we take the service for granted. It's much the same with television – the viewers are only concerned with the end product, not how the programme was put together and who agonised over what.

As usual, I have a cupboard for video tapes of all the teams, which is gradually filling up. Even more so this coming weekend, when the play-offs will be covered by a variety of channels, offering coverage of a further five teams who will join the ten nations already qualified, and hosts Portugal, in the finals next June.

THURSDAY, NOVEMBER 13TH

Had things worked out differently, I would have been going to Latvia today. All year long we were geared up for the possibility of England being in the Euro 2004 play-offs this coming week, but that draw in Turkey means a welcome change of direction – instead it will be Old Trafford and a friendly against fellow group winners Denmark.

The built-in bonus for me is that I can now snatch one day's racing at Cheltenham, where the three-day November meeting featuring the Paddy Power Gold Cup marks the proper start of the jump season. We don't get as much time together as a family as I would like, so it's doubly rewarding to be able to take Anne and Fred to the Dormy House Hotel for a couple of nights.

Soon after we arrived, Jon Champion picked us up and took us out to dinner at his local pub, The Churchill Arms in the Cotswold village of Paxford. Jon had also invited Bryan Richardson, the former chairman of Coventry City, who lives nearby. Bryan's brother Peter was England's opening batsman with Colin Cowdrey when I used to follow cricket as a schoolboy, so for once the conversation did not revolve around football. We agreed that from tomorrow we would be talking more about rugby. England's World Cup semi-final against France takes place on Sunday morning, and the nation is starting to get so excited they are comparing Clive Woodward, potentially anyway, with Sir Alf Ramsey.

FRIDAY, NOVEMBER 14TH

Twice a year at Cheltenham our two racing partnerships get together. Five members of the Corroboree syndicate and three from Polar Summit set out for the course this morning, having absorbed the *Racing Post* at breakfast time.

On the course we went our separate ways – Anne, Fred and I were guests in the Ladbrokes box – but most of the chaps preferred to stick together and watch from the lawn. When we reassembled in the evening, everybody had managed to pick up a couple of winners so we were in good heart for a rather raucous dinner.

Every year we submit individual lines in the 'Ten to Follow' competition, run nationwide by the *Racing Post*. In our own private contest, the member who collects the fewest points from his four lines over the season has to buy a loser's lunch or dinner for the rest. This year our Scottish representative Terry Williams was in the chair, and no sooner had we sat down than the three younger lads from the North, Al Morris, Dave Neilson and Peter Williams (no relation) suggested we should phone through a few bets on the evening's greyhound racing at Wimbledon.

Now I have been to the dogs at Walthamstow a number of times, but betting on races I cannot see, based purely on trap numbers, is not my idea of a wise investment. Despite a note of caution from the older trio, Bob Sims, Ian Robinson and myself, the table chose to press ahead, and within 45 minutes we had won on all three races. The accumulator brought in no less than £350, whereupon, with the red wine now flowing freely, it was agreed Al would place the whole lot on Corroboree the first time he runs over fences. Are we crazy or what?

SATURDAY, NOVEMBER 15TH

Back to sanity today. Charlie Debono, the football department's regular driver, picked me up at the hotel this morning and whisked me up north, where I decided to take in the Rochdale v Kidderminster match *en route* to our BBC hotel in Manchester. We were just past Knutsford Services on the M6 around noon when I persuaded Charlie to veer off to a nearby hotel, where we commandeered the television in the bar to watch *Football Focus*.

It was a good job we did. The build-up to the England game had centred around an episode involving Alan Smith which, hard on the back of the Rio Ferdinand incident, had caused banner headlines castigating the FA's disciplinary structure – or lack of it.

Smith had been interviewed by the police at two o'clock last Thursday over a bottle throwing incident in a recent match against Manchester United; called up by Sven Goran Eriksson three hours later as a late replacement in the squad; then sent home again at nine o'clock when the FA discovered he might still be facing charges.

Garth Crooks had news of a statement from the players and coaching staff, who were clearly confused and angry about the way the matter had been handled. Mark Palios, the chief executive, was again the target getting the blame. David Beckham said at a later press conference it would be nice to get back to the football, which was exactly how I felt when I moved on to Spotland, home of Rochdale and the last but one of the 92 grounds I still have to visit.

Now Rochdale themselves would admit their recent history has been unspectacular. They were relegated to the old fourth division in 1974, and have played in the bottom league ever since.

Back in 1962 they were losers in only the second Football League Cup final – to Norwich City over two legs – but apart from one promotion from the fourth division to the third in 1969, there hasn't been too much to shout about. There wasn't a lot today, either, in that they lost 1–0 at home to Kidderminster, but as with most of the lower division clubs I have visited, the welcome was warm and genuine.

Manager Alan Buckley, who I first met when he played at Walsall, was also following events in the England camp. 'It would help if all the players behaved properly,' he said with a wry smile. GMR, the BBC local radio station in Manchester, grabbed me for a quick interview on the subject. By now the names of other players who had been interviewed by police, like Nicky Butt over a nightclub incident (later cleared) and James Beattie for a drink-driving offence (long since dealt with), were being dragged into the row over inconsistency. The real irony of all this is that if Aston Villa hadn't chosen to take Darius Vassell to Dubai for a friendly in which he got injured, Alan Smith would never have been called up in the first place.

None of which fazed Rochdale's charming and industrious secretary, Hilary Molyneux-Dearden, as she brought my bags upstairs afterwards having kept them in her office all afternoon. I pointed out that her name was almost aristocratic in the unpretentious surroundings of Rochdale.

'I just put all my husbands on the end,' she said.

Football can be fun after all.

SUNDAY, NOVEMBER 16TH

It's not often that an England football match becomes an afterthought, but it nearly did today. For a start, Scotland and Wales both achieved unexpectedly good results yesterday in the first leg of their play-offs. If either one can finish off the job next Wednesday – against Holland and Russia respectively – what a boost that will be for our Euro 2004 coverage next summer.

More pertinently perhaps, this morning's rugby from Australia gripped all of us. I broke off from my Old Trafford homework to marvel at the kicking of Jonny Wilkinson, as England overcame France to reach next weekend's final. A couple of months ago, when somebody said it hadn't been a great year for sport so far, I placed a bet on Wilkinson at 7 to 1 to be voted BBC Sports Personality of the Year. I have no input into that award, which is solely voted for by viewers, but the way he's going he must stand a decent chance.

Jonny's compatriot in the place-kicking commercial currently doing the rounds, David Beckham, must have been relieved to get back to football when he led England out before a 64,000 crowd at his old stomping ground. Where else in the world would a routine friendly sell out to so many spectators? Trevor Brooking and I got back into the commentary groove after a two-month lapse – 15 substitutes coming on in the course of the 90 minutes tested our mettle.

In that respect, I'll always prefer a competitive match where they can only make a maximum of six changes. Roll on Portugal next June.

MONDAY, NOVEMBER 17TH

Many years ago I was on a panel every Christmas judging the best football book of the year, a competition organised by the Association of Football Statisticians, whose then secretary Ray Spiller used to entertain us in a London hotel where we decided which authors should win prizes. Since then, the prestigious William Hill Sports Book of the Year Award has become something of a Holy Grail for football literature, as well as offerings from other sports.

Behind the Network by Bob Wilson – which I mentioned the other day – is on the shortlist for this year's winners, and a number of other titles have come my way from the publishers in the last few days.

Graham Sharpe, who actually works for William Hill as director of media relations, is too modest to vote for his own work, but I much enjoyed *Free the Manchester United One*, a carefully researched investigation into an alleged match fixing scandal in 1915. Enoch 'Knocker' West of Manchester United, and a number of Liverpool players, were accused of arranging a Good Friday fixture to finish 2–0 in United's favour and thereby help them avoid relegation. West's suspension was not lifted until 30 years later, and Sharpe has gone to some lengths to try to get him a posthumous pardon from the Football Association.

So fashionable has football become that the market is currently flooded with books of all shapes and sizes. Heroes of the recent past like Nobby Stiles, Denis Law and Jimmy Greaves have all been updating their life stories. No need for wives or mothers to worry too much about Christmas presents this year.

TUESDAY, NOVEMBER 18TH

Two London nightspots in one evening – something of a rarity for me, but both invitations had a particular appeal for different reasons. The BBC contributors' party was held in what I am led to believe is now one of London's trendier venues, Sketch, just off Regent Street.

Working exclusively in sport, you don't get too many chances to meet informally with those across the rest of the network, although the music was so loud that it proved difficult to hold a sensible conversation of any length. A gentleman whose name I failed to catch claimed he had composed some music for Radio Three and used my commentary as a background. 'You deliver your words so rhythmically,' he murmured, which was news to me, and even if he had been shouting I don't think I would have grasped quite what he was trying to say.

Peter Salmon, our director of sport, had the right idea. Like me, he had been invited by Comic Relief to a private showing of the new Richard Curtis movie *Love Actually* starring Hugh Grant. So off we went to Whiteleys in Queensway, where half a century ago my late mother used to take me to see Father Christmas. The way the store is set out now, you are quite likely to find him before you reach the cinema, but we got there eventually and I spent an enjoyable evening in the company of my agent, Jane Morgan, and her two able assistants, Sara Alliss and Lucinda Lovelace.

It is a sweet, sentimental film where the ten different love affairs take a bit of following. Rather like most things these days, it could do with being about 20 minutes shorter.

WEDNESDAY, NOVEMBER 19TH

No match for England, so I am in the role of armchair critic with Fred tonight as Wales attempt to beat Russia and Scotland defend their narrow lead in Holland.

First though, I drove over to Totteridge to see my lunch companion Steve Nicholas, who has been literally on his back for a month with a disc problem. It makes my facet joint seem a minor matter. We compared injury notes and decided that our lifestyle, eating and drinking habits, and general lack of discipline, might have contributed to these warning signals from our bodies. Or something like that.

When the football started, Saturday's euphoria disappeared almost at once. Wales and Scotland had their respective limitations exposed – brutally in the case of the Scots who were overwhelmed 6–0 by Holland. The Welsh coach Mark Hughes, whose team never looked like getting the two goals they needed once Russia scored, was non-commital about his future afterwards. But his body language suggested that it would be no surprise to see him resign and take up a club post. Scotland's Bertie Vogts may not have the choice. The size of the defeat means a lot of the support that was beginning to come his way will now evaporate.

Spain and Croatia got through as expected, both winning comfortably away from home, but Latvia kept the dream of the underdog alive with a remarkable comeback in Turkey. Two goals down, they recovered to draw 2–2 and go through on aggregate. So why were we in England so nervous about Turkey? And will they go down as the great over-achievers of the 2002 World Cup?

THURSDAY, NOVEMBER 20TH

In my radio commentary at Chelsea a couple of weeks ago, I made reference to their only League Championship in 1955 without realising that a book I received today, *Stamford Bridge Legends* by David Lane, has just been published to commemorate that achievement. There are 17 chapters, each devoted to one of the players in Ted Drake's squad that won the title in Chelsea's Golden Jubilee year.

Typical of how different the game was then are the recollections of the England outside-left Frank Blunstone, who was doing his National Service at the same time as collecting a First Division Championship medal.

'People talk about how many games the modern-day footballers are forced to play, but at the time I was playing four games a week. I had to play for my depot team, the Southern Command team, the army team, plus Chelsea on a Saturday. Quite often we had a depot match on a Friday after-noon too, less than 24 hours before I was due to be playing in the first division.

'I was being paid one pound eight shillings per week by the army, and another pound by Chelsea, plus six pounds per match – provided I played. There were a number of times I played for Chelsea when I was injured, because I wanted to keep my place and needed the extra six pounds.'

I remember watching Blunstone play in Tommy Docherty's Chelsea side of the early sixties, when my father and I had season tickets at Stamford Bridge. I have always retained some affection for Chelsea, even though the club and the ground are unrecognisable from how they were then. So when my old radio colleague Phil King, whose company produce Chelsea's in-house TV channel, asked me to host one of their regular phone-ins, it had a certain appeal. Mind you, I need to re-read Albert Sewell's original *Chelsea Champions*, published in 1955, to polish up on the club's first 50 years.

FRIDAY, NOVEMBER 21ST

The news that Denis Law, who I met at Huddersfield only a month ago, is suffering from prostate cancer had a poignant ring to it, because I was scheduled to have lunch today with Joe Melling, the vigorous football editor of the *Mail on Sunday*, who has been fighting his own battle against cancer for several months now. Keith Pinner of Arena International was hosting the table, with Vic Wakeling, managing director of Sky Sports, Steve Curry of the *Daily Mail* and myself as guests. Sadly Joe was unable to attend, and although we drank a toast to absent friends and thoroughly enjoyed each other's company, his boisterous presence was much missed.

Boisterous would be as good a word as any to describe the atmosphere in Oxford's Apollo Theatre, where I spent the evening watching Status Quo in concert. Showtime singer Lisa Faye and the group's sound engineer Andy May arranged for me to go backstage and meet Francis Rossi, Rick Parfitt and the rest of the band. It's always a thrill to meet stars you have admired from a distance, especially when they are of your own generation!

After having some photographs taken, we went to the back of the auditorium and watched the show alongside the sound and lighting boys. Quo were on stage for the best part of two hours without a break, and the audience never sat down once. I suppose you could say much the same about crowds at football matches in modern stadiums, where the seats are more or less redundant when the game gets exciting. All in all, with football talk this afternoon, rock 'n' roll tonight and a little red wine along the way, it has been quite a day.

SATURDAY, NOVEMBER 22ND

But it was nothing to compare with the morning after. Never has the nation been gripped by a sporting event in modern times as it was by the Rugby World Cup final between England and Australia. All right, you could argue that some of the football matches I have covered in the World Cup between England and, say, Germany or Argentina, have pulled in massive audiences, but to be cast in the role of viewer and supporter this morning was nothing short of a lifetime privilege. I couldn't help thinking about the betting slip in my office drawer with my wager on Jonny

Wilkinson to be Sports Personality of the Year. After his performance today, who else is there for goodness' sake?

For once football took second place in the news and sports bulletins, and no bad thing either. I took Fred to see Millwall and Derby County battle out a 0–0 draw and, after my references to cancer battles yesterday, was delighted to present a cheque to Millwall's Neil Harris, himself fully recovered from testicular cancer, towards the Everyman Appeal he set up two years ago.

It is always nice to spot a good young player in the making, and the Derby goalkeeper Lee Grant had an outstanding game. Millwall as a club have had to counter an unenviable reputation, and New Cross on a dismal November afternoon certainly won't make the holiday brochures, but the warm welcome I have experienced at so many Nationwide League grounds this season was evident again at The Den. Perhaps they should amend that chant to, 'We are Millwall – and we care'.

SUNDAY, NOVEMBER 23RD

M y first call today came from David Pleat, who knew I was going to White Hart Lane to cover the Tottenham v Aston Villa match for Radio Five Live. He was disturbed over some recent publicity he had been getting from the press, and wanted to get a reply off his chest.

I contacted the *Sport on Five* producer who was delighted to find a slot for a Pleat interview an hour before the kick-off. Not all Premiership managers would make themselves available at that time, so it suited both parties. It also gave me the chance to press David on the direction Spurs are going in to appoint a new manager. It looks as though he will be given the title Sporting Director, and hand first-team affairs over to a coach with a two-year contract – very much the way they do things on the continent.

Pleat insisted they were in no hurry, which led me to conclude that the man they really want is not available at the present time, but he did himself no harm with a couple of second-half substitutions which helped Tottenham to come from behind and win 2–1.

The result left Aston Villa – another club under-achieving for their reputation and tradition – in the bottom three in the Premiership. Their octagenarian chairman Doug Ellis, having sacked his deputy chief executive a few days ago, was preparing himself for some more heavy flak from supporters. 'There are usually 200 demonstrating against me at a home game,' Doug said to me ruefully. 'Next week there will be 2000.'

I'll be able to see that first hand when I go to Villa Park next Saturday.

MONDAY, NOVEMBER 24TH

Fittingly perhaps, I had lunch today with Keith Burkinshaw – the last manager who can claim to have had sustained success at Tottenham. His parting shot when he left after winning the UEFA Cup in 1984 was: 'There used to be a football club here.'

Tottenham under Irving Scholar was the first club to go public on the stock market, but his innovative ideas failed to take off and when Alan Sugar stepped in with Terry Venables in 1991, Spurs were some £20 million in debt and facing financial meltdown.

Twenty years on, Burkinshaw takes no pleasure in seeing the club lose its position in what used to be called 'the big five', but sees football clubs turning themselves into PLCs as a contradiction in terms. When they were privately owned with a low-key board of directors and a manager who was allowed to manage the club on a day-to-day basis, how many times did we hear the words debt, administration or receivership? Yet now many of them have gone public, with chairmen, directors and chief executives taking a large salary in some cases, they seem to have forgotten how to run themselves as a business.

Even clubs who used to pride themselves on their good housekeeping, like Arsenal, Ipswich and West Ham, have succumbed to the shuddering impact of outrageous wages out of proportion to income. Arsene Wenger, asked whether he would be adding to his squad in the January transfer window, was quoted as saying: 'No, because we are bankrupt.' In Arsenal's case, it is the proposed new stadium at Ashburton Grove that has swallowed up all the available finance. Restricted by the size of Highbury, they are speculating to accumulate later. One hopes that they don't get caught out chasing the dream.

TUESDAY, NOVEMBER 25TH

It is exactly 50 years to the day since that pivotal England v Hungary match, but it was another clip of old football footage that flickered across the big screen when I spoke at Leicester City's second sportsmen's lunch at the Walkers Stadium. Nineteen years ago, in the fourth round of the FA Cup, then first division Leicester were trailing Isthmian League Leatherhead by two goals to nil at Filbert Street, before recovering to win 3–2. Chris Kelly, the Leatherhead Lip, could have made the score 3–0 just after half-time. He rounded goalkeeper Mark Wallington and, had Malcolm Munro not cleared off the line, we would have had a cup shock to rival Hereford beating Newcastle three years earlier.

Alan Birchenall, who hosted the lunch, and the question and answer session that followed my short address, was in his usual jovial form. 'Munro was in such a state of shock he left the club that summer, went abroad and was never heard of again. Leicester probably still have his registration.' Birch has never left Leicester. He played in that Leatherhead game, and after retiring came back to front up the club's public relations. He remains more instantly recognisable than many of the current players.

The same could be said of another Leicester hero, former England goalkeeper Gordon Banks, who I met later in the day when I attended Stoke City's first-division match with Crystal Palace. Gordon has been well quoted these last few days over the comparisons between England's last-minute rugby triumph in Australia and the 1966 World Cup final in which he played against West Germany. He regrets there was no commercial spin-off for him and his team, but they still get together for a reunion every year. 'Banksy' will be 66 next month, but looked fit enough for a lot more reunions to come.

WEDNESDAY, NOVEMBER 26TH

Arsenal's 5–1 demolition of Internazionale in the San Siro stadium last night has grabbed the sports headlines back from the rugby boys, at least for today. But the colossal reception Jonny Wilkinson and company received when they returned home – 7000 people at Heathrow at five o'clock in the morning – meant the conversation soon turned back their way when I attended Sir Peter O'Sullevan's annual award lunch at The Savoy in aid of his racing charities.

Brough Scott and the *Racing Post* had kindly invited me to join their table, and Bob 'The Cat' Bevan, whose career as a comedian I played a small part in helping along, was also among the guests. Bob said his friend John Taylor had been hurt by some of the criticism he had received in the press for his commentary on the rugby World Cup final for ITV. Brough promised to drop him a line, and I said they could link me with it – having done the World Cup final five times in my sport, I've been there and know only too well how scary it can be.

On a lighter note, Sir John Mortimer gave a charming, witty speech and the 12 auction lots raised a welcome £89,000 to be distributed among the six welfare charities supported by Sir Peter's Charitable Trust. The special Annual Award went to retired jockey Pat Eddery, who joined the distinguished company of previous recipients including Her Majesty The Queen, the late Queen Elizabeth the Queen Mother, and Lester Piggott.

Nigel Payne, who organised the whole event quite seamlessly, just about had time to tell me our new horse, Henry the Great, would go straight over hurdles in the near future. Meanwhile, the owners and trainers in the warmth of the Savoy again welcomed the downpour in London.

THURSDAY, NOVEMBER 27TH

And still they come, football books of all shapes and sizes. But none better than *Football Days* – 350 pages of classic football photographs by Peter Robinson, who I have bumped into all over the world these last 30 years. With his distinctive style and unprecedented access, Robinson has captured some of the game's most challenging and intimate moments. It would be an injustice to call this a 'coffee table' book – I would never want anything spilt on such a work of art.

On a more literary front came *One Hell of a Season* by Graeme Lloyd, the story of how two Lincolnshire neighbours, Boston United and Lincoln City, faced up to the 2002/03 season, following the collapse of ITV Digital and Boston's four-point deduction for financial irregularities.

Then there were two books for the historian. Jim Brown's *Huddersfield Town – Champions of England* is a well-researched account of the club's three successive championships in the 1920s. It was in that period that Stan Rickaby was born. Now the former West Bromwich Albion and England right-back has marked his forthcoming 80th birthday with his life story – all 220,000 words of it.

Believe me, you could spend 18 hours a day reading football books and the other six watching it on television. No doubt some people do, but I sometimes wonder how much else they're missing. Having said all that, congratulations go to Tom Bower, whose *Broken Dreams – Vanity, Greed and the Souring of British Football* has won the 15th William Hill Sports Book of the Year award. What a pity the Football Association's compliance unit seems unable to act on it.

FRIDAY, NOVEMBER 28TH

Trevor Brooking phoned me before the news hit the headlines. His appointment today as Director of Football Development at the Football Association was almost unique, not just with regard to the job title, but because it showed the FA are moving in a different direction.

I've always felt a connection with Trevor since he scored the winning goal in the 1980 Cup final for West Ham against Arsenal. He remembers it as a rare header; I remember it as a difficult goalscorer to spot in the sunshine as the ball ricocheted across the six-yard box. I went to Upton Park for Trevor's last League game against Everton in 1984, and within five years he was back at Wembley for the FA Cup final, this time as my co-commentator. He has done nearly every one since.

Whether a dual role for Brooking in future will meet with the approval of his new employers and the BBC remains to be seen. We discussed it briefly on the telephone, ruling out his involvement in England matches for obvious reasons, but would there still be a conflict of interests when we cover the FA Cup?

I always resented and rejected the popular image of Brooking as bland and non-commital. His voice and accent sometimes masked the forcefulness of the point he was making, but as chairman of Sport England and acting manager of West Ham, he was perfectly prepared to bang the table and get his point across with passion and self-belief. That non-prejudicial mask could sometimes drop to reveal an inner strength that, forgiving the pun, brooked no argument.

You can see him becoming a powerful presence inside Soho Square, and after the choppy waters the FA have been in recently, they may soon find themselves rowing in the right direction with Brooking as the cox.

SATURDAY, NOVEMBER 29TH

Doug Ellis wasn't wrong when he spoke at Tottenham last Sunday about the demonstration awaiting him at Villa Park today. As he walked past me to his seat in the front row of the directors' box, he could not fail to notice the thousands of placards – mainly at the Holte End where the Villa faithful gather – demanding 'Ellis Out'.

As so often happens in football, the team chose this day to perform as well as they have this season. Dion Dublin's overhead kick – he was playing centre-half and made Man of the Match – won the game for Villa, who would have scored more goals but for the agility of Antti Niemi in the Southampton goal.

The victory took Villa out of the bottom three, but Doug was not entirely comfortable with the three points or with the non-appearance of the placards after the kick-off. 'The police have warned me that the demonstrators may turn up outside my house,' he told me over a drink afterwards.

One seat on the other side of the gangway from his remained vacant today. The death was announced this week, at the age of 85, of Ted Bates, such a loyal and distinguished servant to Southampton Football Club since 1937. In his 66 years at the club, Ted went from player to president, with a sterling spell as manager in between. On a day when Bobby Robson and three more managers were inducted into the Football Hall of Fame, it was a reminder that those who have served the game for so long should never be forgotten. In spite of what some of the Villa fans think, Doug Ellis has no intention of resigning as chairman. He will be 80 in January on the weekend of the FA Cup third round. A good cup run might see a few of those banners disappear.

SUNDAY, NOVEMBER 30TH

I was in the studio this morning with Gary Lineker, Alan Hansen and Peter Schmeichel, to comment on the draw for the Euro 2004 Finals from Lisbon. Live programmes in the studio are not usually my scene, and they keep you on the edge of your seat in a different way to commentary. Until the teams came out of the pots, all the research and notes we had been given amounted to very little, and even when the draw was made it was 'think on your feet' time as we tried to put England's group opponents into context.

The match against France in Lisbon's new Stadium of Light on June 13th is the one everybody will want to see – on which channel we don't yet know and the split between BBC and ITV is going to be closely monitored over the next few days. At this range, Switzerland and Croatia are less formidable opponents, but if the group goes to the wire I can't see England brushing the Croats aside as easily as they did in the August friendly at Ipswich. They were somewhat flattered by the 3–1 scoreline that night.

Running alongside the draw, inevitably, was the ongoing saga over Sven Goran Eriksson's future. The FA's decision to offer him an extended contract until 2008 – made on the same day as they announced the Brooking appointment – could be seen as their way of flushing out the persistent rumours that he is bound for Chelsea after the summer. Eriksson told Garth Crooks in Lisbon that early discussions would take place on the subject. Two other questions remain unanswered: what happens if England fail badly in Portugal, and where do we find his successor?

DECEMBER

MONDAY, DECEMBER 1ST

I have mentioned my friend Roger Ball and the tragic loss of his son, Kester, who was killed in the Hillsborough disaster 15 years ago. Roger himself survived with shock and injuries and the months and years that followed, with the public inquiry, the inquest, and the efforts of support groups to gain legal redress, took their toll on all the families involved.

Three or four times a year Roger, his friend Mike Hide and I get together for lunch. They are Liverpool season ticket holders so the conversation swiftly moves to the Premiership, where they saw Liverpool beat Birmingham at Anfield yesterday.

A few years ago Liverpool would have led the sports pages; a few months ago either Arsenal or Manchester United would have made this morning's headlines. But today it's Chelsea, Chelsea all the way. Just how much of a seminal result yesterday's victory over United was in Chelsea's revolution, only the rest of the season will tell us. The fact is they now lead the championship race, and it could just be a pivotal moment in the season.

Ferguson and Wenger will insist that results in November have little bearing on the outcome of the title, compared to those in March and April, but it was the manner of Chelsea's victory that caught the eye. They have ironed out last season's inconsistent streak, have kept six consecutive clean sheets, and yesterday they took the sting out of the champions' attack for the better part of 90 minutes.

As for Liverpool, I wonder whether they have got the balance right between home and overseas players – something Chelsea also seem to have achieved. Roger says the fans who sit around him believe only three, or at the most four, of the current Liverpool side would have won a place in the great Shankly and Paisley teams of the past.

TUESDAY, DECEMBER 2ND

The only surviving relative on my mother's side of the family is Enid Harrison, my 81-year-old auntie who lives alone in Spalding. We don't see a lot of her these days, although she was a participating guest when I was featured on *This Is Your Life* in 1996 and came to Buckingham Palace with Anne, Fred and me when I received my OBE two years ago.

Every December I drive up to Spalding to take her a box of Christmas presents from our family, and come back with three carrier bags, one for each of us to open on Christmas morning. I always stop off at Stamford on the way back to stay a night at one of my favourite hotels, The George. At this time of year, it is like something off a Christmas card: warm, comfortable and welcoming.

It also gives me a chance to meet up with Dexter Adams and his wife Sheila. They moved north to be nearer their daughters and now live within ten minutes of The George. Dexter was a distinguished England centre-half in the halcyon days of amateur football, playing at Wembley more than once and guesting in the Tottenham first team during friendlies alongside Alf Ramsey and Bill Nicholson. As a manager, he was revered by the players at Barnet – then one of the country's top amateur clubs – and respected throughout the game for his knowledge and integrity.

WEDNESDAY, DECEMBER 3RD

Robert Adcock is joint managing director of Sporting Memorys Worldwide Auctions Ltd, based in Castle Bromwich. They specialise in buying and selling programmes and other football memorabilia. They once sold a replica of a small urinal outside Birmingham City's ground at St Andrew's, but their more serious business is to identify rare and specialist collectors' items which can run into several thousands of pounds.

Robert was at our house today carrying out a detailed valuation of my collection for insurance purposes. I was genuinely surprised at the value of one or two things I had put away years ago and almost forgotten about. For example, the FA Cup semi-final programme in 1915 between Everton and Chelsea at Villa Park is worth more than £1,000; and the first-ever European Cup final programme – Real Madrid v Reims in 1956 – would fetch in excess of £3,000.

By the end of the afternoon, I decided to let Robert take some of my pre-war programmes for his next auction. He also relieved me of about 50 books that were just cluttering up the shelves.

Collectors all over the country and many from abroad receive Robert's and other catalogues on a regular basis. The market in football memorabilia is a vibrant and profitable one. Curiously, I wonder whether the glossy, magazine-style programme published by most clubs today will be as eagerly sought after in years to come as the modest productions from earlier days are now. Somehow, there was a quaintness about them that today's all-singing, all-dancing, 50-page extravaganzas will never replace.

THURSDAY DECEMBER 4TH

Bob Wilson doesn't do anything by halves and never has, so it was no surprise to see him throwing himself so wholeheartedly into the London Football Coaches' Association annual dinner at Highbury tonight. As chairman of this thriving organisation, Bob gets a full house and a powerful top table into his old club's banqueting suite on this night every year. Managers and coaches from the top London clubs usually attend, but the event is really designed for all those full-time or part-time coaches and teachers who spend hours on the playing field improving players of all ages and levels.

Terry Venables was great value in a question and answer session, especially on the subjects of Barcelona, Paul Gascoigne and England in Euro 96. The one thing Terry will never have is a sense of humour failure.

Henry Winter of the *Daily Telegraph* proposed the toast to the guests, and when he had finished the clock was already showing 11.30pm and the main speaker, Bob 'The Cat' Bevan, hadn't even got on to his feet. I hope he wasn't offended when David Pleat and I slipped away into the night. Football dinners invariably overrun, partly because they always start late – a reluctance to sit down on the part of some guests – and usually overload the list of speakers. Not that I can talk. The programme had me listed as a previous guest speaker, and I can't remember a thing about it.

FRIDAY, DECEMBER 5TH

Owning or part owning a racehorse is rather like following your favourite football team – it will send you through the whole range of emotions, from elation to absolute despair.

The joint owners in the Corroboree partnership were hopeful of a second successive win when we assembled at Sandown Park today. After our success over hurdles at Kempton a month ago, we thought he would comfortably cope with his first test over fences. Robert Biddlecombe had Corroboree going nicely round the first circuit, but second time round something was obviously wrong. We were soon to discover the horse had torn a ligament in a hind leg and would be out for the rest of the season – at least.

The rest of the day went by in a bit of a daze. Anne and I drove down to Bournemouth for our first weekend together in our flat overlooking the sea, and I tried to take my mind off the disappointment at the racecourse by starting some homework for Sunday's Five Live commentary at Southampton.

We will know more about Corroboree's state of health once he has been closely inspected by the vet at Naunton. But I fear the news from the yard will not be very good.

SATURDAY, DECEMBER 6TH

The boot was on the other foot this morning. For many years I was able to rely on Lawrie McMenemy to give me an insight into his team and tactics before any number of Southampton games that I covered for *Match of the Day*. Now I had the chance to return the favour. Lawrie phoned to say he was a Sky Sports panellist on tomorrow's Premiership match at St Mary's. He was well up on Southampton (no surprise there) but asked if I could fill him in on a few facts about Charlton.

You would have thought it was All Saints' Day. No sooner had I got to the Fitness First Stadium to watch Bournemouth play Accrington Stanley in the second round of the FA Cup, than Radio Solent grabbed me for a discussion with Alan Ball, a resident studio guest who gives his opinions on Portsmouth, Southampton and Bournemouth as readily as he ran himself into the ground for club and country over 20 years. Peter Phillips, the

Bournemouth chairman, joined the debate, which focused on a World Cup draw that had put England, Wales and Northern Ireland in the same qualifying group for 2006. 'Bring back the home internationals' seemed a popular request.

I was not so sure about the recurring proposal to admit Celtic and Rangers to the Premiership. Alan Ball and I agreed it was a great idea in theory, but littered with snags in practice. What happens about European placings? What sort of security would be needed if thousands of fans were crossing the border every Saturday (and I don't just mean from north to south)? And how would you persuade the present members of the Premiership to give up two more places?

The giant-killers from Accrington belied their part-time status to earn a draw and a replay. Bournemouth's goal was scored by Marcus Browning, a player I have always liked and who, but for injury, would probably have made the top grade.

SUNDAY, DECEMBER 7TH

A new flat means a new running route, and I survived a fierce headwind blowing across the Bournemouth sea front to complete six miles at what can only be described as a leisurely pace. My referred pain is still nagging away at the top of my right leg, but if I stop I may never start again.

The first sign of an anti-Brooking lobby reared its head in the *Sunday Express*. There appear to be a few dissenters in coaching circles who question Trevor's qualifications. Leaving BBC bias aside, I can't figure out where certificates and badges come into this – Brooking has been employed as a policy maker primarily, and putting a long-term plan into place for the benefit of the game at all levels is surely the major part of his brief.

Anne rarely comes to football with me, but today was an exception. She was a guest of Rupert Lowe, the Southampton chairman, while I struggled with those difficult numbers on the red and white stripes in the Radio Five commentary position. It turned out to be one of the most exciting games of the season so far, with Charlton coming back from two goals down before losing to a Brett Ormerod goal (his second) four minutes from time.

Scott Parker scored two beauties for Charlton, and with Sven Goran Eriksson present, made out a case for inclusion in the next England starting line-up. As Charlton chairman Richard Murray suggested, if friendlies are going to serve a useful purpose, why not start with Sven's fringe players or newcomers and give them the greater share of the game, rather than the other way round?

That's all rather academic at the moment. Sven's next match is more than two months away.

MONDAY, DECEMBER 8TH

Hey presto – as they used to say in the boy's annuals – the Christmas lunching season has begun!

The *Match of the Day* Christmas bash doesn't just belong to Alan Hansen, Ray Stubbs, Mark Lawrenson and yours truly – even though we were all there today – but our number now approaches 100 when you consider the editors, producers, technicians, drivers, autocue girls, statisticians and everybody who makes the programme work along the way. They all make a contribution and when you look round the room you realise we are all dependent on each other.

Our organiser Clare Donohoe had this year selected The Embassy Club in Old Burlington Street as our venue, but she had no way of knowing when she booked the event that the England rugby team would be parading the Webb Ellis Trophy through the West End of London on the morning we were due to assemble. But try keeping our lot away from a party. By the time we sat down to lunch, we were quite prepared to believe it was our celebration, as much as it was the rugby boys' who had filled the streets outside. A good joke for the speakers, who added to the entertainment along with a quiz and a few presents to brighten up proceedings.

At some point in the late afternoon (or was it the early evening?) most of the stayers had drifted on to the Strawberry Moon bar in Heddon Street, where I remember having a mumbled conversation with Lee Dixon and Mark Bright before identifying a worried-looking figure at the door. It was my driver. My only defence is that I survived until half-past nine. Our editor Paul Armstrong really lasted the pace; rumour has it he was still there at one in the morning.

TUESDAY, DECEMBER 9TH

I was trying to explain to Ricky George about the team ethic that made yesterday so good – and by definition extends to the spirit that keeps *Match of the Day* on the rails – when he reminded me that we were minutes away from one of the other lively Christmas occasions, the *Daily Telegraph* function at another very plausible West End venue, the Dover Street Wine Bar.

Here, you are privileged to be in the company of Sebastian Coe, Kate Hoey, Colin Montgomerie, Lucinda Green, Graham Taylor and many more. The basis for this lunch is the *Telegraph Sport* supplement – the first of its kind more than a decade ago – which we all read avidly, or at least we do if we care about sport and what goes on around it. I can speak freely since I am not a regular contributor – unlike Rick and most of the others on our table hosted by Keith Perry, the assistant sports editor, who had quietly designed the pages for tomorrow's paper before he started to pour the red wine.

The big story today is that Arsenal seem to have overcome the final hurdle in their financial commitment to a new stadium at Ashburton Grove. Mihir Bose, so often the closest to the inside track on football finance, asked me where I thought that left Tottenham. Exactly where they are, at White Hart Lane, I ventured. Any ground share plan, be it at Wembley or anywhere else in north London, now seems to be history.

Mind you, in football you never know. Nothing is sacred. On the way home I saw an advertisement for a new DVD called *Goalkeeping Nightmares*. It is presented, apparently, by David Seaman.

WEDNESDAY, DECEMBER 10TH

Seaman's old club Arsenal qualified tonight for the second round of the Champions League – some achievement when you consider they had just one point after three games. After referring to Harry Redknapp's views on the competition a few weeks ago, I will be accused of being churlish if I question the merits of a competition for which the BBC does not have a contract. Having said that, I think anyone could have comfortably predicted at the start the names of 14 of the 16 qualifiers from the group stage. You don't need to be an expert to forecast that Manchester United, Real

Madrid, AC Milan, Bayern Munich, Stuttgart, Porto, Celta Vigo, Arsenal, Chelsea, Juventus, Deportivo La Coruna, Monaco, Real Sociedad and Lyon would advance to the knock-out stage.

So what were the six 'match days' about? Money, basically. A device to satisfy the television partners' expensive contracts, irrespective of the size of the crowd in the stadium. Only 12,000 saw Juventus run up a record 7–0 victory tonight.

Having said that, there was immense drama in Celtic's late exit and you can't help getting excited about the next round. When they make the draw on Friday we will be back to a European Cup the way we used to know it.

The highlight of my day was meeting Sir Peter O'Sullevan at a Christmas lunch party hosted by Sunderland's the bookmakers. Would that we could all have the sharpness of mind, sense of humour and courteous nature that Sir Peter retains in his mid-eighties. A broadcasting legend if ever there was one.

THURSDAY, DECEMBER 11TH

After the disappointment of Corroboree last Friday, the return to the racecourse of Polar Summit after two years' absence through injury was something to look forward to.

Until he fell, that is. Our seven-year-old slipped after jumping the penultimate fence on the first circuit of the three-mile Weatherbys Insurance Novices Handicap Chase at Huntingdon. Both horse and jockey Carl Llewellyn survived unscathed, although Polar Summit had to be cornered by his handlers to stop him running out of the course and down the A1(M).

He has now been unplaced in six starts, and Carl says he needs two or three more outings sooner rather than later, to find out whether we should allow him to pursue his racing career.

Better news today was that Fred had survived a severe test of his own – a two-day interview programme at Oxford University where he has applied to study politics. He has already been accepted by five other good universities, so we don't want him to feel any pressure about getting to Oxford.

When he got home he was more concerned about Derby County's new signing. They have arranged a loan deal for the Spanish striker Manel Martinez Fernandez from Espanyol. He will arrive in January until the end of the season and comes with a good goal-scoring pedigree.

The Nationwide League are seeking assurances that they can continue to trade outside the transfer window. Just as critical to the future of club football in this country is the imminent announcement from the European Commission, who have been examining BSkyB's continued dominance of the Premier League broadcast contracts. If they insist on challenging collective bargaining, the game could collapse into crisis.

FRIDAY, DECEMBER 12TH

As Carl Llewellyn said to me yesterday soon after being dismounted by Polar Summit, you need to know your football these days, otherwise you get left out of a lot of conversations. After taking little interest for many years, Carl is now up with the latest results and developments. Today threw up a good example. After all my earlier reservations about the tedious group stage of the Champions League, I am the first to say that the draw for the second round created as much interest as the recent Euro 2004 and World Cup 2006 groupings.

Sky Sports News and Radio Five Live both covered the event at UEFA headquarters – there was plenty of drawn-out pomp and ceremony before Chelsea were paired with Stuttgart, Manchester United with Porto, and Arsenal with Celta Vigo. Because they were all group winners, the three English clubs will play the away leg first.

Half an hour later, Newcastle, Liverpool and Celtic found out their third-round opponents in the UEFA Cup. I fancy all six British clubs to get through, and nearer the February match dates intend to find out what sort of price the bookmakers will offer against that.

The start of the Christmas function period means the pounds start to go on in another sense, and the fitness session with Dean Austin this morning was my hardest yet. Dean consoled me by saying he has doubled the weights I am lifting since we started working together three months ago. All things are relative. I had never so much as picked one up in my life before I started these fitness sessions.

SATURDAY, DECEMBER 13TH

Neville Chamberlain was Prime Minister the last time Queens Park Rangers met Hartlepool, and after today's match in west London, the North East club will probably wish it will be as long before they meet again. Rangers charged into a three-goal lead in no time at all, justifying their position as leaders of division two. They are one of many clubs to have gone in and out of administration, but Ian Holloway has kept the dressing-room morale high throughout, even absorbing the disappointment of defeat at the hands of Cardiff City in last season's play-offs.

My own memories of Loftus Road go back to the early seventies, when Stan Bowles was strutting his stuff and Dave Sexton arrived to develop a team that included Gerry Francis, Don Masson, Frank McLintock and David Webb. Rangers finished second to Liverpool in the old first division in 1976 – the Merseysiders only beat them to the title by winning their final game – and Francis later had two spells as manager, guiding Rangers to fifth place in the first season of the Premier League.

Nick Blackburn, their genial chairman, pointed out that the present side has lost only five games in this calendar year. I enjoyed the atmosphere of a 15,000 crowd in this tight, well-appointed stadium, situated between BBC Television Centre on the one side and the busy flyover of London's Westway on the other.

With the excellent road and underground links, I also find it the easiest of the London grounds to get away from by car, which was particularly helpful today because Anne and I were guests at a 50th birthday party for my agent Jane Morgan. A dinner-dress occasion in the private room at The Ivy was a welcome change from my normal Saturday night routine, which doesn't usually extend beyond a local pub and the Premiership highlights. Des Lynam came armed with the Red Book à la Michael Aspel, to conduct a highly amusing *This is Your Life* on a rare Saturday off for him.

It won't be like that next season for Des. He told me tonight he was definitely retiring from ITV football at the end of Euro 2004. 'I came for three years and stayed for five,' he said. Come to that, it won't be like this for me next season, either. Those long journeys back from Middlesbrough and Newcastle are getting ever nearer.

SUNDAY, DECEMBER 14TH

The BBC Sports Personality of the Year celebrated its 50th birthday tonight, and of those 50 programmes I have been lucky enough to have been in the studio – albeit mainly as a non-participating guest – for at least 30. Her Royal Highness Princess Anne was voted the winner the first time I attended in 1971. The programme then was rather different in format to what it is now – colour television had not long started, and most of the content was a straight, fairly serious review of the sporting year. The present editor, Philip Bernie, has moved the show into the modern era with a bold, imaginative approach which has made it, in my view anyway, less predictable and more entertaining.

What *was* predictable, however, was where the main awards went this year. Our World Cup rugby heroes swept the board, and deservedly so. Quite apart from my own successful wager on Jonny Wilkinson, there were prizes for Clive Woodward, Martin Johnson and the whole team. But what made an even greater impression on me was the way the rugby boys conducted themselves. They seemed as delighted to be there as we were with their performance. No false modesty here, and no semblance of the laddish behaviour which tarnishes the image of football all too often these days.

Our 1971 winner – now known as the Princess Royal – presented Wilkinson with his Sports Personality of the Year award, the first time in 50 years it has gone to a rugby player. Already these boys are back playing for their clubs, and Woodward has them focused on the Six Nations in the new year. Their attitude and behaviour gave the evening a nice warm feel: 'Can we come back next year?' one of them asked.

MONDAY, DECEMBER 15TH

After all I was saying about last night's programme, the reaction of others, both viewers and critics, varied enormously. A lot of people thought there were too many gimmicks, too much light entertainment, too many awards, too many reminders of the voting phone numbers... in short, not enough sport.

Now, I am old enough to remember the way *Sports Review* used to be done. The mandatory five- or six-minute review of the year in the major sports, the pictures dutifully talked over by the appropriate commentator. I voiced the football for many years. In the end that formula became dull and predictable. As I said yesterday, the programme needed an imaginative facelift, but now perhaps the element of surprise needs reining in a bit. Balance is a difficult thing to achieve when you are trying to please ten million people. You only had to walk into a room today and you could easily find three different opinions about the programme.

Desmond Lynam came out publicly, having fronted the show himself 16 times, and suggested they should hire the Royal Albert Hall and invite the public to buy tickets.

My winning ticket was quickly acknowledged by Ladbrokes. That £50 on Jonny Wilkinson in August returned £350 at 7 to 1. Together with another winning bet – I had backed Arsenal to qualify from their Champions League group when they only had one point – meant that the monthly cheque was coming in my direction for once.

But Ally McCoist, with whom I linked up again today on our computer game, is looking even further ahead. He has long-standing wagers on France and Italy to win Euro 2004. Something tells me he will be collecting too, come the summer.

TUESDAY, DECEMBER 16TH

The death earlier this year of television entrepreneur Mike Murphy left a gap in our industry that will never be filled. 'Murf' was a unique character, and his memory was suitably toasted today when the Gentlemen's Lunch, of which he was an integral part was held in west London.

Niall Sloane, one of this year's hosts, memorably described Murphy as the 'unofficial ringmaster' of our business – his views and contacts transversed all channels and made him one of sport's most identifiable media figures. Poignantly, Mike was in the chair for last year's lunch – the last time I saw him – and the empty chair at the table today said a lot about the camaraderie he shared with producers, editors and commentators who made up the party.

Terry Venables, who helped me inaugurate the event 13 years ago, shared many a London rendezvous with Mike and, like the rest of us, often sought his counsel. After lunching at Edera in Holland Park, we adjourned to one of Murphy's favourite haunts, the Windsor Castle in Notting Hill.

Terry, whose late father Fred was a publican, fits comfortably into a scene like this and nobody bothered us as we talked well into the evening.

Niall and his opposite number at ITV, Brian Barwick, were contacted on their mobile phones with the news that Sky have been ordered by the European Commission to release eight Premiership matches for live terrestrial coverage under the new contract. Club chairmen will be relieved. The potential crisis I referred to last Thursday has been averted.

WEDNESDAY, DECEMBER 17TH

Rebecca Lees is the latest in a long line of physiotherapists to lay her tender hands on an unflaterring part of the Motson anatomy. And she believes she can get to grips, in more ways than one, with my ongoing referral pain in the upper part of my right leg.

The referral, in Rebecca's case, came from Health and Fitness Solutions in the City of London, where I was sent by Lester Wilson, the surgeon who originally identified my back problem. Rebecca, who originates from Clitheroe but is married to a Norwegian, practises at the Lister Hospital in Stevenage, half an hour from our house. Her day job there is with the National Health Service, but after hours she finds time to see a selected number of private patients.

Snatching a line from Paul Simon, she confirmed, 'You can call me Becky,' as she gave me the most thorough examination of the many I have had so far. She also gave me two exercises that I must try to make a regular part of my daily routine.

All this is geared towards three running events in the New Year. Although my retirement from half marathons is final, there are a couple of ten-mile runs and a 10k I would like to be fit enough to attempt over the next three months.

We do get locked into our own little world, don't we? Outside it, two major events have dominated the headlines – the arrest of Saddam in Iraq and the Soham murder trial verdict on Ian Huntley and Maxine Carr have consumed more television time and newsprint than I can long remember. For the parents of those poor girls, Jessica and Holly, Christmas can never be the same again.

THURSDAY, DECEMBER 18TH

Memories of that famous FA Cup tie at Hereford were stirred today when I got a call from Colin Addison, who was a young player-manager in the side that knocked out Newcastle. Colin is still a manager – the BBC covered his Forest Green Rovers side in the FA Cup last season – and we have kept in touch with one another ever since our paths first crossed.

Indeed, Colin and his wife Jean have never moved from the house in Hereford where I once stayed with them before a match in the seventies. Their daughters Rachel and Lisa were very small then, but both have grown into smart young ladies and Lisa was after some tickets for the rugby international between our new World Champions and the New Zealand Barbarians. I suggested that Colin contacted our mutual friend Ricky George, whose winning goal propelled Addison's Hereford into the headlines all those years ago. Ricky has a knack of coming up with tickets for big events.

By a curious coincidence, this was also the day when Ricky and I staged our annual Christmas lunch for friends and associates who have helped us in different ways during the year. He was pleased to hear from Colin, who also had better news of Ronnie Radford, who had not been too well. Radford's goal, as Rick would admit, was the turning point in that game and gets played so many times at this point in the season that I keep expecting Newcastle goalkeeper Ian McFaul to save that 35-yard screamer one of these days.

As a surprise present for Rick, I drew up a commentary board for the game (quite what my notes must have been like in 1972 I cannot remember) and had it framed and presented to him at the lunch. Which was all very well, until our taxi home dropped Rick about two miles from his house and he had to carry the cumbersome item along the streets of Barnet at nearly midnight. Just another adventure to add to the many we have shared over the years.

FRIDAY, DECEMBER 19TH

Tony Blair and Rio Ferdinand finished neck and neck in grabbing the evening headlines. The assurances from Libya about dismantling weapons of mass destruction just about edged Ferdinand's eight-month ban for missing his drugs test when it came to the main item on the ten o'clock news. The cynic in me suggests that what Manchester United have called a 'savage' punishment will be reduced on appeal, but for the moment the independent commission appointed by the Football Association have laid down a marker with regard to discipline in general and drug taking in particular.

Despite the reams of newsprint and countless opinions from those not directly involved, there are still a few unanswered questions about this case. What credence did the commission give to Ferdinand's explanation that he genuinely forgot about the test? We await further clarification.

One thing is certain, the underlying feud between the FA and Manchester United shows no sign of abating. Sir Alex Ferguson said before the verdict that whatever happened, Ferdinand would play at Tottenham on Sunday. The fact that the ban does not start until January 12th means he can also take part in the Christmas programme and the third round of the FA Cup. Had the ban started immediately, Ferdinand's eight months would expire in time for him to start next season.

As things stand at present, he will miss the Euro 2004 Finals in Portugal. The whole affair has dragged on far too long and never was there a more urgent need for Brendan Batson and his committee to come up with their recommendations for speeding up the FA's disciplinary procedure. But let this also be a warning that footballers are not a special case when it comes to rules and regulations.

SATURDAY, DECEMBER 20TH

Mark Lawrenson on *Football Focus* echoed my own thoughts about the Ferdinand affair. How do we know precisely what evidence the commission heard, and what interpretation they placed upon it?

Even without that information, everybody today has an opinion. Was the sentence 'draconian', as Gordon Taylor of the PFA maintained? Was it suitable, or was it soft? The *Focus* audience, with hundreds of texts and e-mails, were more or less evenly split between the three. But after all that has been said about speeding up the disciplinary system, it now appears that Manchester United can drag the case on for as long as it takes for an appeal, or more than one appeal, to be heard.

A straw poll among the fans and members of the public I encountered today suggests Ferdinand might have received a lesser sentence had he put his hands up and offered an apology for missing the test, rather than surrounding himself with Manchester United's expensive array of lawyers. Was he best advised?

After all this, it was nice to get back to some football. As long as you weren't going to St Andrews or Molineux that is. The Premiership matches at those grounds were called off because of waterlogged pitches – have we not sorted out how to cope with sudden inclement weather yet, or are referees being too fussy? As I was at Charlton, I have no first-hand view, but it seems a pity that the Premiership and Nationwide programme has now been cut up by postponements that surely could have been avoided.

Torrential rain did not detract from the surface or the entertainment at The Valley, where all that was missing between Charlton and Newcastle was a goal. I went mainly to run my eye over Sir Bobby Robson's team prior to our live FA Cup tie at Southampton in two weeks' time. I was relieved to establish that they would wear a change strip that day – the numbers on striped shirts are still a commentator's nightmare, especially when it could have been both teams!

SUNDAY, DECEMBER 21ST

I pride myself on never having missed a match through illness, but that record would have gone had I been scheduled to work today. A streaming cold picked up somewhere during last week meant I had to cancel my usual Sunday run, and instead stayed in the warm to watch the staple diet of two televised games. In between, Fred showed me the completion of our garage conversion into a properly appointed bar and pool room. The fixtures and fittings are very much in keeping with your local pub, and there will certainly be a convivial evening on offer in future without leaving our drive.

Somebody suggested we should hang up a sign outside saying 'Motty's', but curiously somebody in our home town of Harpenden has already beaten me to it. A new coffee shop has opened bearing that name, but any accusations of plagiarism were put to one side when we discovered that not only did the owner not know I lived locally, he also had no idea who I was and took not the slightest interest in football!

One way of passing the time while staying in the warm was to start my

2004 diary. It suddenly hit me just what a busy year it is going to be for football, especially at the BBC. Heavy FA Cup coverage from early January; the finals of Euro 2004 as soon as the domestic season ends; then the return of *Match of the Day*. Hopefully I can still fit in some matches for Radio Five Live.

So if the first part of this season has read rather like a social whirl, the New Year promises to be just the opposite. Hopefully a few pounds in weight can be shed in the process.

MONDAY, DECEMBER 22ND

I first knew Kevin Blackwell as a young goalkeeper with Boston United, my parents' home town, and Barnet, and if that wasn't coincidental enough, he had a building business in Luton not far from where we live. Our paths crossed again last season, when Kevin was coach to Neil Warnock at Sheffield United. He marked my card meticulously before their semi-final against Arsenal at Old Trafford, which the Blades were somewhat unlucky to lose.

Nobody stands still very long in football, and within a few months Kevin was appointed coach at Leeds United by Peter Reid, a position he maintained when Eddie Gray took over as caretaker-manager at the low point in Leeds' season. Tonight Eddie was absent from the City of Manchester Stadium, attending his daughter's wedding, when Leeds extended their unbeaten run to four games, their best sequence of the season. Kevin was in charge of the team and carried off the managerial duties, including the mandatory live interview on Sky, with a cheerful conviction. Hopefully the new, if temporary, management team will get a decent mention at tomorrow's annual meeting of Leeds United PLC, when questions will doubtless be raised as to why the club find themselves paying expensive and ongoing compensation to three previous managers.

I have never yet seen a successful football club without stability. Maybe Leeds' survival depends on that very factor.

TUESDAY, DECEMBER 23RD

Stability is something Crystal Palace need more than most. My former neighbour Iain Dowie started his first day as their manager, knowing he was the seventh occupant of that seat in three years. My reasons for thinking Dowie will be successful hinge very much on his decision to give up the sumptuous house he developed in Hertfordshire to move lock, stock and barrel with his family to the North West when he took up the poisoned chalice of managing Oldham.

Dowie doesn't do things by halves. He threw himself into a job that promised a future – he guided them to the second-division play-offs last season – but collapsed in his face when the club sank into administration and sold their best players. Iain has strong connections with our part of the world. He did an engineering degree at Hatfield University and Luton Town were the first of his many professional clubs. Somehow I doubt whether he will buy back his old house. The new occupants have put their mark on the neighbourhood with a vivid and slightly scary display of Christmas lights across the front of the property. They scare our dog even more than Iain did.

WEDNESDAY, DECEMBER 24TH

Even as we try to wrap our Christmas presents, the Rio Ferdinand debate grinds on. *Telegraph Sport* columnist Jim White praised veteran pundit Jimmy Hill for 'going just about as far as any lawyer would allow in his attempt to get to the heart of the matter'. In his *Sunday Supplement* programme on Sky Sports, Jimmy had proved again that his 75 years have not dulled one of the sharpest minds on the box; by speculating on a possible reason why Rio missed the drugs test. Whether that theory (which I am not going to repeat here) holds water or not, it bears out what I said about the case the other day. How can any of us express a view on the length of the ban without knowing precisely what evidence the commission had put in front of them?

Meanwhile, the *Telegraph*'s football correspondent Henry Winter, normally the voice of reason amid no little chaos, bucked the trend of most of his colleagues and mounted a stout defence of Manchester United and Alex Ferguson. Quite simply, the only guilty party was Ferdinand, he said.

TOP: With Alastair Campbell before the Great North Run.
ABOVE: At Buckingham Palace after receiving the OBE in 2001. With Fred, Anne and me is my auntie Enid.

ABOVE: A party hosted by then director general Greg Dyke to mark my 30th year with *Match of the Day*.
RIGHT: Wolves secretary Richard Skirrow shows me round the new Molineux. The club will be hoping to bounce back after relegation.

TOP RIGHT: Looking at a different sport. One of my few speaking engagements was at Derbyshire County Cricket Club.
OPPOSITE: With Rick Parfitt of Status Quo before their concert at Oxford.
FAR RIGHT: Leslie Azoulay, who made me a sheepskin coat, at his Station Tavern bar in Cannes.

TOP: Trevor Brooking – now Sir Trevor – spent 15 years keeping me out of trouble in the commentary box.

ABOVE LEFT: My agent Jane Morgan also looks after Des Lynam, Clare Balding, Steve Wilson and many others.

ABOVE RIGHT: Hard not to smile when you're with 'The Birch'. Alan Birchenall cheers me up before a Radio Five commentary at Leicester.

OPPOSITE TOP: A lifelong friendship. Ricky George and I celebrating 40 years since our first meeting in Barnet.

FAR RIGHT: Receiving an honorary degree at Luton University from Professor David Barrett.

TOP: Waiting to do my report for *Grandstand* – but who's the other commentator who got in ahead of me?
ABOVE LEFT: 28 years is a long time to put up with me. But Anne has still to see Newcastle win a trophy in that time!
RIGHT: With Roger Jones, my old chum from the *Barnet Press* days.

OPPOSITE TOP: It was a privilege to host a tribute evening for Bill Nicholson at Tottenham.
FAR RIGHT: Gigg Lane, Bury, was my last stop as I completed the 92 league grounds.

OVERLEAF: Thanks to the boys at William Hunt in Savile Row for keeping me warm.

The fact that Winter revealed Ferdinand's income from Manchester United alone was £3.6 million suggested he was on an inside track, and it was that figure that made me think again about the appalling way professional football has allowed the disparity between rich and poor not just to widen, but to become morally indefensible. No reflection on Ferdinand, but if that's what he's worth, where does that leave the best centre-back in the Nationwide League? On £150,000 a year I would suggest. So Ferdinand is a better player 24 times over? Think about it.

THURSDAY, DECEMBER 25TH

When you get to my stage in life, an original Christmas present comes as a big surprise among the after shave, the socks and the diaries. Fred had ordered on the internet from Germany a framed poster advertising one of Muhammad Ali's early fights, a world title defence against the German Karl Mildenberger in Frankfurt in September 1966. It will look perfect on the wall of our newly converted bar and games room.

Fittingly, one of the books I was given by my brother-in-law Alan belonged to a similar era. It was the year England won the World Cup without Jimmy Greaves – a disappointment he puts into perspective in his new autobiography *Greavsie*. Jimmy puts his descent into alcoholism – now thankfully a quarter of a century behind him – down to his premature retirement from full-time professional football in 1971 at the age of 31. But there was far more of interest in his book than his account of the World Cup and his drinking. I particularly liked his recollections of playing football at Christmas in his early days at Chelsea.

On Christmas morning 1957, my late father took me to Stamford Bridge to see Chelsea play Portsmouth in the old first division. A 17-year-old Jimmy Greaves scored four goals in Chelsea's 7–4 win, a prelude to my dad and me taking two season tickets at Stamford Bridge for the next six years.

In those days, as Greaves recounts, clubs played the reverse fixture the following day. Often, the Boxing Day match enabled the team beaten on Christmas day to turn the tables. In his case, Portsmouth won 3–0 at Fratton Park.

Despite what happened to him later, nothing clouds the clarity of Jimmy's memory of what it was like to play at top level 45 years ago. What strikes him most is the contrast in how supporters then behaved towards each other compared to the hostility that came later. They would appreciate the opposition more, rather than abusing them, and would be prepared to acknowledge and enjoy a good game, even though their own team might have lost.

Greaves went on to recover so well from his illness that he spent 17 years working as a presenter and pundit for Central Television, notably as a double act with Ian St John in the popular ITV Saturday lunchtime show *Saint and Greavsie*. We never worked on the same channel, otherwise I might have embarrassed him by showing him some of the scrapbooks I kept of Chelsea in the fifties.

Brian Clough, a great goalscorer himself before injury ended his career and he took to management, once said to me in an interview that Jimmy Greaves was the best goalscorer of all time. You don't have to be a Chelsea or a Spurs fan to agree with that. Greaves played 516 matches in the old first division, and scored 357 goals. Enough said.

FRIDAY, DECEMBER 26TH

I t was only a small piece on page 12 of the *Sun*, and bearing in mind it appeared on Boxing Day when most football fans were either recovering from the previous day's festivities or else on their way to a Bank Holiday fixture, it probably went largely unnoticed by the football community. Under the headline 'Soccer clubs face cash crackdown', Gary O'Shea reported that new government proposals could force clubs to open their books to the public and show them exactly how they spend their cash – including revealing details of players' wages.

'Proposals, including an independent watchdog to regulate the sport and implement the changes, are part of a report to be published in February by the all-party parliamentary football group. They have been hearing submissions for months and will hand a dossier to Chancellor Gordon Brown and Culture Secretary Tessa Jowell for approval.'

An unnamed Member of Parliament was then quoted as saying: 'Football is in huge financial crisis. Some of it is self-inflicted, but much of it is because the small clubs are not getting a fair deal compared to the giants.'

Without being smug, I seem to have heard a bit about this before. Quite recently in fact, in these pages.

SATURDAY, DECEMBER 27TH

What's this – a Saturday without football? The way Christmas fell this year, the Premiership and Nationwide leagues played on Friday and Sunday, giving Anne and me the opportunity to go racing at Kempton Park. Although the crowd was not as big as it was yesterday for the King George, won by the outsider Edredon Bleu, there was a real buzz about Kempton as we enjoyed a picnic in a very cold car park with some friends of ours, Simon and Sally Dudley and their family.

Once inside, Anne wandered off to look at the horses in the paddock and came back to the Members' Bar in company with Mel Davies, a big sponsor and owner whose company Fawcetts, which he has now sold, entertained us on a number of occasions at Cheltenham. Mel's horse, Itsonlyme, was running in the third race – a three-mile handicap chase for five-year-olds and over – and very nearly came in at 16 to 1. He finished second to Kelami, whose French owner Francois Doumen joined us in Mel's box after the race.

Saturday night television has always meant football for me for obvious reasons, but tonight was different. We settled down to watch *One Hundred Greatest Musicals* on Channel 4, which brought back a lot of memories of shows seen in the past but not forgotten. I am not sure I agreed with *Grease* and John Travolta actually coming top, but there were some great songs interspersed with the usual recollections and views from participants and critics.

Here again there was a generation gap. John Peel and Anita Dobson meant more to me than Judge Jools and Matt Lucas, but there you go.

SUNDAY, DECEMBER 28TH

Delia Smith greeted me with a big hug when I got to Derby to watch the new first-division leaders Norwich City. This was not entirely due to a director's delight at City's recent form, nor was it down to the fact that Delia wants me to follow Anne Robinson and Alan Hansen as the next speaker at her Carrow Road celebrity nights. No, Delia and I go back quite a long way. Although a BBC Worldwide mega-earner with her cookery books and videos, she has always taken a passionate interest in football and at one time wanted us to collaborate on a coaching video for children.

That particular project never came off, but soon afterwards Delia and her husband Michael got heavily involved with Norwich and their recently increased investment now seems to be paying off. They have bought three new strikers in the last two weeks – Darren Huckerby, Leon McKenzie and Mathias Svensson – which sounds to me like a real pitch for promotion to the Premiership. Certainly, to Fred's dismay, they overwhelmed Derby. Four second-half goals sent Norwich six points clear at the top of division one and at present nobody else is showing enough consistency to overtake them.

As for Delia, her influence off the field is there for all to see. The club turned over £2.5 million in catering income alone last year – a clear profit of £600,000. When the fourth stand at Carrow Road is completed early in the New Year, there will be five restaurants on the ground. Surely she can't do the cooking in all of them?

MONDAY, DECEMBER 29TH

The last match of the old year brought the Premiership to its halfway stage, with Arsenal's victory at Southampton taking them back to within a point of Manchester United, with Chelsea a further three points behind.

The top three would seem to be cast in stone, which means the seven of us involved in our annual pub bet are really fighting to be right about fourth place and who goes down. The popular vote seems to be for Liverpool or Newcastle to finish fourth, and the three promoted clubs, Wolves, Portsmouth and Leicester, to grapple with Leeds in the relegation struggle.

I am not so sure. Charlton are defying their patchy home form to hold on to fourth place for the moment, and any one of ten clubs could find themselves flirting with the drop zone.

The Premiership has a rest over the New Year while the clubs sniff glory in the FA Cup. Sadly, that competition is struggling to regain its former prominence, but try telling that to the likes of Accrington, Kidderminster and Tranmere, who all have a chance of carrying the giant-killers' mantle this coming weekend.

At the BBC we have pinned our hopes on Yeovil living up to their 50-year cup tradition by extending Liverpool next Sunday. I still believe the third round of the FA Cup is potentially the most exciting weekend of the season, and as usual Ladbrokes have asked me to put my head on the block and pick four teams who could go all the way. I have chosen Chelsea (the favourites at 7 to 2), Liverpool (8 to 1) and two 'value' bets, Middlesbrough at 18 to 1 and Manchester City at 25 to 1. I just hope two or three of them are still in the draw a week today.

TUESDAY, DECEMBER 30TH

The *Match of the Day* office collapsed in uproar today as we watched a video profile of Jimmy Hill, made by one of our young producers for viewing at a Football Writers' Association dinner in honour of Jimmy in January. It is quite difficult to tell the story of Jimmy's colourful life in football in the space of seven minutes, but there were a few clips that were new even to those of us who worked alongside him in his 25 years with the BBC. From his remonstrations with the referee over a free-kick in his early days at Fulham, to his hilarious defence of the Romanians' dyed hair in the 1998 World Cup, Jimmy's infectious personality and passion for the game came over in every sequence.

Today's players can be grateful to him for leading the abolition of the maximum wage in 1961; Coventry fans will never forget the way he took them from the third division to the first; when he left the manager's office there to join London Weekend Television, he more or less invented football analysis on the screen. When he joined our firm in 1973, he doubled up as a presenter and pundit, always rising to his best I thought, when England were playing.

Terry Venables, Desmond Lynam, Malcolm Allison and the late Brian Moore all figured in the tribute, but none of them were in the four-seater plane with Jimmy and me when we flew to Merseyside for an Everton match in the mid-seventies.

In those days, the *Match of the Day* producer Alec Weeks used to hire a small private aircraft to whisk the presenter – it was David Coleman before Jimmy – up to a match and back, returning in time for him to host the show in the studio. That particular Saturday the gusty weather blew our plane all over the place. As we were about to land at Liverpool's Speke Airport, Jimmy was convinced we were going to finish up in the Mersey. A couple of port and lemons were his medicine before we left the airport. The return journey was less eventful, but when he introduced the programme that evening, Jimmy actually said good evening by telling the story of his dramatic flight and his still-heaving stomach.

All very amusing, except that it was the time of the three-day week and petrol was severely rationed. The BBC duty office was inundated with hundreds of calls, all complaining about the indefensible waste of fuel that the BBC had sanctioned by chartering a private plane.

We never flew to a match on that tiny plane again.

WEDNESDAY, DECEMBER 31ST

I celebrated New Year's Eve by going to collect my new sheepskin coat. The old one is nearing its sell-by date, and I am still under orders to donate it to the National Football Museum at Preston. This time, I am going upmarket and having one custom-made by a Savile Row tailor. Not quite as ostentatious as it sounds, because this particular fitting and transaction came about by sheer chance.

Back in August, when Spurs beat Leeds at White Hart Lane, I shared a lunch table in the sponsors' lounge with John Regal and David Dervish, partners with William Hunt in the clothing business that they opened in London's West End in 1998. When William Hunt first opened its doors in Savile Row, they were met with a fair amount of suspicion and cynicism by its longer-serving tailors – sharp, modern and on the edge with their fashion, they got used to being frowned upon.

Not so much now. Having supplied David Beckham with the suits he wore to Buckingham Palace and Downing Street, and attracted the custom of Dwight Yorke, Harry Kewell and the Neville brothers, they are pushing ahead with their ambition to dress the England team, rather than leaving them to the mercy of overseas designers.

Anyway, the new Motty sheepskin was the warmest, the longest and the most fashionable I have so far worn. It felt as though it was wearing me. 'We've given you shoulders,' joked John Regal.

The *Daily Mirror* arrived on the scene, alerted by the BBC publicity department, to slant a new angle on this weekend's FA Cup third round. The coat will make its debut at St Mary's on Saturday when Southampton and Newcastle kick off our live coverage.

JANUARY

THURSDAY, JANUARY 1ST

Having spent a comparatively quiet New Year's Eve with the family at our local, I was quite chirpy as I picked up Ricky George to take in the Nationwide fixture between Barnet and Woking at Underhill. As former player and reporter in the town, we still have a mutual affection for our local club – especially when they serve egg, bacon and sausages, not to mention smoked salmon, before the lunchtime kick-off.

It was the first time I had been to Barnet this season, and Martin Allen had obviously done a more than decent job with an almost entirely new squad, most of them signed on free transfers from league clubs, and now pitching for a place in the play-offs which could take the club back into the Football League.

Even with the advantage of the famous Underhill 'slope' in the first half, Barnet and their free-scoring striker Giuliano Grazioli could not break down a stubborn Woking defence, and the clubs drew for the second time over the holiday period.

The Conference, which next season will have a second division, is now virtually a full-time professional league. Later today Chester, under former England centre-half Mark Wright, won 6–2 at Leigh RMI to go six points clear at the top and stake their claim for automatic promotion. Former league clubs Hereford, Aldershot and Shrewsbury are in the chasing pack and today the Conference had the football scene all to themselves. The proximity of the FA Cup third round in two days' time meant there were no fixtures in the Premiership or in the Football League.

A time for reflection? The *Daily Telegraph* compiled a table of transfer expenditure during the calendar year 2003 – and guess who were hidden away in 15th place? Arsenal, with a modest outlay of £4 million compared to the £111 million spent by Chelsea.

The transfer window opens today, but I still don't see Arsene Wenger getting the cheque book out.

FRIDAY, JANUARY 2ND

Funny how a cup tie picked in all innocence four weeks ago suddenly becomes a news story. Freddy Shepherd, Newcastle United's chairman, took issue with everybody from 'the management downwards' earlier this week when he expressed his displeasure at the way the team have been performing. Preparing today for my commentary on Newcastle's third-round cup tie at Southampton, I wondered how those words had gone down in the dressing room and what effect they might have tomorrow.

Sir Bobby Robson was sanguine about it when I spoke to him, although he may have been feeling rather different underneath. He certainly didn't want reminding about Newcastle's record at Southampton – they haven't won there for 32 years.

Listening to Ricky George previewing the 32 ties on Five Live tonight, it brought back yet again memories of our Hereford experience 32 years ago, if only because Newcastle bounced off that humiliation and promptly won away games at Manchester United and... Southampton. Robson told me the chief reason for their indifferent recent form was that Alan Shearer was having to shoulder the burden very much on his own, due to the injuries to Craig Bellamy and Shola Ameobi. Tomorrow Robson intends to play Kieron Dyer as a striker. My research tells me he hasn't scored for nearly a year, so who knows what might happen?

The bookmakers' odds against the smaller teams are quite appealing, according to Ricky. I decide to have a 'yankee' on four draws, backing Accrington, Scarborough, Telford and Kidderminster to live to fight another day.

SATURDAY, JANUARY 3RD

Whatever they tell you about the FA Cup and its place in football's priorities these days, I still woke up today to what some of us still believe is the most exciting weekend of the season. I hadn't intended to start by going shopping, but I realised I had come down to the south coast yesterday without any decent shoes, so a quick drive into Bournemouth left me a lot lighter on the credit card. A suit and a jacket were quick additions to the wardrobe. Out of it, making its debut on a cold night at St Mary's, came the new sheepskin coat. One or two people had seen the zany picture in the *Daily Mirror* so I was quite ready for a few ribald comments when I arrived at the ground.

Interviewing the two managers before the game, I was struck by Robson's awareness of how much the FA Cup means to the people of Newcastle. More than to supporters of other clubs, he suggested.

His team went out and played that way. The 3,200 who had made the 300-mile trip from the North East had a convincing 3–0 victory to cheer. Dyer responded to his new position with two goals, and Freddy Shepherd must have heard the reaction out in Dubai.

I found myself a few pounds richer when I got home. Three of my potential giant-killers had got the draw I predicted, so the shoes were paid for even though Telford went one better and produced the result of the day by winning at Crewe. Not far behind was Gillingham's victory over Charlton, a fitting start for the *Match of the Day* highlights programme, which managed to show every goal scored in the third round.

SUNDAY, JANUARY 4TH

Having covered the live game last evening, I was cast in the role of viewer today and tried to repeat my 'draw bets' success without any return this time. Yeovil held Liverpool until half-time, but then fell away; Cheltenham were giving me a return at 5 to 1 until Fulham's last-minute winner; Aston Villa led Manchester United until Paul Scholes came up with two quick goals; and as for Leeds – they started as 4 to 1 outsiders to beat Arsenal at Elland Road, and lost, appropriately, by four goals to one!

One tailpiece to this FA Cup weekend was bumping into Neil McNab, the former Tottenham midfielder who was manager of Exeter City when I covered their first-round tie against Forest Green Rovers last season. Neil has since gone to America to take up a coaching post in Atlanta – he probably wanted to get as far away from the trials and tribulations at Exeter as he could – but it was another example of how the FA Cup throws up characters and connections from way back.

One thing that still puzzles me about the Sunday papers – especially the broadsheets – is how much they know about the habits of their readers. Today there were full-page previews of the matches at Yeovil and Villa Park, yet by the time the late risers had picked up the paper the games would be half over. Certain newspapers have cravenly followed the lead set by dedicated sports channels on television and radio – an almost obsessive desire to spend more time previewing an event than actually reporting it – a trend I find contrary to real journalistic principles. In the business, we call it space filling.

MONDAY, JANUARY 5TH

They say football is a game of opinion, and there was no better example of that than today. I experienced both sides of the debate over video technology to settle difficult decisions for the referee, but the two schools of thought coming from different camps were wholly in reverse to what I would have expected.

As a guest on Jonathan Pearce's *Sport on Five* evening show, I joined Alan Curbishley, Frank Lampard senior and Steve Claridge in a wide-ranging discussion which took in today's draw for the fourth round of the FA Cup, this week's Premiership programme, and a look back to the weekend.

Jonathan was commentating at Watford when Heidar Helguson's header came back off the underside of the crossbar, and the officials gave a goal. Replays showed conclusively that the ball did not cross the line.

Everybody knows I am dead against the use of video evidence and the presence of another referee in the stand, as happens in cricket. It would slow the game down, frustrate the crowd, take the human error out of football, and above all lead to too many grey areas. For example, if you introduce the technology on the goal line, within a matter of weeks managers would be asking for video evidence for offside, diving offences and the validity of red and yellow cards.

I was fully expecting the three professionals round the table to take me to task, but to my surprise they all agreed with me. Leave the game the way it is, and leave it to the referee and his three assistants, was the message loud and clear.

Imagine my surprise then when I dropped in at our local on the way home, to hear a table of four supporters of senior age, all appealing for the introduction of instant replays to help the referee make his decision. Now, Alan Curbishley had made the point on the air that supporters in general love to go home arguing after a game – it's part of football, he said. But these fans thought otherwise. I resisted the temptation to join the debate and slipped out of the pub quietly. One discussion is quite enough for tonight.

TUESDAY, JANUARY 6TH

After covering a live match, you can rest assured as a commentator that your postbag will contain some critical letters. Such was the case when I got to the *Match of the Day* office today. One viewer was incensed by my referring early in the game at St Mary's to Cup shocks during the afternoon. As far as he was concerned, news of Gillingham, Telford and Kidderminster upsetting the odds had spoilt his enjoyment of *Match of the Day* highlights later that evening.

Now I quite appreciate that in time gone by, when there was no Ceefax, no Five Live and no Sky Television, many BBC viewers deliberately avoided listening to the results so that they could enjoy the programme in the evening without knowing the outcome of the televised highlights. Time moves on, and rightly or wrongly most of us assume that it is now practically impossible to avoid all the sources of information – including news bulletins – that refer to football. So much so, that the editor of our programme from Southampton was inclined to use a few of the goals from the afternoon during our half-time sequence, purely as a 'taster' for what was to come later.

Having been accused of 'crass stupidity' by that correspondent, I was next taken to task by an amateur referee for misinterpreting the law regarding a shoulder charge. I always make a point of replying personally to these letters – indeed from time to time I have surprised the sender by phoning them up if they have left a number – but to all intents and purposes there is no time to clarify these things on the air. We are too busy planning the next match.

That was why the office was so busy today. As soon as the cup draw is announced, BBC and Sky Sports select their live matches. Our first choice was not difficult this time round – Liverpool v Newcastle leapt off the page – but we had to wait for police approval for the 5.35pm kick-off time on Saturday evening. Once this was granted, Sky selected the away matches involving Manchester United and Chelsea, whose opponents in each case depend on replays.

Back came the BBC with our live Sunday lunchtime game – Leicester or Manchester City against Tottenham. That's where I got lucky. It's my turn for the Sunday job, and as it happens I am covering the replay a week on Wednesday, and three days earlier commentating for Five Live on Leicester's Premiership match against Chelsea.

Couldn't be better from the homework point of view, and just to cover all eventualities I shall pop down to Portsmouth next Saturday to see Manchester City.

WEDNESDAY, JANUARY 7TH

Tonight the Barclaycard Premiership midweek programme meant most clubs were starting on the second half of the season. Their 20th fixture was the reverse of those played on the opening weekend back in August, and in the only game played last night Aston Villa had reversed their 2–1 defeat at Fratton Park.

A group of us in The Hollybush decided to spice up the evening by forecasting how we each thought the nine matches would finish. Not one of us forecast Liverpool to win at Chelsea – their first victory at Stamford Bridge in more than 14 years – but I sneaked home by forecasting five correct results to my nearest challenger's four.

In many ways tonight's results were a possible guide to the second half of the season. I fully anticipate a Liverpool revival – if they beat Newcastle I think they could win the FA Cup – the championship looks beyond Chelsea, and all three promoted clubs, Wolves, Leicester and Portsmouth, are going to be fighting relegation all the way to the finishing line.

Neither do Leeds United look like pulling clear. If they don't find a buyer in the next 12 days, they will go into administration, with the threat of having to sell what remain of their chief assets, Robinson, Smith and Viduka.

ITV's *Premiership* programme packed in all the night's action, but once again their football team were let down by the schedulers. The show finished at twenty to one in the morning. No wonder Des Lynam took the night off. People of our vintage should be tucked up in bed well before midnight.

THURSDAY, JANUARY 8TH

France Football, in my view the best weekly magazine of its kind in the world, published a feature today to mark the eighth anniversary of the Bosman ruling – the change in law authorised by the European Commission which means players can now walk away at the end of their contract, often without a penny in compensation for the club that may have discovered and trained them.

I have always believed the judgement is fundamentally flawed. If I worked on a car assembly line and exercised my right to leave and seek employment with a rival plant down the road, I am entitled to take my labour elsewhere, but I leave the cars themselves behind. In football the players *are* the product. Apart from the ground, which is often rented or leased anyway, the clubs own nothing else of material value. Every player has been identified and developed somewhere, so why should his original employers lose his services and value when he and his agent decide?

This, together with the decision allowing the home club to keep all the gate receipts from league matches, has driven a huge wedge between the 'haves' and the 'have nots'. The Manchester Uniteds can now cherry pick more or less any player they fancy – young Liam Miller from Celtic being an example today – by paying him wages that nobody else can afford.

You only have to look at the Premiership table, where an enormous gap has now developed between third and fourth place, to realise the English game is in serious danger of eroding the competition that was once its lifeblood. Can you ever envisage a Nottingham Forest or a Derby County winning the championship again?

Sadly, neither can I.

FRIDAY, JANUARY 9TH

For once, football took second place in the sport headlines today. Greg Rusedski, Britain's No 2 tennis player, has been tested positive for the drug nandrolone. Rusedski and his advisers protested his innocence on the grounds that he was given nutritional tablets by the Association of Tennis Professionals' trainers, before they were banned after subsequently being found to be contaminated. He protested that 46 other players among the world's top 120 had been shown to have elevated levels of nandrolone in their system. 'The ATP did not pursue those cases, so why are they singling me out?' asked Rusedski.

He expects the charges to be dropped at a hearing in Montreal early next month. In the meantime, the scandal has taken the heat off Rio Ferdinand, who is now into a 14-day period when he has to decide whether to appeal against his eight-month ban. Not that Ferdinand failed a test – he just forgot to take one, according to his evidence.

Nothing grabs more space in the national press than a drugs story. There were pages and pages devoted to the Rusedski case today. My reaction, having heard his passionate denials in front of the television cameras in Australia where he is currently playing, is that this will eventually amount to a storm in a teacup, or perhaps in a test tube. What would a tennis player have to gain by knowingly taking such a substance? It is hardly going to enhance his performance, and we all have the capacity to produce a supply of nandrolone in our system by natural means.

It may sound naive, or perhaps cynical, but my gut feeling is that somebody somewhere has set Rusedski up. Time will no doubt tell.

SATURDAY, JANUARY 10TH

The first Premiership Saturday of the New Year was a personal version of Groundhog Day. The same journey as I made on the opening day of the season – to Fratton Park to watch Portsmouth; the same assignment – to interview Harry Redknapp for *Football Focus*; Sarah the same producer waiting while I missed the junction on the M27 and had to turn round and come back the other way. It only needed Teddy Sheringham to score and the whole scene would be exactly repeated, with a Portsmouth victory of course. Teddy duly obliged with the third goal in a 4–2 win over Manchester City.

John Jenkins, the steward in the directors' lounge who had befriended me back in August, had since celebrated his 85th birthday. It is 70 years ago that he left school at Portsmouth to join the Cunard liner *Mauritania* as a 14-year-old bellboy, for its last voyage from Southampton to the West Indies and back.

But it wasn't that aspect of John's graphic memory that struck a chord with me today. He was also present that year at the FA Cup final at Wembley in which Manchester City, with Matt Busby at right-half, defeated Portsmouth 2–1.

'The only thing I can recall about the game was Frank Swift collapsing under the crossbar at the final whistle,' he said. The story of City's then 20-year-old goalkeeper fainting at the end of the game is carved in football folklore. I never dreamt I would meet anybody who actually saw it happen.

Curiously, the City goalkeeper had to be helped off the pitch again today. David Seaman, twice the age that Swift was then, hurt his shoulder after 12 minutes. Bearing in mind they then hit the bar three times in the first half, as well as leading 2–1 at half-time, it was hardly City's day. This was their 14th consecutive game in league and cup without a win. Judging by the grim expression on the faces of their directors as they left the ground, I wondered how safe the jobs of Kevin Keegan and his coaching staff were.

SUNDAY, JANUARY 11TH

I only found out this morning that the private plane taking those Manchester City directors and their guests back from the south coast was forced to make an emergency landing in Hampshire only a few minutes after taking off. Thankfully the pilot did the necessary and they survived the scare.

A less scary form of transport perhaps was the stretch limousine in which Roman Abramovich and his associates pulled into the car park at Leicester's Walkers Stadium. Chelsea had taken a bit of a pounding since their defeat by Liverpool four days ago, but Ranieri made six changes and got the response he wanted. Four-nil was a shade harsh on Leicester, but with Manchester United dropping two home points to Newcastle, the championship is still a three-cornered contest.

Anybody who doubts Abramovich's interest in the game should have seen him glued to the Old Trafford television coverage after his own team had completed their victory. He and his travelling companions kept the limousine waiting until the match between the two Uniteds was over.

Our Five Live commentary passed without incident. Steve Wilson, Mark Bright and I are now television colleagues as well, although I got the usual ribbing when three of the four goals fell in my period of commentary.

MONDAY, JANUARY 12TH

It looks as though I have done my last commentary with Trevor
Brooking. After 15 years alongside me at the main games, including
World Cups, FA Cup finals and big England matches, Trevor's new role at
the Football Association would mean a potential conflict of interests if he
continued at the microphone.

The meeting between Trevor and the BBC to clarify his position
sounded far more amicable than some of the noises emanating from
leading managers with regard to Brooking's appointment at Soho Square.
Sam Allardyce, among others, expressed concern today about Trevor's lack
of the mandatory coaching qualifications which the FA's former technical
director, Howard Wilkinson, put in place to apply to all leading coaches.

It's not because I am wearing my BBC hat that I think Sam may have
missed the point. Brooking's new job has a far wider brief than the
coaching area, and in any event he does have his routine badges. He needs
to update the qualification on a refresher course and that is something he
has put in hand.

What concerns me more is whom I will be working with in the future.
The chemistry between the commentator and his summariser is one that
takes time to develop. I believe Trevor and I are better broadcasting partners
now than when we started. Mark Lawrenson has proved he can fill the role
more than adequately – he and I did the Euro 2000 final together – but
Mark has studio commitments too, and his links with the Republic of Ireland
mean he might not be acceptable to the audience for England games.

The same would apply to Mick McCarthy, another candidate who has
worked for us at major events. Then there are Mick's club commitments at
Sunderland to consider. Some of the younger football names who might be
worth a try are still playing, and it might take two years to get them ready
with the necessary experience for a major championship. It's a case of
watch this space.

TUESDAY, JANUARY 13TH

If co-commentators don't exactly grow on trees, neither do English
goalkeepers, not those of international quality anyway. I didn't realise
when I saw David Seaman helped off the Fratton Park pitch holding his

injured shoulder early in Saturday's match, that this was the last time we would see the 40-year-old in a jersey. Seaman announced his retirement today, at about the same time as Manchester City signed his England successor, David James, from first-division West Ham.

I suppose my generation were spoilt when we were brought up on Gordon Banks, Peter Shilton, Ray Clemence, Joe Corrigan and Phil Parkes. In those days home-grown goalkeepers were supreme at their craft, and overseas keepers frequently derided as lacking confidence, bravery and consistency.

Not so now. In the Premiership last Saturday, Seaman apart, there were only four English goalkeepers out of 20 on duty. Nigel Martyn of Everton – himself 38 later this year – his Leeds successor Paul Robinson, Leicester's Ian Walker and Michael Oakes at Wolves. The others play for the following countries: The United States of America (3), Finland (2), The Republic of Ireland (2), Germany, Denmark, Italy, Northern Ireland, Holland, Poland, Australia and Trinidad and Tobago.

If anything should go wrong with his current choice of keepers in the England squad – James, Robinson and Walker – then Sven Goran Eriksson might find himself in an embarrassing position. Liverpool's Chris Kirkland is injured again, as is Everton's first choice Richard Wright. Martyn's performances in his place have prompted David Moyes, the Everton manager, to suggest he could get a recall. In the meantime, where are the young English goalkeepers of the future?

WEDNESDAY, JANUARY 14TH

This is the working day in the season that I hate most. The third-round replays of the FA Cup usually take place on a bitterly cold night, with the possibility of postponement always in the air, and usually involve a journey not without a weather-related incident. Ask me about commentaries I have not enjoyed – and there aren't many – and most of them will have fallen around this time of the year, especially in the evening. Maybe it's my imagination, but I still believe the players look less familiar in the middle of January.

Before I get carried away with paranoia or superstition, let me say I got the better of the draw in our three-match programme tonight. Another trip to Leicester was the next best thing to a London match in terms of distance and did not involve an overnight stay, while Simon Brotherton had to move his base camp to North Yorkshire for the replay between Scarborough and Southend.

Simon got his reward with the big story of the night. The Conference side won with a late goal and now host Chelsea, with all their expensive trappings and trimmings, in the next round. And my evening could have been a lot worse too. The recently acquired sheepskin coat was only just coping with the freezing conditions when extra time loomed between Leicester and Manchester City. But along came Nicolas Anelka and Jonathan Macken with two goals in the closing minutes to spare us an extra half hour.

Despite their disappointment, the Leicester chairman Jim McCahill cracked open a bottle of Champagne in the boardroom while the Manchester directors rubbed their hands at the thought of a live television fee for the next round against Tottenham.

Garth Crooks and I got a lift back down the M1 and a bottle of wine mysteriously appeared in the back of the car. Not a great mixer with champagne, and when I got home I found my white shirt covered in ugly red stains. Garth never could pour properly at 70 miles an hour.

THURSDAY, JANUARY 15TH

Thanks to Dominic Hart, the deputy sports editor of the *Daily Mirror*, I received this morning a splendid portfolio of colour prints from my recent coat fitting at William Hunt. Some are less flattering than others, but there are a couple of me being measured up which I shall drop in to the boys in the shop. It won't put me up there with their star customers like David Beckham, but the coat was much admired last night at Leicester.

Footballers, when I started, weren't really into fashion. There was the odd exception like the late Bobby Keetch, but for most of the players in the early seventies a mohair suit was about as far as it went. Now they step out of the pages of the trendy men's magazines. Ian Walker, Leicester's goalkeeper who I knew well when he played for Tottenham, nodded sagely when I told him where the coat had come from. 'I'll get in that place myself when I'm in London,' he said.

The coat situation is now getting quite complicated. Leslie Azoulay down in Cannes is expecting me to take my old one when I fly to Nice a week on Monday, with a view to making me a new coat himself. So I could have two by the end of the season. As for the photographs, Fred has mischievously put the most embarrassing one up on the notice board in the bar in our garage. The most respectable ones are being saved for my publisher. You never know, one of them might appear somewhere in this book.

FRIDAY, JANUARY 16TH

Today I officially became a shareholder in Ipswich Town Football Club. No need for alarm, or accusations of bias. I already have a small handful of shares in Charlton Athletic, and my wife Anne has guarded her Newcastle shares jealously having been born, lived and gone to university in the city.

The BBC had no problem with my decision to respond modestly to the prospectus that came with the new Ipswich share issue. The club needs a serious re-flotation after going into administration following relegation and the collapse of ITV Digital, not to mention the transfer window which effectively robbed them of the two big fees that would have kept them solvent.

The financial reporters were wise to what was happening. Within minutes of signing my cheque, I received calls from the business department of BBC *Breakfast Time* and Five Live news, asking me to join in an early morning discussion next Monday – the day the share issue at Ipswich is due to close.

Easy answer to this. I am not an early morning person and once made a pact with myself never to go on the air before breakfast time – which for me is nine o'clock or later. Apart from which, my contribution is largely a sentimental one and I have no wish to join a debate which will obviously compare Ipswich to Leeds United – whose deadline date for a takeover or administration is also next Monday.

Mind you, the Ipswich story was a mere dot on the landscape compared to today's official launch of Great Britain's (sorry, London's) bid to stage the 2012 Olympics. Any hope of a Great Britain team in the Olympic football tournament?

Not a chance. Picking the team will be confined to pub games. And London's chances of staging the Games? Slightly better than our 2006 World Cup bid I would say. And what a waste of public money that was.

SATURDAY, JANUARY 17TH

It is 32 weeks today until the return of *Match of the Day*, and it is with no disrespect to my ITV colleagues and competitors that more and more people in football are counting the days.

Not that *The Premiership* as a programme in itself is being targeted as inadequate. It is a combination of the inevitable advertising breaks, the commercial necessity to promote the big clubs and reduce coverage of the others, and the late finish to the programme, that over the last two-and-a-half years have attracted criticism from viewers.

There is nothing Des Lynam and his lively panellists can really do about this. The agenda at ITV is utterly different to that at the BBC, and I am sure we shall find next season that there is a limited, defined audience for recorded highlights now that we have been spoilt by so much live football. I can also accept that some of the people who speak fondly of *Match of the Day* are influenced partly by the fact that they more or less grew up with the programme, and partly because, when in a conversation with someone like me, they are hardly likely to take the opposite view.

All that taken into account, the likes of Alan Sugar and Gérard Houllier are neither sentimentalists nor prone to wasting words. At Tottenham today, both made unprompted references to the return of the programme. 'When do you come back?' Sugar asked me at half-time. There was no need to ask what he meant. 'Good,' he grunted when I told him August.

As for Houllier, the trenchant remarks of Messrs Lawrenson and Hansen about Liverpool from time to time have obviously not affected his affection for the programme. After all, he was only the second person I remember to have the *Match of the Day* signature tune on his mobile phone.

The first was Gary Lineker.

SUNDAY, JANUARY 18TH

The Fred Hughes Memorial is a ten-mile run organised by St Alban's Striders running club every January in memory of one of their leading members who was, sadly, killed riding his bicycle some years ago. I have taken part in most of the past eight or nine events, but today was different. I had not attempted the distance since I stumbled through the Great North Run four months ago.

It wasn't a lot easier today. Although it was a nice, dry January morning and the course was fairly flat, every mile after the halfway mark felt like two. Anyway, I finished in one piece and received the statutory medal to go with the other mementoes of a very modest running career.

In football, the major event of the day was that Arsenal went back to the top of the Premiership and now lead Manchester United by two points. The bookmakers obviously think they will stay top, having made them odds-on favourites after the price against the Gunners had drifted out beyond 2 to 1 just a couple of weeks ago.

MONDAY, JANUARY 19TH

The headline above Alan Hansen's column in *Telegraph Sport* this morning said it all: 'When the biggest clubs set their sights on a player, smart money says he always leaves.'

In the case of Louis Saha, for quite a *lot* of money. Fulham have finally given way to Saha's wish to play for Manchester United, and with the transfer market the way it is, a reported £12 million is not to be sniffed at. But there is a wider issue here. Scott Parker has made it clear to Charlton that he has been unsettled by Chelsea's interest in him. So much so that Alan Curbishley left him out of the team that won at Everton on Saturday.

Then there is the case of Jermain Defoe, linked with Premiership clubs ever since he put in an ill-advised transfer request as soon as West Ham were relegated. If Hansen is right, and current events suggest he is, then what will happen when word reaches the agents of Southampton's James Beattie, or Everton's Wayne Rooney, that one of the top five clubs are prepared to pay the asking price for them?

What we are really saying is that contracts don't mean very much anymore, except as a device that can be broken to suit the player, or in some cases the selling club, and sometimes both – though more often the former.

The worrying aspect of all this is that sooner or later the top talent will be playing exclusively for the leading three or four clubs. It is another example of how the rich are becoming more powerful, and how the rest of the Premiership – not to mention the Nationwide League – are struggling to keep up.

You may have noticed I haven't mentioned the word loyalty. That's because it no longer has a place in football's vocabulary.

TUESDAY, JANUARY 20TH

I was halfway through lunch with a former *Barnet Press* colleague of mine when Steve Perryman rang my mobile. As captain of the Tottenham side that won the FA Cup two years running in 1981 and 1982, he is organising a reunion in Enfield next Sunday. It hadn't escaped Steve's notice that Spurs' current side would be playing Manchester City while Keith Burkinshaw and the rest of Steve's party were enjoying themselves. He invited me to join them, and then realised that I would be working at the City of Manchester Stadium.

But the conversation did not end there. I asked Steve whether Ossie Ardiles and Ricky Villa would be coming, and he said he hoped both would be travelling halfway across the world to attend. What a good photo opportunity, I thought, with memories of the 1981 final against the same opponents on Sunday. I suggested a possible televised 'up link' for the start of *Match of the Day*, and also told Ricky George to alert the *Daily Telegraph*, in case it made a good picture for Monday morning.

Ricky Villa's winning goal at Wembley will always live in the memory when the two clubs meet, but I remember another match between Spurs and Manchester City, at Maine Road, when Ardiles was Tottenham manager. It was in October 1994, shortly after Jürgen Klinsmann had first signed for Tottenham, and attack-minded Ardiles was fielding his 'famous five' forward line: Jason Dozell, Nick Barmby, Klinsmann, Teddy Sheringham and Ilie Dumitrescu.

Maybe not surprising that Spurs, with such an attacking line-up, lost 5–2, with one of their former players, Paul Walsh, scoring two goals. The match was played in pouring rain and City provided plastic covers for the spectators on the popular side, where the new Kippax Stand was still unfinished.

Happy days.

WEDNESDAY, JANUARY 21ST

The Football League Cup was originally invented by the late Alan Hardaker as a way of complimenting a new format of five divisions of 20 clubs. He got the new cup, but never the revised league format. From its inception in 1960 until 1981, it ticked along as the FA Cup's poor relation.

The final moved to Wembley in 1967, then the bigger clubs began to take more of an interest.

By the time sponsorship kicked into football, the League Cup was not only a target – it was a moveable feast. From 1982 until 1986 it was known as the Milk Cup; then for four years it was the Littlewoods Cup; Rumbelows lasted two years as the next sponsor; between 1993 and 1998 we knew it as the Coca-Cola Cup; it turned alcoholic then, with the Worthington Cup its title from 1999 until last year, when the Carling brand took over.

The competition has been streamlined in recent seasons. The old two-leg format for the first and second rounds has gone; so have all replays, with matches now settled on the night by penalties if necessary; those clubs involved in Europe don't join until the third round; but the prize for the winners is still an automatic place in the UEFA Cup.

Tonight's semi-final first leg between Bolton and Aston Villa was one of the most dramatic games of the season. Jay Jay Okocha produced two sublime free-kicks before jetting off to the African Nations Cup, as Bolton won the first leg 5–2. Sam Allardyce clearly put this competition higher in his priorities than the FA Cup, where his under-strength team lost to Tranmere last week.

Arsene Wenger, on the other hand, thinks differently. He gave his youngsters a chance in their semi-final against Middlesbrough (they lost the first leg 1–0) and kept his heavy guns back for the FA Cup against the same opponents on Saturday. I am not sure what conclusions to draw for this piece of history. Probably because I was more concerned with taking my wife out for her birthday.

THURSDAY, JANUARY 22ND

People sometimes ask how long it takes to prepare a commentary. How long is a piece of string? It depends very much on the game, the teams involved, whether a lot of travelling is required and how often the commentator has seen the teams in question. But however many videos I sit through, whether or not I see fit to watch a training session, however many hours I spend on the motorway to attend midweek games, the most important two hours are those spent in my office at home summarising all the information I have gathered on to what I have come to call, for want of a better description, my 'commentary chart'.

Always stick your notes on cardboard, I was told when I first started as a radio commentator. Then they won't blow away. And put a piece of perspex over them. Then they won't get wet and the colours won't run.

On one side of the board I have a list of both squads, hopefully with the starting eleven listed first. Each team I code in a different colour, as close as possible to the shirts they are playing in. Christian names and numbers require two further felt tip pens, while the biographical notes alongside each player are written in smaller letters in red, blue or black biro.

On the back of the chart I print in capital letters ten or twelve 'bullet points', one underneath the other. These are general sequences applying to one team or the other: games without a win, scoring records, past meetings etc. At the bottom I list all the scorers for the current season.

When the game is over, most of the information on the chart is out of date and of no further relevance to me. Which is why I keep a stack to send to auctions and charities. My board for the Germany v England match in Munich fetched just under £2000 for a good cause. Mind you, England did win 5–1.

FRIDAY, JANUARY 23RD

Further to my thoughts about commentary preparation yesterday, I should have added that unforeseen circumstances can throw those carefully crafted notes up in the air at a stroke.

It became clear as today wore on, that neither Arsenal nor Middlesbrough were going to show a full hand at Highbury tomorrow. Both managers were playing cagey with their Carling Cup semi-final second leg coming up, and by mid-afternoon I tore up my first draft of the line-ups and started again.

Knowing there would be no time tomorrow to prepare for Sunday's game, the Manchester City v Tottenham homework would have to take care of itself for now. I have seen both teams this season and don't expect too many surprises. Even so, all four squads are likely to include players I have not seen before. Arsenal are certain to include on the bench one or two teenagers who did well in a weakened team in midweek; pronunciations are always worth checking – Quincy Owusu-Abeyie in the No. 54 shirt will be a real mouthful if he plays. Even the Highbury staff have decided to simplify things and call him Quincy.

When it gets to five o'clock on Friday I always put the pens away, go out to buy the *Evening Standard* and retire to the pub. Only this week, the pub was our garage. As I have mentioned, Fred has converted it into his own tavern, with fully fitted bar, pool table and darts board. A handful of his friends and mine turned up for the 'official opening' and they all seemed to enjoy the evening. It was a nice way to relax before my busiest weekend so far this season.

SATURDAY, JANUARY 24TH

There's always something you forget. On my drive to Highbury, I couldn't remember how many FA Cup medals Ray Parlour had won. He played in Arsenal's successful teams of 1998, 2002 and 2003 but in 1993 he was dropped after the first drawn match against Sheffield Wednesday and did not figure in the replay. Did he still receive a medal?

It may sound trivial, but among modern players David Seaman and Mark Hughes lead the way with four winners' medals, and should Arsenal win the cup again this year, Parlour could become the first man since the 19th century to have five winners' medals on his mantelpiece.

I made mobile calls to Arsenal's two senior press officers, Amanda Doherty and Dan Tollhurst, and to the great amusement of the three of us, they came up with different answers. At half-past two, after much debate, Amanda marched into the Arsenal dressing room and established with the man himself that he *did* get a medal in 1993.

As soon as the match ended in a routine Arsenal victory, it was hotfoot to Heathrow for the evening flight to Manchester, where I linked up with Gary Lineker and the team at the hotel. They had arrived from Anfield where Liverpool had won the first BBC live match of the round against Newcastle.

It was a busy weekend for BBC football. As well as the two live games and *Match of the Day* highlights, we started coverage of the African Nations Cup. I had rung Steve Wilson and Simon Brotherton in Tunisia to wish them well for their month-long stint. In their absence, Radio Five's John Murray was scheduled for his television debut – but his heart must have sunk when the Telford v Millwall match was postponed this morning. The cameras were quickly shunted across the Midlands and in the most trying of circumstances John had a splendid debut on Birmingham v Millwall.

As I found at Hereford all those years ago, an unexpected postponement can kick-start a new career.

SUNDAY, JANUARY 25TH

One of the reasons Steve Perryman had invited me to the Spurs reunion party today was that more than 20 years ago, when he was Tottenham captain, they sometimes afforded me the privilege of travelling back from the North on the team coach. In those days players were more accessible and less defensive towards the media, so I believed the days of the commentator 'hitching a ride' were long gone.

I was wrong. In fact, the whole day was littered with memories. Just like their 1981 final, City and Spurs drew 1–1, with Tottenham coming from behind to force a replay. On the way out, I bumped into the sprightly figure of Tommy Docherty – now 75 – the winning manager when I did my first Cup final commentary in 1977.

The mild satisfaction of having completed two commentaries in 24 hours without mishap did not last long. When I arrived at the airport, British Midland announced a long delay in the flight to London, due to technical trouble.

At that moment, Chris Hughton, who had played in the 1981 final, came through the departure lounge with the tracksuited Tottenham squad. A brief consultation with David Pleat, and a spare seat on Spurs' private jet back to Stansted was put my way.

The FA Cup coincidences did not end there. I found myself sitting next to Clive Allen – like Hughton, now on the Spurs coaching staff – who figured in two Wembley finals in the eighties. Clive limped off injured playing for Queens Park Rangers against Spurs, then five years later put Tottenham ahead inside two minutes against Coventry, who went on to win 3–2. Allen now also works for ITV as a pundit and co-commentator. Fate does funny things. I wonder whether that fortuitous flight with Spurs may one day lead to us working on the same channel.

MONDAY, JANUARY 26TH

Three years ago, Mark Lawrenson told me the best time for commentators to take a 'mini mid-winter break' was straight after the fourth round of the FA Cup. There's too much football over Christmas and the New Year to get away before that; more cup rounds, replays and internationals blocking the February diary. Which is why Ricky George and I were on the easyJet flight from Luton to Nice this morning for three days' rest and relaxation in La Napoule just outside Cannes.

The main reason we are revisiting last year's venue is that Leslie Azoulay at the Station Tavern in Cannes is still determined to fulfil last year's promise and make me a sheepskin coat. The new one from William Hunt was much admired in Manchester yesterday, but I desperately need a spare if my original – which I am taking on the flight for Leslie to measure and copy – is to be donated as promised to the National Football Museum.

The Cote D'Azur looked anything but a European playground when we arrived. It was pouring with rain, nearly as cold as it was in England, and a grey mist hung over the Mediterranean. A mist also seems to have come over one of our leading sports writers, Jim White of the *Daily Telegraph*. He picked up on the Manchester City v Spurs angle over the weekend and quoted the BBC commentary that accompanied Ricky Villa's winning goal in the 1981 FA Cup final replay. 'Villa, Villa, and still Villa,' didn't sound quite like what I said at the time, especially as Jeffrey Zemell, a Tottenham fan and keen student of commentary, has been quoting me word for word for the last 20 years.

When I read Jim's piece more thoroughly I realised he was quoting Barry Davies – or so he thought. I know Barry will find this as wryly amusing as I do – we get used to our roles sometimes being confused. Bearing in mind we have completed a joint total of 66 years' service with *Match of the Day*, we don't take this too seriously.

At least Jim got the right channel.

TUESDAY, JANUARY 27TH

Don Wayne Patterson of Jet Records in Montreal knows nothing about football. So when I met him over breakfast in the Sofitel Royal Casino at Mandelieu this morning, it was refreshing to talk about something completely different. Don was one of hundreds of music publishers, buyers, sellers and agents attending Midem, the music festival staged every year in Cannes by the Reed Organisation, who are also responsible for the famous film festival. Britney Spears and Madonna had both put in an appearance, but what made Patterson an interesting character was that he is researching his family history – something I once did many years ago. This has led him to England where he recently tracked down the grave of his great grandmother in Chingford Cemetery in Essex. She died in the 19th century, and Don was granted permission to erect a stone at her tomb, which was previously marked only by a number.

But just when football was furthest from my mind, the news came through of the BBC/ITV 'split' for coverage of Euro 2004 in Portugal in the summer. At first sight it looked as though our competitors were off to a flyer, with exclusive coverage of the first two England matches, but the BBC have the third and potentially decisive group match against Croatia, and if Eriksson's men progress, we will be with them all the way after that.

Some of the other BBC matches have great appeal too, but initially the press reaction will spin things ITV's way. We get used to that, even though the audience ratio towards the end of the last World Cup was better than 4 to 1 in the BBC's favour.

WEDNESDAY, JANUARY 28TH

Looking out over the sea from my hotel balcony this morning, with the sun shining while snow fell back home, I should have been writing a favourable review of our visit last night to what is reputedly one of the classiest restaurants in Europe, the Colombe d'Or at St-Paul-de-Vence.

Sadly, it did not live up to my expectations. Maybe I was carried away by the long list of world-famous celebrities who have eaten there, maybe it was the time of year, maybe I was just unlucky, but rather than the intimate surroundings in the brochure, I was made to feel I was gate-crashing a family party.

Actually, there were three large groups eating at separate tables, clearly with no dress code, and one of them included a baby in a highchair whose cries were eventually stemmed by a dummy. I know the French love their children, but we were past nine o'clock in the evening. It's a good job I am not a restaurant critic, because I would be too hard to please. The food was cooked more in the English style than French, the wine was acceptable when the waiter remembered to pour it, or when they weren't carrying dirty dishes past our table.

Anyway, enough of that. Tonight we finally caught up with Leslie Azoulay. The Carling Cup match we had hoped to watch on his giant screen at the Station Tavern was postponed, but he was in no mood to delay the making of the new coat. To the amusement of his regulars, Leslie measured me up in no time at all, and told me he would have the coat ready within a month.

Another excuse to go down to France? Possibly, but if Sven Goran Eriksson has his way after his meeting with Premiership managers, we might all get a much longer break this time next year.

THURSDAY, JANUARY 29TH

Emma from Sunderland saved the day. Or at least, with her sense of humour she made it a whole lot better.

For the second year running, my return from the south of France was complicated by the atrocious weather conditions in England. Roads were blocked, snow and ice made travelling hazardous and inevitably many flights were cancelled or delayed. My only argument with easyJet is that they are not as forthcoming as they might be with information – not at the French end anyway. Their departure desks at Nice airport were flooded with worried customers wondering whether their flights home were ever going to happen. Having been given several different versions as to whether or when our plane had actually left Luton to get to Nice, we eventually took off more than three hours late. Some of the passengers, Rick and myself included, were not in the best of spirits.

That's when Emma took over. I am not sure her role as an easyJet stewardess is meant to include her being a comedienne, sweet talker, nursemaid and humorist, but she certainly had the plane rocking with her announcements over the Tannoy. She even made turning off your mobile phone a hoot.

Neither were we short of lively conversation. The lady who sat next to Rick turned out to be Jane Pasternak – a great niece of Boris – who lives in Monaco. We finished our trip by helping her do the crossword. It was reassuring to know the brain was still working.

FRIDAY, JANUARY 30TH

The resignations of Gavyn Davies and Greg Dyke over the Hutton report dominated the news on my return. When the Chairman of the Governors and the Director General both fall on their sword in the space of 24 hours, I guess you can forgive the headline 'BBC in Crisis'.

Contributors like myself on long-term contracts have no say in the running of the BBC, and nor should we. Management is a totally different career to performance and presentation, but I could understand the affection in which Greg Dyke was held by a lot of the workforce. Selfishly from the sports department point of view, he certainly made more money available for football and was a genuine fan, often appearing in the stand to watch games and joining the BBC team for a drink afterwards.

My favourite encounter with Greg was after England had beaten Germany 5–1 in that unforgettable match in Munich in 2001. As we checked in at the airport on the morning after, I was sharing the enthusiasm of the Director General for England's performance. 'We'll get a fantastic audience,' he said. 'We will, but how about those people who missed it? Pity we can't show it again,' I said.

'That's a bloody great idea,' he said. 'We'll do it tonight. How the hell do we cancel *Panorama?*'

Within minutes Greg had summoned a couple of other BBC executives who were checking in for the flight home. *Panorama* was moved, and the repeat showing of the England match got another significant audience rating.

SATURDAY, JANUARY 31ST

Bumping into Trevor Brooking at West Ham today, I was reminded of something he said when he retired in 1984. Even then, Trevor doubted whether players of the future would remain with one club, as he did, for their whole career. His 18 years spent at Upton Park seems like an anachronism in these days of the Bosman ruling.

Scanning the West Ham programme before today's match with Rotherham, I counted 12 players on their squad list who were not there last season. Trevor himself had brought three of them in when he was caretaker manager, and Alan Pardew had signed a further nine since taking over just four months ago. What a contrast with Wimbledon, whose administrator was sitting next to me in the stand. Four of their former players are among the West Ham newcomers, and the Dons have sold eight more to other clubs while fighting for their future existence.

So the Hammers have reinvented their staff while Wimbledon's, in the words of their manager Stuart Murdoch, have been 'raped'.

But looked at from another angle, they share similar problems. The Hammers lost a number of established stars when they were relegated from the Premiership, and were forced to rebuild. Wimbledon are still counting the cost of their relegation and will almost certainly go down again. In their case, the seemingly endless supply of youngsters from the scheme put in place by their former youth development manager, Roger Smith, means they will resurface stronger next season in division two.

That is the way it is in football now. With all the loan deals being rushed through before the transfer window closes again this weekend, some supporters will see players they hardly recognise wearing the shirt next weekend. The testimonial for ten years' service is a thing of the past.

FEBRUARY 2004

Having covered the Arsenal v Manchester City match at Highbury for Five Live today, I am starting to believe we shall see something that hasn't happened since the 19th century: a team going through a league season in the top division unbeaten.

Today Arsene Wenger's team equalled the record set by George Graham's championship side in 1990–91: a run of 23 unbeaten matches since the start of the season. In their sights now, the record of 29 set by Leeds in 1973–74 and equalled by Liverpool in 1987–88. But can Arsenal surpass even that and avoid defeat in their remaining 15 games? One or two breaks went their way with borderline decisions today, which is always the case when a team is on a roll, and the signing of Jose Antonio Reyes can only add to the Gunners' armoury.

When Reyes conversed with Steve McManaman in Spanish as they both warmed up off the substitutes bench, it was the only language the two clubs were sharing today. While Arsenal remain unbeaten, Manchester City have won only one of their last 18 games... and that was a cup tie.

I was just leaving a restaurant with three former Tottenham stalwarts this afternoon, when news came through right on the transfer window deadline that Tottenham had signed Jermain Defoe from West Ham for seven million pounds. There was no warning of this last-gasp deal. The morning papers had not had even a sniff of it, neither had the well-connected London evening newspaper that usually gets the first whispers from Upton Park.

My West Ham statistics from Saturday needed a rapid update. Defoe was the 17th player to leave the Hammers since they were relegated nine months ago, and Bobby Zamora, who left Spurs in part exchange, must now be the 13th new signing in that time.

Mind you, it was former West Ham boss Harry Redknapp, now in charge at Portsmouth, who was the busiest manager on the last day for transfer business. He completed his seventh recent incoming deal – the Pompey fans will hardly recognise their team next weekend.

All these changes were a world away from the landscape my lunch companions were used to some 25 years ago. Yet it was Keith Burkinshaw, manager at White Hart Lane at the time, who broke new ground when he brought over the two Argentines, Ossie Ardiles and Ricky Villa, after the 1978 World Cup.

Keith, his former assistant Peter Shreeves, who later twice managed Spurs, and the cup-winning captain of the early eighties Steve Perryman were all in jovial mood as we discussed the way the game had changed. On the day after a game in those days, Keith and Steve would spend two hours on the telephone on a Sunday discussing the whys and wherefores of the Spurs performance, and the things they needed to work on in the week ahead.

I wonder how much Premiership managers take their captain as seriously into their confidence today.

TUESDAY, FEBRUARY 3RD

Martell are in their 13th and last year of Grand National sponsorship, and they were determined to make the annual 'weights lunch' one to remember. I was placed on the 'Earth Summit' table, named after the 1998 winner in which I was once offered a share. Six years ago I turned the proposal from Bob Sims down on the grounds that I then had little interest in racing. Ricky George joined Bob's partnership instead, and the rest, as they say, is history. Earth Summit became the only horse ever to win the English, Scottish and Welsh nationals. His trainer, Nigel Twiston-Davies, has six national medals on his table, having won twice at Aintree, the second time two years ago with Bindaree.

Nigel Payne, the Aintree press officer who organised today's event, was also in the partnership. He got all the members together on the same table and was kind enough to include me. Also in our group was Gerry Morrison, who this year will direct the pictures at the National for the BBC for the first time. Our regular producer Malcolm Kemp is sadly seriously ill.

Although the BBC has franchised out the greater share of our racing coverage to an independent production company, in accordance with government guidelines, the Grand National remains in-house, along with The Derby and Royal Ascot. In a week when the BBC is under the cosh from all sides, following the resignation of the chairman and the director general, it was reassuring to be reminded that you might take certain people out of the BBC, but you can't stop the BBC belonging to the people.

WEDNESDAY, FEBRUARY 4TH

It was nearly midnight, and David Pleat and I were the last to leave the Tottenham boardroom after watching the BBC highlights of one of the greatest FA Cup comebacks of all time.

It was a case of, 'Will the last person to leave switch off the lights?' and Pleat didn't need asking twice. His team had led 3–0 at half-time in their fourth round replay against Manchester City, yet somehow contrived to lose 4–3 against ten men – City had their top goalscorer taken off early in the game through injury, and a midfield player was shown a red card as the teams left the field at half-time.

'How fickle football can be,' mused Pleat. 'I have now had my best and worst moments as a manager against the same club."

He was referring to that unforgettable afternoon in 1983 when his Luton side escaped relegation at Maine Road with a late Raddy Antic goal that sent Manchester City down. Pleat's ecstatic, loping run across the pitch at the final whistle to embrace his captain, Brian Horton, is one of the most captivating moments in the history of televised football.

But the history Manchester City made tonight left him dazed and in despair. Had his Spurs side capitalised on their first-half superiority, his opposite number Kevin Keegan would, by his own admission, have been out of a job tomorrow morning. His City side had won only one of their previous 18 games.

I had to go home and watch the video to remind myself of what really happened, but even after a third viewing there was no logic to it. As a commentator, you can shake your head in disbelief, but there is no comeback as long as you have done your job properly. But for those who were involved, however gigantic their salaries, it must rankle for weeks. I saw the Tottenham captain Steve Carr on the way out. He was literally speechless.

THURSDAY, FEBRUARY 5TH

So where did the Spurs/Manchester City epic stand in the panoply of great Cup matches? It certainly brought back memories of their stirring replay in the 1981 final, but in terms of sheer comebacks, today's papers tried in vain to find a direct comparison.

I was in the commentary box at Stamford Bridge in the same fourth round in January 1997, when Chelsea were two down at half-time to Liverpool (it should have been three) and came back to win 4–2, with Mark Hughes proving to be a devastating second-half substitute. Then there were two games in Euro 2000 in Belgium. Slovenia led Yugoslavia 3–0 in Charleroi, and with Mihajlovic sent off the ten men came back to draw 3–3. In the same group, Yugoslavia led Spain 3–2 four minutes into injury time, only for the Spaniards to score twice within a minute and rescue their place in the competition. But in none of these cases had a side come from three down to win with ten men. Everywhere I went today, people were talking about last night's match, something I had not noticed so obviously since England won 5–1 in Germany three years ago.

From the BBC's point of view, the game may have come a year too soon. Although several million would have seen our edited highlights, the game was seen live on Sky by a smaller audience. When the new FA contract kicks in next season, the BBC will screen live coverage of all FA Cup replays, and have access to three live games in every round.

Which reminds me: Fulham's replay win over Everton last night – almost overlooked in all the excitement at White Hart Lane – means I will be covering two London derbies in the next round – Fulham v West Ham on the Saturday and Arsenal v Chelsea on the Sunday.

FRIDAY, FEBRUARY 6TH

While I am busy writing this book, a successful freelance writer by the name of Adam Ward is putting one together called *Motson's National Obsession* for Sanctuary Publishing. It is one in a series of neat, popular hardbacks that take a subject and pander to its anoraks with facts, figures, lists, statistics and sequences.

Sounds right up my street, so it didn't take much persuading to get me to put my name to the football version, especially as I know Adam as a historian who has meticulously researched and written the story of several of our leading clubs. Breakfast meetings are not normally my style, but this one was at the civilised time of ten o'clock and I found myself sharing toast and orange juice in Kensington with Adam and his publisher Iain MacGregor. *Obsession* will come out in May, at the end of the domestic season, but my other obsession, *Motty's Year*, is scheduled to take in the finals of Euro 2004 before hitting the shops in September. Lunch today with BBC Books commissioning editor Ben Dunn and his editor revolved mainly around which photograph should go on the front cover. Ben was convinced that the time-honoured shot of Motty in his sheepskin coat in the snow at Wycombe should be on the jacket.

'But it was taken over 13 years ago,' I protested. 'Yes, but it's iconic. It's more "you" than any of the others,' he said earnestly.

So that's it then. Stuart Clarke never realised when he clicked his camera on that cold December lunchtime in 1990 that, not only would it feature on a postcard in his *Homes of Football* series, but that it would establish me and my coat in the minds of so many people.

Thanks Stuart. You did more for me than any of my commentaries could manage.

SATURDAY, FEBRUARY 7TH

This was the first Saturday of the season that I was not to be found at a football match. There was a very good reason. The events of the week, notably the remarkable match at Tottenham on Wednesday, meant I was required to be in the BBC studio for an appearance on *Football Focus* and *Final Score*.

Studio work never appealed to me when I joined television. The camera never liked me that much, and I was far more comfortable behind the microphone where you don't have to worry about your appearance or what is happening on cameras and monitors all around you. However, as an occasional guest of an accomplished presenter like Ray Stubbs, I can just about get away with it. He has the ability to listen to the studio director in one ear, the editor in the other, and still address people on the sofa with relevant questions.

Peter Schmeichel was alongside me at lunchtime and new though he is to the role, it was me who needed the broadcasting coach more than the international goalkeeper. Rather than talking to moving pictures in the commentary box, I was responding to Peter's opinions and Ray's frantic hand signals. At teatime, Gavin Peacock moved in to field the results as they came in on the teleprinter. Sorry, that was the name given to the 'tickertape' service many years ago. Now they call it the 'vidiprinter'.

It was only later I learnt that Gavin was making his studio debut in that slot. We had worked together on Radio Five Live matches, and somehow Ray steered us through an hour-long sequence that seemed like ten minutes.

My head was still spinning when Anne and I attended a 50th birthday bash for a mutual friend, Elaine Darvell, later that evening. In the meantime, Fred and his friends were celebrating his 18th birthday at Walthamstow Greyhound Stadium.

It was another reminder that for most people, Saturday night out is a natural release as part of the weekend. For me, over the last thirty-something years, it has always been an endurance test after my hardest day of the week. Never mind. Everybody else works hard from Monday to Friday.

SUNDAY, FEBRUARY 8TH

Ken Bates has been the Lord and Master of Stamford Bridge for more than 20 years. Everybody knows the story of how he bought Chelsea Football Club for a pound, took on the debts, and fought the world and a lot of people in it to develop the ground and the club as it exists today. Ken has revelled in a reputation that could justifiably be described as confrontational, controversial, even cantankerous, but he has never asked for sympathy. As a result, I felt a tiny bit guilty about feeling sorry for him today. I was not alone. Having given me a piece of his mind many times over the years, Ken and his wife Susannah invited me for a glass of champagne before the match against Charlton. But in the plush surroundings of his directors' restaurant in the redeveloped West Stand at Stamford Bridge, I quickly realised all was not well.

Certainly Ken wasn't. He was coughing alarmingly, and it was without realising the implications that I spotted, while he was welcoming other guests, that his regular provocative column was missing from the Chelsea programme. 'First time I've missed writing it in 22 years,' he explained. 'The new owners told me they didn't want it today.'

Times are changing. Peter Kenyon had taken up his duties at Chelsea as chief executive after moving from Manchester United, and a feature on his arrival had replaced the Bates blast. Knowing Ken, he won't take kindly to that, although his sense of humour certainly didn't disappear with his programme notes. 'Interest rates are up to four and a half per cent this week, and they will be five by the end of the season,' he smiled.

Everything has its price. And Ken Bates, deservedly, got his for Chelsea from his Russian successor.

MONDAY, FEBRUARY 9TH

It was on my mind all weekend, but it was only today that I was able to reflect on the life and achievement of Bob Stokoe, who died last week. The enduring memory of Geordie Bob will, for most people, be his dash across the Wembley pitch to embrace his goalkeeper Jim Montgomery, whose amazing double save won the FA Cup for Sunderland in 1973.

My memories of Bob are rather different. When I started at *Match of the Day* in 1971, some of my early matches were at Blackpool, where he was manager. His kindness to a rookie commentator is something I will never forget.

When Stokoe left Bloomfield Road to take over as Sunderland manager in November 1972, I drove with him across the North of England at six o'clock in the morning to film his arrival at Roker Park and his introduction to the Sunderland players. I stood outside the door of the manager's office while he sacked another member of staff, and walked with him on to the pitch where he made himself known to the likes of Montgomery, Dennis Tueart and Dave Watson. Within six months, a second-division side had won the FA Cup at the expense of mighty Leeds, but my association with Stokoe did not end there.

In February 1985, I was hastily rerouted from Liverpool to Manchester one frosty Saturday morning, when a game at Anfield was postponed and the BBC cameras were swiftly installed at Maine Road for a second-division match against Carlisle United. Arriving only an hour before kick-off, I hardly knew a single Carlisle player, but Bob took me into the dressing room and personally introduced me to his entire team.

We both got lucky. Carlisle won 3–1 and I got away with the commentary. No wonder they prolonged the minute's silence for Bob Stokoe at St James' Park last Saturday. He was a giant of a centre-half for Newcastle and much loved at two North East clubs

TUESDAY, FEBRUARY 10TH

Next August, *Match of the Day* not only returns to the nation's television screens, but also celebrates its 40th anniversary. I can honestly remember watching the first programme on August 22nd 1964, when I was among an audience of just 22,000 who tuned in to BBC2 at 6.30pm to watch the extended highlights of Liverpool's opening match as defending champions, against Arsenal at Anfield.

At the time, I was a local reporter on the *Barnet Press*, and rushed back from covering Finchley's match in the Athenian League in time to watch Kenneth Wolstenholme introduce the new football programme from the side of the pitch in what he described as 'Beatleville'. These memories were stirred today by Paul Wright, the producer charged with making an anniversary programme, and Martyn Smith, who is writing a book on the 40-year history.

I won't steal the thunder for either of them by dwelling on my personal highlights – seven years after being one of the first viewers, I joined as a young commentator – but I know that the affection in which the programme is held will be suitably reflected in what they are planning.

Sixties nostalgia was maintained tonight when I joined the veterans of my old Sunday league side, Roving Reporters, at our twice-yearly gathering. Not for the first time we enjoyed a convivial evening at Walthamstow Greyhound Stadium. Along with the club chairman Roger Jones, I was one of the founder members in 1965, a year after *Match of the Day* started. So next year it will be our 40th anniversary, and Roger is already planning a celebration dinner.

WEDNESDAY, FEBRUARY 11TH

It was time today to revisit my Harley Street physician John Newman, to find out the results of my four-month battle with the worrying cholesterol count. Fortunately, the news was good. The statin tablets John had prescribed had brought my level down from over seven to under five, and he seemed satisfied with that. He wasn't so pleased when I got on the scales. I protested that the increase in my weight was partly due to fat turning to muscle after my modest efforts in Dean Austin's gym, but Newman wasn't having any of that. Cut down on the saturated fats and drink more water, was the verdict.

That advice quickly went to the back of my mind when I arrived at Loftus Road tonight to see Fulham play Aston Villa. It is customary for the home side to welcome their boardroom guests with a glass of champagne, or two glasses if you get there early. Not for the first time I found myself sitting close to Sven's assistant Tord Grip, who insisted that England would field as close a side as they could in next week's friendly in Portugal to the one that will start in Euro 2004 against France.

It took all of a minute from kick-off to see why England need to be careful in Faro. Luis Boa Morte, named in Portugal's squad today, scored in the first minute. Aston Villa came back to win 2–1 and looked a far better outfit than when I saw them earlier in the season. But my mind was focused on Fulham, who play West Ham in the first of my two FA Cup ties this coming weekend. Hammers' manager Alan Pardew was running the rule over their opponents, so it was a useful night in terms of collecting background information.

I don't think I'll tell John Newman about the cheeseburger I ate outside the ground.

THURSDAY, FEBRUARY 12TH

Mike Dillon, the unmistakable face of Ladbrokes racing, is also a committed football fan. In FA Cup weeks we touch base when I offer my brave, and sometimes wildly inaccurate, forecasts for the coming weekend's fixtures. Before the third round I was asked to pick four teams who might do well this year – not necessarily the favourites, but one or two whose price might appeal to the punter at the outset. After two rounds I have three still running – Chelsea, Liverpool and Manchester City. My excuse for losing out on Middlesbrough is they were concentrating on the Carling Cup, where they have reached the final. All well and good, until Mike reminded me that Chelsea are away to Arsenal, who have beaten

them in the competition for the last three years, and Manchester City –
having won only two matches out of the last 21 – are at Old Trafford.

I skirted round those two games as best I could – at least Chelsea and
City will be a good price to win – and reminded everybody that my major
tip was Liverpool, who I backed myself at 8 to 1. Just to keep Mike happy,
or it could have been the other way round, we struck a separate bet on what
I called my 'Italian yankee'. Dillon offered me decent prices on Juventus to
win the Champions League, Roma for the UEFA Cup, AC Milan for the
Serie A title, and Italy to win the European Championship. If all those four
come in, I will be buying drinks all round. But just two results out of the
four would show a profit.

I need a bit of luck with the bookies. My each-way bet on Nigeria to
win the African Nations Cup went out of the window when they lost on
penalties to Tunisia in the semi-final.

FRIDAY, FEBRUARY 13TH

Friday the 13th – and certainly unlucky when it came to our horse
ownership. Nigel Payne, the driving force behind our syndicates, rang
to say that Polar Summit has broken down again and will have to be
prematurely retired as a racehorse. This comes hard on the back of the
long-term injury to Corroboree, which will keep him out for this season
and next. Ironically, the photographs of his win at Kempton in the early
part of this season arrived only this morning. The only other interest I
have, the horse Nigel christened 'Henry the Great', has not made an
auspicious start to his racing career, and word from the stables is not
encouraging.

The footballing hero of Nigel's, after whom the horse was named,
didn't have a great day on the fitness front either. Word reached me from
the Arsenal training ground that Thierry has a bad foot and is doubtful for
Sunday's fifth-round FA Cup tie against Chelsea. Before then, I have to
cover another London derby, Fulham against West Ham, tomorrow
afternoon for the *Match of the Day* highlights programme: another double
bill which will keep me busy for most of the day with preparation.

I did remember, though, to pop out and buy my wife her Valentine
card. I don't think we have ever missed popping one under each other's
pillow since the year we were married.

SATURDAY, FEBRUARY 14TH

Valentine's Day did not get off to a friendly start. Rarely have I ever encountered problems on the M1 travelling south from my junction into London on a weekend, but maintenance work between the City exit and the end of the motorway meant a two-mile tailback which delayed my arrival at Loftus Road.

I needn't have worried. Fulham's manager Chris Coleman had also been overtaken by events and the planned interview for *Football Focus* was cancelled. Fortunately they had plenty of material and our input was not critical.

It was a few years since I had climbed the steps to the camera platform at Queens Park Rangers' ground (rather like most Fulham supporters, I still associate them with Craven Cottage) and I had forgotten just how tight it was, having been constructed in the early days of televised football. In order to accommodate two of our overseas colleagues, I had to squeeze up between two cameras and my view of the nearside of the pitch was severely restricted. Not that there was much to be missed. Fulham were below form, and even without six ineligible players West Ham looked the better side without being able to make it tell.

Nor was there a romantic end to the day. Anne was running a fund-raising dinner for Barnardo's as the chairperson of our local group, and the early kick-off at Highbury tomorrow meant I had to get my head down over some more homework tonight. My old colleague and friend Bill Hamilton and my son Fred combined to handle the auction, and I don't think my absence was noticed.

Sven Goran Eriksson, who I had met at the Fulham match earlier, announced his squad for next Wednesday's match in Portugal. It included Sol Campbell, but my information is that he is struggling even to make tomorrow's game.

SUNDAY, FEBRUARY 15TH

When I got to Highbury, Campbell had passed his fitness test and both line-ups were as I expected, with Jose Antonio Reyes getting his chance because of Henry's injury. The ladies who organise the food in the directors' suite served up a fantastic cooked breakfast, which meant I was their first customer soon after ten o'clock. A bonus when the kick-off was so early.

Chelsea's bonus, having not beaten Arsenal in the FA Cup since Clement Attlee was Prime Minister, was a first-half goal by Adrian Mutu which suggested they might at last lay to rest their hoodoo against the Gunners in the FA Cup. Not so. Mutu's goal was overshadowed by an even better one from Reyes, who then got the winner. Once Arsenal got in front, Chelsea seemed to lose their desire and, with the notable exception of John Terry, a few heads went down.

There was the usual 38,000 crowd at Highbury, but mention was again made of the empty seats at some of the other FA Cup ties over the weekend. A lot of clubs still seem to have missed the point. By not including FA Cup vouchers in season-ticket books, they are asking supporters to pay through the nose again to watch Cup ties.

The All-Party Football Committee who came out with their report last week might have usefully raised the issue. Sadly, their findings seem to have made little impression, which (even more sadly) was only to be expected. They can make as many recommendations as they like, but ultimately they have no power.

MONDAY, FEBRUARY 16TH

Because dinosaurs like me still exist in this world of technological advancement, John Rolt still services portable typewriters. He called this morning to take my beloved 'Olympia Traveller de Luxe S' away for a couple of days while I am in Portugal. It will come back in sparkling condition, Tipp-Ex stains removed and a nice new black ribbon fitted.

When he arrived I was glued to the video recorder again, watching a tape of Portugal's 8–0 victory over Kuwait in their last international. Until a couple of years ago, commentators would agonise (some more than others) over which players from the respective squads would line up for an international. Now, thanks mainly to Sven, the game plan has changed. We know that he and sometimes his opposite number are likely to field an entirely new team in the second half. Thus, some 44 names have to be listed, and FIFA president Sepp Blatter has plans to change a system which he believes is unfair on the paying spectator.

Eriksson's argument, which he reiterated to me last Saturday, is that the club managers will co-operate better with him if he uses the leading players sparingly. And how often does he get a chance to look at the rest in match conditions? Personally, I can see the argument resolving itself before long. The extended World Cup qualifying groups over the next two years will mean that friendly dates will be few and far between, and matches like this week's in Faro will be virtually redundant.

I am not sure how much anybody really cares.

TUESDAY, FEBRUARY 17TH

The flight carrying most of the written and broadcast media to Faro for the England friendly was due to leave Gatwick at the unearthly hour of 6.40am, which would have involved my getting up at about three o'clock in the morning. The BBC took pity on me and arranged a civilised British Airways flight in the late afternoon, which gave me time to make a guest appearance on Chelsea TV, the club's dedicated subscription channel.

For nearly an hour, in company with presenter Neil Barnett, I fielded questions from Chelsea supporters still smarting from their second-half performance at Arsenal on Sunday. Most of the time it was me trying to get a word in. The e-mails were never-ending, and the telephone callers were determined to get their point across at some length. You could feel the sense of bitter betrayal they felt after playing so well in the first half.

Neil told me afterwards it was the first time the fans had questioned Ranieri and his tactics. Not the best time for him to pick up the *Daily Express* and read yet another 'exclusive' about Sven Goran Eriksson taking over in the summer.

When I arrived in Faro, the England coach was more concerned about the withdrawals of Sol Campbell, John Terry and Darius Vassell adding to the absence of Jonathan Woodgate, Gary Neville, Rio Ferdinand and Steven Gerrard. Seven missing – nothing new there.

It will be as much a dummy run for this commentator as it will for England. Two nights in a comfortable hotel and a chance to stake out a couple of nice restaurants will stand me in good stead for the summer, when my first match will be between Spain and Russia here on the Algarve...

WEDNESDAY, FEBRUARY 18TH

By then, Joe Royle will have firmly established himself in Trevor Brooking's seat as my co-commentator on England matches. Joe joined me in Faro this morning, and over lunch we caught up on old times, of which there are many.

I have known Joe since he was a young player at Everton; commentated on his early days as an England centre-forward; covered Oldham's cup exploits in his long spell there; witnessed the Everton revival he started in the mid-nineties; and worked briefly with him in Korea at the start of the 2002 World Cup. Having just received my certificate as an Ipswich Town shareholder, I am now entitled to ask a few pertinent questions about how they are coping on coming out of administration. A play-off place is currently on the cards but Joe fears more players will have to leave if they are not promoted.

Easing Joe into Trevor's role was something I had no qualms about. Had we been breaking in a new, inexperienced broadcaster there would have been teething troubles, but Joe has worked for Channel 5 on a semi-regular basis and once I left him in Korea, to join Trevor in Japan, he teamed up with Steve Wilson and became an integral and popular member of the BBC World Cup team.

Although we were only showing recorded highlights tonight, Joe and I treated the match as though it were live. We avoided the trap of both talking at once and I felt his comments brought the required sane analysis in between my frantic version of events.

Not only does Royle's career record speak for itself in terms of his authority at the microphone, he is also a warm social animal and what we call in the broadcasting business a 'team player'. In other words, we didn't get to bed until very late.

THURSDAY, FEBRUARY 19TH

It is three months before Eriksson announces his squad of 23 players for Euro 2004, but most of the media spent today picking *their* version based mainly on the 1–1 draw in Faro last night. Tottenham's Ledley King pushed himself on to the fringe of the selection with an assured display at centre-back. He also scored England's goal, but then again four of Sven's regular centre-backs were missing.

At this stage, the three goalkeepers for Portugal will be David James –
over whom I still have reservations – Paul Robinson and the still uncapped
Chris Kirkland; the four full-backs look like Gary Neville, Ashley Cole,
Wayne Bridge and either Phil Neville, who could double up in midfield, or
Danny Mills.

If Sol Campbell, John Terry and Jonathan Woodgate are all fit, and
assuming Rio Ferdinand is still banned, it looks like a straight fight
between King and Gareth Southgate for the fourth centre-back slot.

At least seven midfield players will go, with David Beckham, Paul
Scholes, Steven Gerrard, Frank Lampard and Nicky Butt looking
certainties. Add to those Joe Cole and Kieron Dyer, and the likes of Owen
Hargreaves, Scott Parker and Jermaine Jenas have a bit to do.

As for the strikers, Michael Owen, Wayne Rooney, Emile Heskey and
Darius Vassell lead the way at present. Were Sven to add a fifth to the list
– bringing up the required total of 23 – Jermain Defoe could be a late
shout now he has moved to Tottenham. I think the likelihood is for an
extra midfield option, in which case the three I have mentioned could be
competing for one place.

Having said all of this, history tells us that one key player at least is
always injured at the last minute, and that one unexpected late arrival gets
his chance. We will see in three months' time.

FRIDAY, FEBRUARY 20TH

Three major matches in five days left me in need of a break, so my first
real weekend off from any television or radio commitments meant I
could enjoy a day's racing with Fred at Sandown Park. Not only that, but
we struck lucky with four winners out of the seven races. Jim Falconer and
Samantha Parfitt, the hosts in the Ladbrokes hospitality area, must have
got a bit concerned when the other guests started asking us for our tips. For
the last winner we had to thank the ubiquitous Mike Dillon, who popped
into the box to say that French trainer Thierry Doumen strongly fancied
his horse Royal Paradise in the last race of the day.

With just three weeks to go now to the National Hunt Festival at
Cheltenham, my enthusiasm for racing is growing again. The ante-post
market is thriving and although I normally leave my investment until I know
what is definitely running, I am reminded by Doumen's success today of

what he said about First Gold when we were at Kempton Park at Christmas.

I was brought down to earth when we got home and I saw the pile of video tapes waiting for me. There was a cluster of international friendlies played all over Europe on Wednesday, many of them involving countries I will be covering in the summer. Somehow I don't think it will be a weekend without football.

SATURDAY, FEBRUARY 21ST

The tributes to William John Charles, who died this morning, were totally in keeping with the stature of a man who could claim to be Britain's most successful football export. He received international acclaim in life and in death.

Charles was as revered in Italy, where he led Juventus to three championships in four years, missing only two games, as he was in Wales, for whom he played in the 1958 World Cup finals, and in Leeds, where 40 years ago he finished the season with 42 goals in 39 league games. John's passion for the game endeared him to everyone he met long after his heyday. After he finished as player-manager at Hereford, he played out the last days of his career with Merthyr Tydfil at the age of 41.

To try to capture just how good Charles was as a young player at Leeds, I turned up the *Playfair Football Annual* for 1955–56. A feature by Eric Stanger of the *Yorkshire Post* described him as, 'Two players in one. There is no better centre-half in the game today. And no better centre-forward.'

The point was proved elsewhere in the same book. A report on England's 3–2 victory over Wales at Wembley in 1954 made Roy Bentley's hat-trick of secondary concern compared to the performance of John Charles, who scored both the Welsh goals. 'A football giant in every sense, Charles was magnificent. The sight of this great footballer bearing down on the England goal with the ball at his feet was sufficient to send the Welsh patriots into a frenzy. Even when an injury to Ray Daniel necessitated Charles taking over at centre-half for a period, he continued to dominate the game.'

Forty years later, the obituaries said very much the same things. The man was a colossus and even though John is no longer with us, his is a legend that will never die.

SUNDAY, FEBRUARY 22ND

So now you know why I am a commentator and not a tipster. Liverpool, my fourth and last hope for a winning FA Cup bet, stumbled out at Portsmouth – sweet revenge for Jim Smith, who saw his Pompey side lose on penalties to the Reds in the semi-final 12 years ago. If you recall, and I can't pretend it was otherwise, my four FA Cup tips were Chelsea, Middlesbrough, Manchester City and Liverpool. Not one will figure in the last eight.

Now there are those who feel the competition loses some of its appeal when the big clubs are toppled, but I am not among them. The fact that Tranmere from division two, Millwall, Sheffield United and possibly Sunderland and West Ham (both still to replay) will be in the sixth round means the cup retains its romance. And we could still have a Manchester United v Arsenal final. Talking of those two clubs, one bet I do look like winning is the one I placed on the Gunners for the Premiership in October. They went seven points clear of United yesterday and I will be amazed if they let it slip again this year.

Going back to the Portsmouth game, if television body language is any guide, Gérard Houllier and Michael Owen may be somewhere else by the time this book comes out. The Liverpool manager wore a doomed expression when they went a goal down, and Owen's penalty would surely have sent the match a different way had he scored. Which way Owen's career goes now will depend even more on Liverpool achieving the fourth Champions League spot. And even then, would he be prepared to sign another long-term contract at Anfield?

MONDAY, FEBRUARY 23RD

Talking as we were about Gérard Houllier's position, how the expectation of a club like Liverpool has grown since the days of Bill Shankly, the original architect of Anfield as we know it. Shankly won his first championship with Liverpool in 1964, and another two years later, with their first FA Cup triumph in between. But in the six seasons that followed, Liverpool won absolutely nothing. Their finishing position in the old first division was 5th, 3rd, 2nd, 5th, 5th and 3rd. They made one losing appearance in the FA Cup final, and that was about it. Would any

PREVIOUS PAGE: The trophy that enabled me to earn my stripes as a commentator.

TOP: Arsenal went through the Premiership unbeaten.
ABOVE: The goalscorers in my 25th FA Cup final for the BBC. Disappointment awaited both at Euro 2004.

TOP: My old neighbour Iain Dowie performed a miracle at Crystal Palace.
LEFT: A happier moment for the England captain before Euro 2004.
ABOVE RIGHT: Thierry Henry was everybody's 'Player of the Year'.

PREVIOUS PAGE: I'm happy to be playing for the best team.

ABOVE: England all set to go in Euro 2004. Just look at the flags – the support in Portugal was the best I have ever seen.

BELOW: One of the highlights of my year was meeting up with Ricky Villa.

RIGHT: Rooney scores against Croatia. England's promise, and their demise, both lay in his feet.

TOP RIGHT: Nuno Gomes (not the footballer) was one of our drivers and fixers in Portugal.

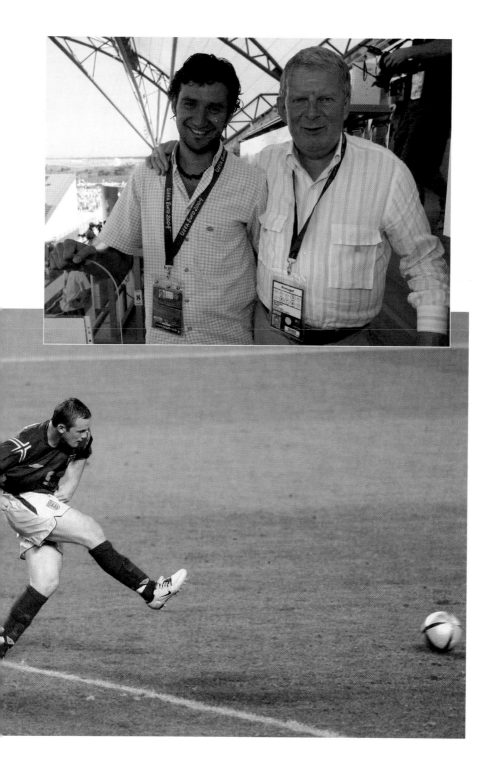

LEFT: At the commentary position in the Faro-Loule stadium on the Algarve, one of the venues for my 16th major championship with the BBC.
BELOW: A Greek odyssey. The 100 to 1 outsiders win Euro 2004.

board of directors stand for that sort of performance today? Not at Liverpool's level certainly, but in those days nobody even thought about questioning Shankly's position.

As it turned out, Liverpool won a double of league and UEFA Cup in 1973, followed by the FA Cup the following year. Shankly then retired, and his legacy was carried on by Bob Paisley, who won just about everything.

So Houllier, who won three major Cup competitions in 2001 and took Liverpool to second in the league the following year, now has to cope with a level of expectancy that would stretch any manager – let alone one who owes his life to a 12-hour heart operation. Even the normally balanced *Telegraph Sport* saw fit to fire the warning gun. Henry Winter in his match report wrote, 'The clouds darken ever angrily over Houllier's head', and columnist Paul Hayward called the Portsmouth defeat 'calamitous' and said Liverpool's fans were in despair.

TUESDAY, FEBRUARY 24TH

I suppose you could say I have had three mini-careers in BBC Radio Sport, quite apart from the 33 years I have spent in television. My first job in the Corporation was as a sports news assistant in the old Radio 2 sports department from 1968 to 1971. I started by writing bulletins and reading the racing results, graduated to presenting and commentating, and by the time I left for *Match of the Day* had covered not just football, but also boxing and tennis.

That prompted my 'recall' from television for the Wimbledon fortnight from 1976 until 1981. I was reporting from Centre Court on all five of Bjorn Borg's singles titles, and worked in the commentary box with the legendary Fred Perry, our last men's singles champion who, well into his eighties, was a skilful broadcaster and smashing colleague.

I was reminded of the late Perry's omnipresence today when I passed one of the clothes shops that still bears his name in Covent Garden. Fittingly, I was on my way to lunch with Bob Shennan, the controller of Radio Five Live. It was Bob who revived my radio career again three years ago. He had briefly come across to head BBC Television Sport in 1998, and a year later gave me a five-year contract for which I shall always be grateful.

By the time Bob got his controller's job, we had lost the Premiership highlights on *Match of the Day* and he asked me to join the Five Live team. The arrangement has worked happily for both parties, and we both hope it will continue in some form when I resume my weekly television role next season.

When I left Bob, I was driven to West Ham for televised highlights of tonight's FA Cup replay against Fulham. Here again, there was a reminder of my past. We went by the East End Mission where my father was Methodist Superintendent for seven years. And for two of those, I lived in a top-floor flat right on Commercial Road in Stepney.

WEDNESDAY, FEBRUARY 25TH

It was only this morning that I was able to reflect on one of the strangest incidents of my commentating career. It was at once bizarre, funny and finally very rewarding to all concerned.

West Ham were good enough to seat me in a new commentary position on the edge of the press box at Upton Park last night – enabling me to get much closer to the action than had I sat with the cameras on the new platform right at the back of the stand. A lady in the row across the gangway was frantically signalling to me while I was commentating in the second half, and it was only when the match was over that I was able to respond to her unusual request.

Helen Cadzow, of Interface Europe Ltd, was a guest of the corporate sponsors, and wanted to present them with the gloves I was wearing. 'I'm happy to pay you £50 for them – they're part of your image,' she insisted. Once I realised she was serious, I said I would only take the money on condition that it went to charity. She produced the cash and I gave her the gloves. I also threw in my commentary card to soften my embarrassment.

As it so happened, I had asked Paul Aldridge, West Ham's managing director, for a Hammers shirt to pass on to my friend Leslie Azoulay down in Cannes. So in the boardroom we came to an agreement that suited everybody. I gave Paul the £50 towards the club's current charity donations, he went down to the dressing room and picked up the shirt Steve Lomas had just worn, and I came home happy.

Not so West Ham. They lost 3–0 and blew the chance of a million-pound payday at Old Trafford in the next round. As for my gloves, they are in a frame somewhere in East London.

THURSDAY, FEBRUARY 26TH

By now, you probably think everything runs far too smoothly for me, that there is never a really bad day, and that everything I do is hugely enjoyable and never puts me in anything other than a good mood. Not so. This morning I got caught in what I can only describe as the 'call centre trap'. Anne has warned me about it many times, and about the frustrations that follow when you are left in a telephone queue, but patience has never been my greatest virtue and to my shame I snapped this morning and left a young man rather shocked and hurt.

A missive from the BBC's contributors' payments department offered a telephone number for queries, but when I dialled I found myself being offered the option of pressing various buttons depending on the type of inquiry. That was just the start of it. The lady who finally answered told me she would have to refer me to somebody else, but clearly their line was busy because I then sat through ten minutes of piped music. As someone brought up on delivering deadlines, I put the phone down and started all over again. The same thing happened, only this time the music lasted longer before I put the receiver back.

At the third attempt, timed at 27 minutes after I first picked up the phone, I got through to a gentleman who said he would have to investigate my inquiry further. I am not proud of the outburst which followed – I suppose you would say I gave him a piece of my mind. It was only when I met Cathy Barrow, the BBC Sports Talent Manager, later in the day, that I realised I wasn't speaking directly to the BBC at all. It was an out-sourced call centre with a franchise to process various payments – including mine! I asked Cathy to apologise to the young man concerned who happened to be at the other end of the line. How much easier it would be if every relevant department had a direct-line telephone which somebody answered when it rang.

FRIDAY, FEBRUARY 27TH

My next television commentary is nine days away, but work starts now. Millwall and Tranmere are not teams you see every week, and the fact that they will be playing for a place in the FA Cup semi-final means the match needs carefully preparing.

Not least in my reservoir of cup memories is the fourth-round tie at Prenton Park four years ago, when Tranmere finished their 1–0 victory over Sunderland with an extra player on the pitch. The confusion arose when referee Rob Harris sent off Tranmere defender Clint Hill, for a second yellow card offence, thereby reducing the home side to ten men just as Sunderland were about to take a free-kick in the dying seconds. Tranmere's manager John Aldridge sent on substitute Steve Frail, who ran on to the pitch before they could withdraw Andy Parkinson, the man he was to replace. Thus, when the free-kick was cleared and the final whistle went, Rovers had eleven men on the field rather than ten.

Sunderland appealed against the result, but the FA decided not to replay the game. Instead, they suspended referee Rob Harris and his assistant Tony Green, on the grounds that the responsibility for the error lay with the match officials.

It was the season the Cup had already been tarnished by playing the third round before Christmas, and persuading Manchester United to take part in the World Club Championship in Brazil, whereby they withdrew from the FA Cup. I received a note from Bob Shennan, then in charge of our department, to the effect that it was a good job I had swerved the South America trip in order to concentrate on the FA Cup. These are the unpredictable incidents which test a commentator's concentration and observation. No amount of research would have prepared you for that little cameo.

SATURDAY, FEBRUARY 28TH

Everybody knows that Hereford is very close to my heart – you would need to have been asleep for 30 years *not* to know – but I certainly didn't expect the Conference team to be top of the agenda when I arrived at Millwall today.

As luck would have it, or maybe it was an earlier return from the pub than usual, I was among those who had nothing better to do last night than tune in out of curiosity to Sky's coverage of the Dagenham and Redbridge v Hereford match on a Friday night. Don't for one moment think I am belittling the Conference – my regular visits to Barnet have been supplemented in the last two years by appearances at a number of other grounds, including Dagenham. But if I needed converting to the live option, then Hereford's 9–0 victory was the perfect persuasion. Not only did it equal the Conference record, but it reminded me of the last time I saw a team score nine away from home – Peterborough at Barnet in the third division in 1998.

There were never going to be nine goals at Millwall, but the two they did score were sufficient to beat Burnley, and their performance gave me a good indication of what to expect next Sunday. Especially that of midfielder Tim Cahill, who looked to me like a player the Premiership scouts had missed out on.

The Saturday night headlines were made by another Alex Ferguson rant at referees – this time because Manchester United were denied a penalty at Fulham. The fact that Arsenal, who beat Charlton, have opened up a nine-point gap in the Premiership title race won't have improved his mood. Frankly, I think it's all over.

SUNDAY, FEBRUARY 29TH

Leap year, the first Sunday in Lent, the Carling Cup final, Liverpool and Newcastle both in action in the Premiership – what more could you ask for on a Sunday?

Certainly not, in my case, the new set of bathroom scales that Mrs Motson produced today. Such is modern technology that they reveal not just my weight – which in itself is bad enough – but my body-fat level and the number of calories I should be eating. My morning run did nothing to dispel the depression which greeted my first reading. There is no escaping the fact that exactly a stone has plonked itself on the Motson stomach in the last four years, and in quiet contemplation in church tonight I vowed to do something about it over the next 40 days and nights.

The Middlesbrough chairman Steve Gibson is one who has never had to worry about his weight. A keen Sunday footballer, he got his reward for 20 years on the board when Boro won their first major trophy in 128 years by beating Bolton at Cardiff today.

Steve was a young director when the club came within minutes of going out of business in 1987. They put a padlock on the gates of Ayresome Park then, but thanks to his investment they found the key to a future which has brought a new stadium, a sustained position in the Premiership, and now a trophy.

Elsewhere, my earlier reservations about loan deals between Premiership clubs were borne out when Lomana Lua Lua struck a late equaliser for Portsmouth against his own club Newcastle. The fact that the Geordies had reportedly forgotten to include a clause in the loan agreement to prevent him playing against them is not the point. His goal could, in theory, deprive Newcastle of a place in the Champions League, yet by the end of the season he could be back at St James' Park.

Don't blame the player. The rule sends out the wrong signal and should be reversed forthwith.

MARCH

MONDAY, MARCH 1ST

The funeral and memorial service for John Charles made moving pictures on the news today, and perhaps reminded the people of Leeds of days when values were slightly better than they are now.

I spent this morning locked in a studio with Ally McCoist, putting the finishing touches to our voiceovers for the PlayStation game *FIFA 2005*. The release date seems to get earlier and earlier. McCoist and I had to find a way of introducing a sequence of some 75 matches over the same pictures, changing our words to suit the occasion, be it a cup tie (first or second leg), a league game or a friendly. Those computer literates who play *FIFA* will know exactly what I mean, although I am not sure whether I do.

One player who did rejoin the scene today was our old friend from Cannes, Leslie Azoulay. He was over to buy a London taxi – yes, a black cab – which he is going to drive around the Côte D'Azur to advertise his bar and restaurant. I met him in a tea shop in Borehamwood with his friends Ray and Jean Phillips, who had negotiated a deal whereby Leslie got the cab for £1,450, rather than the £4,000 he had been quoted.

It must have put him in a generous mood, because the sheepskin coat he had made me, based on the measurements he took in the South of France a month ago, was an absolute steal at £400. It fitted me like a glove, and with two new trademark coats in the wardrobe, I can now fulfil a promise and let the National Football Museum have my old one.

The only thing that spoilt the day was the accusation of racist chanting by Millwall fans towards Burnley's Mo Camara on Saturday. I had noticed some booing directed at the left-back, but put it down to the legacy of a stormy FA Cup tie between the clubs at The Den two weeks earlier. Goodness knows how hard Millwall have tried to live down their battered image over the years – on this occasion I am sure that the abuse was no more or less than any biased set of supporters would direct at a player involved in a previous incident, whatever the colour of his skin.

TUESDAY, MARCH 2ND

Talking to millions of viewers with a microphone is a lot different to being able to see your audience, and this morning I was face to face with the Faber and Faber sales force from all over the country. They are distributing *Motson's National Obsession* when it is published at the beginning of May. The writer, Adam Ward, is two thirds of the way through the copy and the publishers, Sanctuary, are optimistic of sales approaching 100,000. Iain MacGregor, who commissioned the book, wanted me to share a few anecdotes with the sales team, who were gathered together for a brainstorming session on four new titles, one of which was mine.

After a pleasant lunch, it was off to Wimpole Street for the ECG that John Newman had recommended as a routine check-up. My reading of 67 seemed to satisfy the medics, and it was all over in less than ten minutes.

My next appointment took a little longer. I did say the other day that the Hereford saga is never further away than touching distance, and this evening Ricky George and I met up with Keith Hall, who is the public address announcer at Hereford United's ground at Edgar Street. Keith is doing a post-graduate diploma in Broadcast Journalism at Falmouth College of Arts, and as part of his final assessment is putting together a radio documentary called *Moment in Time*.

He was in the crowd the day Hereford beat Newcastle, but wanted to broaden his theme to show how our lives had been intrinsically linked both before and after the event.

Goodness knows what nonsense we talked over two bottles of champagne, but Keith is a lovely fellow and has two hours of nostalgia on his tape recorder to get some sense out of.

WEDNESDAY, MARCH 3RD

I first met Andy King when he was a young player at Luton, but our paths crossed more memorably when he scored the winning goal for Everton in a Merseyside derby at Goodison Park in 1978. It was the first time

Everton had beaten Liverpool in seven years, and midfielder King, appropriately with number seven on his back, scored the only goal of the game with a peach of a volley that left Ray Clemence clutching thin air.

BBC viewers will remember the occasion not only for the goal, but for the way a formidable member of Merseyside Constabulary pushed King and an interviewer unceremoniously off the pitch as Andy was trying to relive his big moment.

King is now manager of Swindon Town, who, after a few fallow years, have surprised a number of people by crashing into the play-off positions in Division Two. My reason for revisiting the County Ground – where I last covered an FA Cup tie against Aston Villa in 1992 when Glenn Hoddle was manager – was to spy on Tranmere Rovers in advance of Sunday's FA Cup game at Millwall.

Sadly, my drive down the M4 was to be rendered unimportant by the shocking news that Adam Ward, the author of *Motson's National Obsession*, had been killed in a car crash on Monday night – something of which the publishers were totally unaware when we met yesterday. Adam was 32 with two young children and much admired in the book trade where he had proved himself a prolific and dedicated professional. I only met him once, but his gentle nature and sense of humour left a marked impression. What a tragedy. It puts life into perspective.

THURSDAY, MARCH 4TH

Sepp Blatter, the FIFA President, has been in town this week, assuring Tony Blair that there is no reason why Great Britain should not enter a football team in the 2012 Olympics, and supervising various law changes made by the international board – some good, some bad. I totally approve of a limited number of six substitutes in international friendlies – forty or more players taking part in one match had become a farce – but I am sorry to see the end of the silver and golden goals. Now we have to resign ourselves to a tedious 30 minutes of extra time – plus penalties maybe – every time a match is drawn in the knock-out phase.

Blatter also spoke with forked tongue when it came to the contentious issue of fixture congestion and demands on players. He suggested that a reduction to 18 clubs in the Premiership and the abolition of FA Cup replays would lighten the load in England and give us a 'proper' winter break, but in the next breath he wanted FIFA to press on with spurious competitions like the Confederation Cup and the World Club Championship. For some time now I have felt we have reached saturation point in football generally, and televised football in particular. Just how many more matches can even the keenest fan absorb?

Personally I would welcome a reduction in the size of all our leagues – not that 18 out of the 20 Premiership chairmen would ever vote for it – but FA Cup replays have always been part of the fabric of the competition. Better to free up another date by playing a one-off semi-final in the Carling Cup. This year's winners, Middlesbrough will be in the UEFA Cup next season, when the plan is to play early rounds in groups of five. Another mistake. More games might mean more money, but we should not ignore the law of diminishing returns.

FRIDAY, MARCH 5TH

The latest in a line of unpalatable football scandals hit the headlines this morning. Nine Leicester City players who were out training in La Manga, have been detained by Spanish police over allegations of sexual impropriety. As the day wore on, it became clear that six of the players were to be released without charge, but the three others – Paul Dickov, Frank Sinclair and Keith Gillespie – were put in prison pending further investigation*.

Over the last three years, there has been a long list of incidents involving highly paid footballers, alcohol and sleaze. The judicial system has to take its course, and they are all innocent until or unless found guilty, but these episodes leave a slur on the game. Sadly, the Football Association, the PFA and the clubs themselves do not often appear either prepared or persuaded to take any action of their own within the game's own code of conduct. You do not have to be found guilty of a criminal offence before being charged with bringing the game into disrepute.

Nobody is saying that because famous footballers are role models to youngsters that they should not be allowed out of the house. But if they are not responsible enough to know where to go, and how to behave, then their clubs should impose suitable fines and suspensions to protect the image of the game. I know it is a forlorn hope. In most cases, all the clubs care about

*All three players were later cleared.

is making sure the players are available to play the following week; neither are the PFA ever heard to criticise or castigate their members; so it should be down to the parent body, the FA, as the guardians of the game, to come down on player and club like a ton of bricks. But rather like their attitude to the bung allegations over transfers, the FA either don't want to get their hands dirty or are worried about the legal implications. In the meantime, a minority of managers and players allegedly believe they can exist above the law.

SATURDAY, MARCH 6TH

Today my faith in the better side of the game was restored. At the invitation of my good friend David Carr, I attended a meeting of the Huddersfield Town Patrons before their match at Oxford. And what a refreshing eye-opener it was. The Patrons formed their own organisation to support the club when Steve Kindon was commercial manager a few years ego. When Huddersfield went into administration, they helped to pay the players' wages and keep the club alive through a survival trust run by Robert Pepper.

Despite Town dropping from 10th in Division One, and on the verge of the play-offs to the Premiership, down to Division Three and near extinction, the loyalty and dedication of these supporters, together with the return of popular manager Peter Jackson, have given Huddersfield new hope. Their victory at Oxford today was their 10th in 12 games and they now have realistic hopes of promotion.

Before the match, chief executive Andrew Watson – himself a boyhood supporter and later a player at the club – spent over an hour with the Patrons discussing a wide range of financial issues affecting the club. No stone was left unturned. He was utterly transparent in what he told them. The fact that 1,500 Town fans then occupied one of the stands at the Kassam Stadium showed the sense of belonging that he personified. That Huddersfield won the match was not really the point – it was a heartening display of support, the way football was meant to be.

Neither are these sentiments confined to Huddersfield. They say the gap between players and supporters is now so wide that one cannot relate to the other. Today I was left with the slightly guilty feeling that some of us in the media have also forgotten what it means to be a devoted and often unrewarded follower of the local team. Thanks to the Huddersfield Patrons, I now know that the true spirit of the game lives on.

SUNDAY, MARCH 7TH

M y reflections on the current state of the game over the last couple of days were given further impetus today when I drove to south-east London to cover Millwall's sixth-round FA Cup tie against Tranmere Rovers. Nobody else would have remembered – and there was no reason why they should – that twice before in my career I had sat in the commentary position at an FA Cup quarter-final involving Millwall.

Back in 1978, at their former ground in Cold Blow Lane, the referee had to take the Millwall and Ipswich players off the pitch while mounted police brought a crowd riot under control. Worse still, at Luton's Kenilworth Road seven years later, I watched petrified from the main stand as supporters at the Millwall end threw seats on to the pitch and one young man was seen repeatedly kicking a policeman in the head.

A few weeks later, the tragic events at Heysel happened, and hooliganism raged wildly out of control. The fall-out from the Hillsborough disaster brought Lord Justice Taylor's report and all-seater stadiums, of which Millwall's 'New Den' was one. Even then, the club's name has been besmirched by bad behaviour outside the ground and their image tarnished by racist abuse from a sinister minority.

Today all passed off peacefully as Millwall's biggest crowd of the season saw an opportunity to reach the semi-final go begging when Kevin Muscat missed a penalty. Contrary to their popular cry, Millwall *do* care, and not everybody dislikes them. Today's draw means they and Tranmere are in the glass bowl for tomorrow's semi-final pairings. Which means it is likely that one of them will face Arsenal or Manchester United.

MONDAY, MARCH 8TH

I was wrong. The two Premiership giants were drawn out together when Sven Goran Eriksson and Mark Palios made the semi-final draw at lunchtime today. I was in a restaurant in west London, nursing my table radio, when the Nationwide teams came out first. One of the three – Sunderland, Tranmere or Millwall – will be in the final and probably in Europe too.

My lunch companion Roger Ball immediately asked me where and when I thought the big match would be played. The BBC has first choice in the semi-final, and I am down to commentate. I knew our schedulers wanted our semi at teatime on Saturday to follow the Grand National, but the FA had already announced that the two venues would be Old Trafford and Villa Park. No way would the Birmingham police allow the Arsenal v Manchester United game to be played in the Midlands at that time.

Like many of our viewers, Roger was unaware of how much the police influence the placing and timing of games of this magnitude, making it difficult for the FA to deliver to the letter the contract they have signed with the broadcaster. Discussions went on throughout the day, with the Millennium Stadium in Cardiff mentioned as a possible alternative – hardly fair on the other semi-finalists surely. Playing both games on the Sunday was also out of the question – Arsenal and Manchester United were still hopeful of being in the Champions League the following week.

I still believe the game will have to be played on Saturday lunchtime, but having been wrong about the draw, I am not going to bet on it.

TUESDAY, MARCH 9TH

As it turned out, I was right this time. The Arsenal v Manchester United game will take place at Villa Park at noon on Saturday, with the Grand National to follow. What a day for BBC Sport – and hopefully we'll get an audience to match.

The scandal sheets are still following the fate of the three Leicester players detained in Spain, but for once football has been wiped out of the front-page headlines by allegations of corruption in horse racing. The new internet betting exchanges, over which punters can back horses to win or lose without going through a recognised bookmaker, were always going to be open to manipulation unless the sport could keep a rigorous check on any suggestions of malpractice. Suspensions to jockeys Kieron Fallon and Sean Fox* are the prelude to a vigorous inquiry by the Jockey Club into inferences concerning bets that were placed on these and on other horses in the races concerned. But just like the Leicester trio, they are innocent until proved otherwise.

The question is nevertheless raised again: are these sports capable of regulating themselves to the point of transparent honesty?

*At the time of going to press, Sean Fox was awaiting the outcome of an appeal against his suspension.

I detected a nervousness on the part of some of my racing colleagues when I attended the 75th anniversary lunch for the Tote in London today. It wasn't quite the publicity the sport was looking for on the eve of the Cheltenham Festival.

WEDNESDAY, MARCH 10TH

A broken tooth, a broken phone and a not quite broken back. Not the best of days, but if things go in threes then certainly today I scored an unwanted hat-trick.

For years I have had two false teeth on a plastic plate in the roof of my mouth, and found it comfortable and convenient. Apart from the day before Euro 2000 started in Holland, when I bit clean through the plate and Mark Lawrenson had to rush my spare out in his luggage. When I heard a snap as I munched a piece of bread today, I thought the same thing had happened again. As it turned out, it was an adjacent filling that had come out. The St Peter's Lodge dental practice in St Albans responded to the emergency and my teeth were back intact by the afternoon.

Then the mobile phone, on which we all now depend so much, just stopped working. I could hear my callers, but they couldn't hear me. Fortunately Fred had kept my old one in a drawer, so I had something to fall back on there.

As for the back, I made another visit to Andy Platts at the Wellington Hospital and he pumped some more cortisone into me, hoping it would get me through the Hemel Hempstead ten-mile run on Sunday. This is an event I have supported for ten years, but the overworked organiser Diane Ratcliffe has herself reached the finishing line. This will be the last event in the series, and I am determined to stagger round before scaling my running down still further.

THURSDAY, MARCH 11TH

One of the most memorable and emotional nights of the season. They rolled back the years at White Hart Lane, as 350 supporters gathered over dinner to honour their greatest-ever manager, the one and only Bill Nicholson. Maybe the fact that Spurs have not won the championship for

43 years has added to the iconic status Bill has always commanded in Tottenham history, but the fact remains he was the architect of the first team to win the League and Cup double this century.

Spurs' achievement came at a time when all the first division clubs operated on a level playing field. They shared their home gate receipts, and until that year they were all governed by a maximum wage of £20 per week. It took Arsenal ten years to match Tottenham's double feat; it was a further 15 years before Liverpool did it; and when Manchester United won their first double in 1994, Nicholson's side had been in the record books for 33 years.

Eight of his 1961 heroes were present to be inducted, behind Bill, in the newly unveiled Tottenham Hotspur Hall of Fame. Full-backs Peter Baker and Ron Henry; half-backs Maurice Norman and Dave Mackay; wingers Cliff Jones and Terry Dyson; and strikers Bobby Smith and Les Allen. Goalkeeper Bill Brown, who now lives in Canada, and Welsh international Terry Medwin, whose appearances in the double season were restricted by injury, were both added to the list of inductees. And so, posthumously, were the late Danny Blanchflower and John White.

Many players who served under Bill after 1961, like Martin Chivers, Pat Jennings and Steve Perryman, were also present to add their tributes. And Nicholson himself, still with a twinkle in his eye at the age of 85, topped the evening off with a moving acceptance speech. It was a privilege to be there.

FRIDAY, MARCH 12TH

Two speaking engagements in consecutive nights is not my style, but after acting as host at Tottenham last night, it was down to Southampton to fulfil a promise to be guest speaker at the annual gourmet dinner organised by their chairman Rupert Lowe. Alan Hansen had preceded me a year earlier for an occasion which is really a compliment to the chefs who provide the food at St Mary's Stadium. I lost count of the number of courses they served with immaculate precision, or was it the number of different wines we were encouraged to sample alongside?

Not that I profess to being a regular on the after-dinner circuit – far from it – but one thing I have learnt is that at these events, as in broadcasting, you can prepare a script as carefully as you like, but always leave room for a spontaneous surprise.

It was halfway through the main course that the chairman contacted Southampton's new manager, Paul Sturrock, and persuaded him to leave his lonely hotel room and make a guest appearance. The welcome he received came close to that accorded to the Tottenham legends 24 hours earlier. Southampton's supporters clearly relished his appointment, many of them having rejected the idea of a return to the club by Glenn Hoddle.

Sturrock, who I had not met since his playing days at Dundee United and Scotland, seemed genuinely moved – overawed even – by the whole occasion. But meeting his well-wishers over dinner is one thing. The real business will start on Sunday when Saints entertain Liverpool in his first match as manager. Will his individual style, so successful at Plymouth, work in the Premiership?

SATURDAY, MARCH 13TH

To be honest, no two managers ever operate in an identical fashion. That I can be sure of, having experienced the whys, wherefores and whims of hundreds of them over the last 30 years.

Take Luton Town, for example. I had not visited the club nearest to my home all season until today, but I go back a long way with their manager Mike Newell and the director of football Mick Harford. Looking at their respective titles, you might expect Harford to be behind a desk and Newell to be barking orders on the training ground. As it turned out, they operate entirely in reverse, and having kept Luton in play-off contention despite being cash-strapped in administration, you have to say it works.

Twenty minutes before kick-off, Newell was still quietly sipping tea with his Blackpool counterpart and former Everton colleague Steve McMahon. Harford was doing the business down in the dressing room. Upstairs in the boardroom, there was no chairman and no directors – simply because Luton don't have any until they come out of administration. 'Makes my job easier in a way,' smiled Newell.

Luton won an entertaining match 3–2, and the crowd at Kenilworth Road have a new hero in the making. Enoch Showunmi scored with a free-kick that would have done justice to David Beckham – just a few weeks earlier he had been playing for Willesden Constantine in the Middlesex County Premier League.

Before the kick-off there was a minute's silence for the 200 victims of the train bombings in Madrid. The shock of that atrocity – the nearest thing in Europe to 9/11 – dominated the week.

SUNDAY MARCH 14TH

Following on from my 'retirement' from half-marathons last autumn, it was time to mark the start of spring by competing for the last time in the annual ten-mile run at nearby Hemel Hempstead. Not only was this scheduled to be my last, despairing effort at this distance, but it marked the closure of the whole event. As I have mentioned, after many years of service, the unflagging organiser Diane Ratcliffe is herself withdrawing from the field and we presented her with a token of our appreciation for keeping us on the road for so many years.

The run itself was uneventful from my point of view. Having squeezed another cortisone injection out of Andy Platts, and grabbed some strong anti-inflammatory tablets from Dean Austin, I never broke into anything more than a gentle jog, and came home in about one hour 35 minutes, a good six or seven minutes slower than four years ago.

My recovery rate was certainly an improvement on the Great North Run, and within a couple of hours I was hotfoot down to the Dormy House Hotel at Broadway, ready for the annual holiday at the Cheltenham Festival. Four key Premiership matches being played today made great listening on Radio Five Live and shortened the journey. The Manchester derby, in which City eclipsed United, more or less handed the title to Arsenal; Newcastle's defeat at Spurs and Southampton's victory over Liverpool in Sturrock's first match as manager meant the battle for the fourth Champions League spot is now more wide open than ever; Aston Villa moved into the reckoning by winning 4–0 at Wolves, who remain in the bottom three.

What did disappoint me was that ITV did not see fit to screen a Premiership highlights programme that evening. Those 12 will goals remain unseen by most of the population for at least another 24 hours.

MONDAY, MARCH 15TH

Bob Sims and I always start the Festival week by going to the Monday meeting at nearby Stratford, but I was a bit taken aback when I collected my tickets at the members' entrance and found a copy of my old school's magazine with a picture of Gary Newbon and yours truly on the cover. It had been taken when we attended the headmaster's lunch before Christmas, but nobody at the school had bothered to send me a copy. By chance, Ilona Barnett, the lady who runs the administration at Stratford, is an Old Culfordian herself, and had kindly left me a magazine with my racing passes.

The coincidence did not end there. After the second race John Poynton, the former Coventry City chairman and racehorse owner, invited me up to the directors' box for a drink. He was sponsoring one of the races before taking his string to Cheltenham. And the first person I bumped into on the balcony was the aforementioned Gary Newbon, a racing enthusiast himself not distracted this year by European football, which normally falls in the same week as Cheltenham.

Gary and his family were enjoying a day at one of their local courses before treading the boards at Cheltenham for the next three days – just like us. It seems Gary had already got a copy of the magazine and the photograph. Which is only to be expected. When we were 11-year-olds in the third form at Culford, he always got the football paper before I did. And that's the way it's been for the last 50 years.

TUESDAY, MARCH 16TH

From a punter's point of view, the Festival started brightly and when Brave Inca came in at 7 to 2 in the opening race – the Supreme Novices Hurdle – it reminded me of what happened in the same race when I first came to Cheltenham ten years ago. It was not only my first visit to the home of National Hunt racing, but also to Nigel Twiston-Davies' yard at Naunton. Peter Scudamore showed me round, and told me to steer clear of a horse called Arctic Kinsman, who he said was hopelessly out of form but was due to run in the first race. Naively, I ignored his advice and placed my first modest Cheltenham bet on the horse. I remember sitting in the grandstand and watching him romp home – my bookmaker had shared Scudamore's view and offered me odds of 66 to 1. Thus my five pounds each way paid out something like £400.

Happy days. Apart from getting me hooked on racing, that experience has never been repeated. Despite the fact that today there were three winners at big prices, I didn't get near any of them. Ricky George, Ian

Robinson and I were guests of the Royal and Sun Alliance, one of the festival's leading sponsors. The hospitality was excellent, the sun was shining, and as always with Cheltenham, the day was as near to a perfect sporting occasion as you can get.

Until the time comes to drive home of course. I don't know how many of the 50,000 racegoers bring their own cars, but it takes at least an hour to get away from the course, and a bad accident tonight meant it was two and a half hours before we found the sanctuary of our hotel. Never mind. We will be back again tomorrow – hoping for a bit more luck. We all had a hole in our pocket after today.

WEDNESDAY, MARCH 17TH

A much better day for the punter and quite a busy one, as it turned out, for the commentator. No sooner had Ricky George and I arrived at the course, than we were whisked into the Festival radio studio for an interview. Cheltenham regulars will know all about this station. It takes to the air during the National Hunt Festival, and can be heard within ten miles of the course. It was surprising how many racegoers told me they had heard our attempts to pick winners later today.

Before racing, I had two other commitments. The BBC are putting together a documentary about Tony McCoy, and wanted me to make a contribution. His affection for Arsenal is well known, and started when he idolised the likes of Pat Jennings and Liam Brady while growing up in Ireland. McCoy is a fully paid-up member of the Thierry Henry fan club – a case of one outstanding, dedicated sportsman admiring the class of another. I also read today that the Irish television station RTE had nominated a jockey as their Sports Personality of the Year – over here it has taken a lot of lobbying to get Tony into the top six!

Cheltenham Racecourse wanted me to contribute to a video they are making about the decision to extend the festival to four days next year, with the Gold Cup on the Friday. I know many people have reservations about this – will our pockets and our livers last out for another day? – but generally I am in favour. Looking at the crowds this week, there is surely a demand for this great event to be widened.

I spent the rest of the afternoon with the Ladbrokes directors and their guests. Managing director Chris Bell always makes a string of awards which he has kindly christened 'The Motties'. This year's prize was a pop-up Motty in a case – a tiny figure complete with sheepskin coat and microphone. Very flattering.

THURSDAY, MARCH 18TH

Gold Cup day, and the opportunity to witness a moment of sporting history. I have been lucky enough to be in the crowd for this event every year for the last decade, but today was something very special. Best Mate equalled Arkle's achievement in winning three successive Gold Cups, a magnificent triumph for trainer Henrietta Knight, owner Jim Lewis and jockey Jim Culloty.

Superstition dictated that Henrietta followed her Gold Cup day routine to the letter, even sitting in the same place at the same table at lunch provided by the sponsors. Rebranding means the Tote is now known as Totesport, but they were careful to meet the trainer's wishes and not change the menu!

The roar that greeted Best Mate's third victory is something that will live with me for a long time. It was a terrific race too, with Sir Rembrandt making a determined bid to catch the champion up the famous hill after the last fence.

Football man first and foremost I may be. But I still believe Cheltenham on Gold Cup day is a sporting experience without parallel.

FRIDAY, MARCH 19TH

At last, six months after he missed a drug test, the Rio Ferdinand saga is over. Not for the player, who won't be able to pull on a Manchester United or England shirt until next season is well under way, but the long, drawn-out appeal process finally came to a halt yesterday when a three-man commission upheld the original eight-month ban. Just about everybody has had their say on the case, and opinions varied from those who expected the ban to be reduced, to those who thought it should be extended. My own view is that they got it just about right. Ferdinand had to be punished in a way that spelt out a warning to others. Missing Euro 2004, the FA Cup semi-final and maybe the final, and the start of next season, adds up to a considerable dent in his career.

Hopefully it is also a sign that Mark Palios, after a jittery start not of his own making, will stamp his authority on a number of issues where the reputation of the game is at stake. For too long the FA have been bystanders when they should have been taking punitive action over some of the misdeeds that everybody knows go on in football – at top level especially. The lead has to come from the top, and the chairman and chief executive have to protect and enforce the FA's role as guardians of the game.

Quite what effect the absence of Ferdinand has had on Manchester United is hard to define. It certainly hasn't helped, and neither has the row between Sir Alex Ferguson and the Irish contingent over Rock of Gibraltar. History tells us it has always been dangerous to write off United or their manager. But their invincibility is now seriously open to question.

SATURDAY, MARCH 20TH

High winds and driving rain made for postponements, abandonments and tragedy at football today. An Everton supporter was killed by flying debris on his way to Leicester's Walkers Stadium, while several games were called off because of the dangerous conditions. My road to Reading was paved with good intentions – Sunderland were the visitors and, as potential FA Cup finalists, ripe for a spot of research – but a bad accident on the M4 meant I almost missed the kick-off at the Madejski Stadium. However, no ground out of the 91 I have so far visited is more accessible from a major route, and none of the new stadiums has a better layout than the one named after Reading's chairman.

John Madejski was being interviewed by a BBC2 camera crew when I arrived – part of a documentary to be screened in May. He seemed nervous – not about the interview, but about the significance of what he considered Reading's most important match of the season. A glance at the first division table – with up to eight clubs battling for play-off positions – confirms that for those involved the stakes are, relatively, as high as those for which Arsenal and Chelsea are playing in the Champions League.

The Sunderland directors looked equally apprehensive, but Mick McCarthy's team upped their tempo in the second half and won by two clear goals. I sense they can squeeze narrowly past Millwall in the FA Cup semi-final, and possibly book a second trip to Cardiff in the play-offs. What a difference a year makes. The 4,000 fans that Sunderland brought south today were in despair 12 months ago when their team lost 18 and drew two of their last 20 matches in the Premiership.

I sat next to a Reading supporter of 60 years' standing, and couldn't disagree when he said neither team could hope to survive on this showing if they were promoted. Madejski is a wealthy man, but would he become Berkshire's answer to Roman Abramovich? I could tell he was dejected by Reading's defeat when we said goodbye. But he was the perfect host, and he was still talking to the camera crew.

SUNDAY, MARCH 21ST

A quiet day at home. My gentle five-mile run went well, especially when a kind resident on Harpenden's East Common came out of his house with a glass of blackcurrant when I took a breather near the golf course.

After meeting Steve McMahon at Luton last week, I turned on the LDV Vans final at the Millennium Stadium to see whether his Blackpool side could win at Cardiff for the third time. They dominated the first half against Southend, taking the lead in the second minute and adding another after half-time. So McMahon achieved something no other manager has so far done – a hat-trick of victories in the four years that the stadium has been used for key finals.

Elsewhere, Millwall threatened to make a nonsense of my semi-final prediction by thrashing West Ham 4–1 in a stormy match at The Den. That just about finishes the Hammers' hopes of automatic promotion. Both clubs are now looking to the play-offs. As to which three clubs make way in the Premiership, Portsmouth's victory over their South Coast rivals Southampton reinforces my view that Leeds and Wolves will go down, despite the 'rescue' of the Yorkshire club announced this weekend. It then looks like a straight fight between Portsmouth and Leicester to avoid the drop. With nine games to go, the season enters its most critical and exciting phase.

Where would we be without football?

MONDAY, MARCH 22ND

The Ipswich Building Society is over 150 years old, but only in the last four years have they tried to add a little spice to their annual general meeting by inviting a guest speaker. Having followed Libby Purves on to that short list of guests tonight, I am pleased to say it was fresh ground for me too. What limited amount of public speaking I have done in the past has usually been at dinners, openings, auctions, charity events or testimonials. It will come as no surprise when I say that at most of these, the audience has had a glass of wine or two, and in some cases were in such a convivial mood that I didn't have to be anything better than ordinary to get a few laughs at my stock of broadcasting anecdotes. However, the building society account holders were there first and foremost to approve the re-election of directors, pass the minutes of last year's meeting, and formally raise their hands to endorse the balance sheet they were shown.

John Edwards, an old school friend of mine who is now the society's chairman, showed how a business meeting should be conducted by concluding all this in the space of 15 minutes. The floor was then mine. The audience did not need a drink. They were responsive and appreciative, even asking a few questions once I had filled my allotted time.

Harold Smith, another old friend who served on the board at Ipswich Town for many years, brought along his first building society passbook. The year of the first entry was 1917, and without asking Harold his age I guessed somebody must have opened an account for him when he was born. Just think of all the interest he must have accrued over the last 87 years! On second thoughts, at the current rate for investors, perhaps not.

TUESDAY, MARCH 23RD

While in Suffolk, I had also agreed to speak to the Saxmundham branch of Ipswich Town supporters. They have a membership of 150, fill at least one coach to every away game, stage various functions during the season, including a dinner dance, and have a meeting of one sort or another every three weeks.

David Sheepshanks, the Ipswich chairman, took me to lunch earlier in the day. He updated me on the new share issue, which has kicked in now the minimum figure has been raised, and warned me that some of the fans

I would be addressing might have a few criticisms to make of him and his board. As it turned out, he need not have worried. The Ipswich fans are a loyal and phlegmatic lot, deeply attached to their club and only too happy to revel with me in a lot of cherished memories – not least of them the 1980–81 season when I commentated on their UEFA Cup triumph and saw them come mighty close to a treble.

Fred came with me for a bit of moral support, slipping out before the end to get the scores of tonight's matches on the car radio. He came back elated that Derby had grabbed a point at Sheffield United, a result that went down well in the hall since the Yorkshire club are one of Ipswich's rivals for a play-off place. We were just congratulating ourselves on surviving another in my limited portfolio of speaking engagements, and looking forward to a late-night drink before watching the European Champions League highlights, when a perfect day came to an imperfect conclusion. The local pub had closed at half-past nine. They obviously go to bed early in Suffolk.

WEDNESDAY, MARCH 24TH

Tonight's Champions League quarter-final between Chelsea and Arsenal brought back memories for me of the last time two English clubs met in Europe's premier competition. You have to wind the tape back more than 15 years, but I can still vividly remember being at Anfield the night Nottingham Forest, the English champions, knocked out Liverpool, the European Cup holders, in the first round of the competition when it was a straight knock-out format from the start. Forest were then in a sequence of 42 league games unbeaten – spread across two seasons – and Liverpool had won the European Cup two years running. Whether the tie attracted the amount of newsprint devoted to the two London clubs this year, I really can't remember, but I do recall how unexpected the result was. For a start, Forest's goals in the first leg at the City Ground were scored by Garry Birtles, who had only just got into the first team, and full-back Colin Barrett, who rarely got into scoring positions. In the second leg at Anfield, I remember my commentary being dominated by constant plaudits for Peter Shilton, who kept Liverpool at bay time after time.

After the game, which ended 0–0 and an aggregate victory of 2–0 to Forest, Brian Clough came out on to the pitch for me to conduct a *Sport-*

snight interview. There were no media areas and sponsors' boards in those days – blimey, the game wasn't even shown live! Clough was at his most assertive and unflinching. 'Maybe people like you, John, will now start to realise we are quite a good side,' he intoned in that unmistakable accent. Little did I know it, but Forest would go on to win the trophy that season, and retain it the year after. No English club has done that since.

And by the way, Chelsea and Arsenal drew 1–1 at Stamford Bridge. I must confess, having never covered a game in the re-named Champions League, I wouldn't mind doing the second leg again –15 years on.

THURSDAY, MARCH 25TH

Today I was given my schedule of matches for the first round of Euro 2004 in Portugal in June. If you think I've had an easy time of it so far this season, then that is about to change. Seven matches in twelve days, nine different countries involved, a lot of travelling between venues. Nothing new in that, when you consider this will be my eighth European Championship, matching the eight World Cups I have covered for the BBC.

It doesn't get any easier, even with experience. Working abroad is a different challenge for a commentator – generally speaking you are seated further away from the pitch, you are working to pictures directed by the host nation's coverage, and however much homework you do the players are not as familiar as those at home. Having said that, there is nothing to beat the big tournaments when it comes to importance and impact. Each of these events only comes along once every four years, the audience at home is glued to the England games at least, and the terrestrial battleground with ITV is at its keenest.

All season I have been collecting video tapes of the countries involved, although there are still some gaps in my library. While I am in Gothenburg next week covering England's friendly against Sweden, the family will be searching the Eurosport schedules to record any other relevant games. It is also time to re-establish contact with fellow commentators on the continent – guys like Eddy Poelmann from Holland (a friend for nearly 30 years) and Stefan Lindeberg from Sweden, who I shall meet when I go there next week.

Gothenberg will also be the venue for the UEFA Cup final, and tonight Martin O'Neill's stock rose even higher when Celtic, fielding an under-strength side, put out Barcelona thanks to a 0—0 draw in the Nou Camp. It was also a pivotal night for some of his contemporaries – for other reasons.

FRIDAY, MARCH 26TH

Gérard Houllier's future, along with that of Claudio Ranieri, has been the subject of ongoing debate all season – but Liverpool's defeat in Marseille last night means they will definitely end the season without a trophy and the call for a change on Merseyside will become a clamour if they don't finish in the top four. Elsewhere in Europe, Newcastle marked a one-year extension to Bobby Robson's contract by waltzing past Real Mallorca and earning a UEFA quarter-final against the manager's old club PSV Eindhoven.

Which brings us back to Sven Goran Eriksson, and the speculation linking him to Chelsea, Real Madrid and anybody else with a possible vacancy. No doubt he will now merit a mention in the Anfield rumour mill, along with Martin O'Neill, who has now been elevated to near papal status by the Celtic following. He could enhance his reputation still further if they get to the final of UEFA for the second year running. O'Neill has even been connected with the England job should Eriksson depart; it would appear the Swede is keeping his options open – maybe he has studied the history of the European Championship and realised it has been something of a graveyard for England managers.

Way back in 1972, Sir Alf Ramsey's World Cup achievements were overtaken by a quarter-final defeat in Europe by West Germany. He was sacked a year later. Twenty years later, Graham Taylor's decision to substitute Gary Lineker and England's failure in Sweden, were the start of a slippery slope for him. Four years on, Terry Venables led England to the semi-finals of Euro 96, but never took charge again. The FA refused to extend his deal before the tournament, and he was succeeded by Glenn Hoddle. Kevin Keegan lasted for just two games after Euro 2000, where England failed to reach the quarter-finals.

No wonder Eriksson is sitting on the fence. If England flop in Portugal, would public opinion still be on his side?

SATURDAY, MARCH 27TH

It was very thoughtless of the England coach to get caught out by the press talking to Chelsea on the morning I set out to visit my 92nd and last League ground. Didn't he realise that the speculation over his future and that of the England team was a serious distraction when I was trying to concentrate on Bury's third division match against Boston United?

Joking apart, the photographs and disclosures in *The Sun*, picked up in the later editions of the other dailies, made my appearance on *Football Focus* this morning take on a completely unexpected slant. No sooner had I left for the airport at 8am than the editor was on the phone asking me to take up my camera position at Gigg Lane for the start of the programme.

Ray Stubbs asked me where I thought this left Sven and his position with the FA. There was no time to make any meaningful telephone calls to clarify the situation, which appeared very fluid anyway. What I did say was that on the continent, national coaches rarely get contracts as long as Eriksson's and nobody therefore seems too disturbed if they leave at the end of a given tournament.

However, Sven's ongoing conversations with Chelsea – and other clubs it seems – have reached the point where the FA now find themselves in a profoundly embarrassing position. The match with Sweden is only four days away, the finals of Euro 2004 just two months ahead, and they cannot afford not to know where their coach stands. One or two newspaper columnists were urging them to sack him here and now for disloyalty.

Amidst all this furore, my last stop on the crusade I had started last August was decidedly small beer. Nationwide kindly presented me with a glass decanter, Bury gave me a shirt with 'Motson 92' on the back, and I had a thoroughly enjoyable day at Gigg Lane. When I got back to Manchester Airport, Ray Stubbs phoned to say his intelligence suggested the FA had been working overtime on the Eriksson issue all day, and they now felt they may persuade him to fulfil and even extend his contract.

It is at times like this when the BBC has to be extremely careful. Our news reporters need to have stories like this verified by at least one reliable source, otherwise we might be facing a football version of the Hutton Report. The evening bulletins were not able to take the story much further and my guess is that the two parties were still talking, possibly late into the night.

In the meantime, my respect for the modern professional footballer was enhanced when the seat next to me on the flight to Heathrow was occupied by Blackburn's Australian international Lucas Neill. Having played for Rovers against Portsmouth at Ewood Park, he was on his way south to link up with the Aussie squad for a friendly against South Africa at Loftus Road on Tuesday.

I'll no doubt embarrass Neill if he ever reads this, but charming, polite and interesting are not adjectives that spring to mind when you consider the popular image of players today. Overpaid, pampered and badly behaved have been words frequently used to describe footballers involved in unsavoury events of late, but Neill restored my faith in those who don't make unwelcome headlines. This despite the fact that his reputation on the pitch has made him sound like some sort of assassin!

He is only 26, and still harbours an ambition to return to his native Australia when he retires, but I can see this young man going a long way later in life. For the moment, it was a bonus to end a most reassuring day in the heartland of football by meeting a man who felt privileged to be in his profession.

SUNDAY, MARCH 28TH

I seem to have written words to this effect before somewhere, but the ink was scarcely dry on some of the Sunday papers before they were spectacularly out of date. 'Sven quits' screamed one, and most of the others said his days with England were numbered. However, the back-page headline on the *News of the World* begged to differ. Eriksson, they said, would sign a new contract until 2008.

Further to my comments yesterday, Garry Richardson and his team on Radio Five Live's *Sportsweek* had checked their sources carefully. At 9am, with the papers lying unopened in many households where the clocks were put forward last night, Garry opened his programme by revealing that Sven was definitely staying with England. A press conference two hours later confirmed it. The fact that 200 media people have to assemble at a hotel 30 miles outside London on a Sunday morning to be told that the status quo prevails, just reflects the crazy world in which we now operate.

Eriksson admitted what they all knew. Yes, he had had talks with Chelsea about their managerial post; and with other clubs about theirs; but he had received no concrete offers, and he was now staying in the England job with an extended contract until 2008. Neither he nor the FA chief executive Mark Palios were prepared to reveal the 'get out' clauses which exist in the new deal. So really, not much has changed, except that a lot of people lost a lot of sleep and for the time being both parties are off the hook.

If yesterday's revelations meant the FA had to act fast, then they have protected the immediate future and stability of the England team. Eriksson will go to Euro 2004 in charge, and after that we wait and see. As some of us have been saying for some time, if England were to flop, what then?

But Sven didn't need to ask himself what happens next. From the press conference, he was hotfoot to Highbury, where he saw Arsenal set a record that may never be broken – 30 games unbeaten from the start of the season in the top division. That great Leeds side of the seventies and that majestic Liverpool team of the eighties had shared a sequence of 29, but despite conceding a late equaliser to Manchester United, Wenger's team re-wrote history as well as virtually taking the Premiership title back.

But anybody preparing an obituary for Ferguson's side was reminded in the last 20 minutes that United are still a dangerously wounded animal. I certainly won't be backing against them when they meet Arsenal again in the FA Cup semi-final at Villa Park next Saturday.

MONDAY, MARCH 29TH

If Sven Goran Eriksson has lost favour with a lot of people over the Chelsea business – and today's papers suggest he has – then he would surely command a lot of support for his plea for a mid-winter break. Not only would it give the players a short rest (although not in La Manga hopefully), it would surely mean everybody could take a deep breath – managers, supporters and even the media.

This week indicates how impossible that is under the current schedule. The dust is still settling after a Premiership weekend which climaxed at Highbury yesterday; the television trucks are on their way north for next weekend's FA Cup semi-finals; but in between we have the little matter of international friendlies for every European nation – not to mention World Cup qualifiers in South America.

For the five home and Irish nations, Wednesday's matches have already descended into farce. Between 40 and 50 players have been declared unavailable, a few sensitively left aside by Sven, but the majority withdrawn by their clubs. England, Scotland, Wales, Northern Ireland and the Republic, deprived of nine or ten first-choice selections, will field what are virtually reserve teams. Now that may mean opportunity for some on the fringe, but international caps should never be handed out cheaply, and more to the point, the managers of these teams see little enough of their best players as it is. Surely they are entitled to what would be only their second get-together since November. The football calendar is a juggernaut close to being out of control. Sven has his own reasons for wanting to slow it down, but it might do us all a favour.

TUESDAY, MARCH 30TH

I had not been to Gothenburg since 1992, when the Ullevi Stadium was one of the main venues for the European Championship. Holland played all their matches there, including the semi-final against Denmark which they lost on penalties, and Schmeichel's team went on to beat Germany in the final in the same stadium, having only been reinstated on the eve of the competition when Yugoslavia were withdrawn.

Some things don't change though. The Brasserie Lipp, one of the main restaurant bars on Gothenburg's main street, was adopted as an evening wind-down retreat by the BBC team 12 years ago, and a few memories came back when a high-profile Football Association management team took three of us to dinner tonight. This engagement was not related to the events of last weekend concerning Mr Eriksson – although Garth Crooks took some good-natured ribbing from ex-BBC man David Davies about his persistent enquiries at the press conference regarding the get-out clauses in the England coach's new contract.

No, the underlying theme of this convivial gathering was the extended role of the BBC next season as the FA's senior television partner. It won't have made much impact in the public domain just yet, but the balance of coverage between Sky and ourselves changes considerably next season when it comes to England matches and the FA Cup. In simple terms, there will be more live matches on our channel. Together with the return of *Match of the Day* on Saturday nights, it means the BBC portfolio will be its strongest ever in football.

It was strange to find myself sitting next to Trevor Brooking in his new capacity. He used to stab his finger across me to point out which player on my commentary card had just been booked; it took me a little while tonight to realise he was just reaching for the salt.

WEDNESDAY, MARCH 31ST

None of us who was in Munich three years ago when England triumphed 5–1 over Germany will ever forget the wave of sadness that cut through the euphoria when the news came through of the death of ITV commentator Brian Moore. Tonight's match in Sweden was shrouded by similar emotions when confirmation came through of what his many friends in both sections of the media had been led to expect – the premature death of Joe Melling, the *Mail on Sunday* football editor.

Thoroughly respected in his trade and by those within the professional game, Melling was a man whose company you automatically sought in press rooms, media centres and hotels. With his provocative sense of humour and his fund of riveting stories from his many sources, Joe was as popular as they come in his profession. He had fought a brave and uncomplaining battle against cancer for over a year, always optimistic when we asked him how he was responding to treatment. He kept his column going almost until the end, and readers would never have known how he was suffering.

Joe would have been too modest to want it mentioned, but his passing overshadowed a forgettable friendly in which England lost 1–0 to Eriksson's home nation. No surprise there then; we haven't beaten Sweden since 1968. Sven spared us the full range of 11 substitutions and only used eight this time. Thank goodness he will be limited to six from the start of next season in friendlies – for commentators it has been an absolute nightmare. Trying to remember who has gone off, let alone identifying those who have come on, became such an ordeal that in the end some of us started to laugh about it. The European Championships can't come soon enough – a maximum of three changes per team will seem a huge relief.

THURSDAY, APRIL 1ST

With Euro 2004 just 73 days away (and bearing in mind it is April Fool's Day), it seems a good moment to play again at being the England coach before Eriksson announces his squad. Most of today's papers had the same idea – nominating those who they think will be in England's 23-man party for Portugal, and writing off those who they don't think will be 'on the plane'. Eriksson has said he will take three goalkeepers, eight defenders, eight midfield men and four strikers. So here goes with my selection – fitness permitting of course.

James, Robinson and Walker; Gary Neville, Campbell, Terry, Ashley Cole, Bridge, Woodgate, Southgate and Phil Neville; Beckham, Scholes, Gerrard, Lampard, Butt, Dyer, Hargreaves and Joe Cole; Owen, Rooney, Heskey and Vassell.

So who have I left out? Chris Kirkland is injured, otherwise he would have been my third goalkeeper. Danny Mills gives way to Phil Neville in my selection because Neville is more versatile. Anthony Gardner, Jamie Carragher, Jermaine Jenas and Scott Parker, all of whom played last night, will now need to look to 2006. Alan Thompson has come into the frame too late to solve the last left-sided problem. The latecomer who some critics think will be last up the aircraft steps is Jermain Defoe, who certainly made a firm impression on his debut in Sweden. However, Eriksson sticks to those who have served him well, and Darius Vassell was in the starting line-up in Japan against Sweden, even though he was injured against the same opposition last night.

But experience has taught me that England invariably lose a key player on the eve of a major tournament. I hope injury doesn't strike this time, but I fear it will.

FRIDAY, APRIL 2ND

There was a big cheer at the BBC today, and not just in the sports department, when Michael Grade was appointed as the new chairman. A former controller of BBC1 and head of the television service, Grade has served the corporation at senior level in the past, as well as holding key positions at ITV, Channel Four and other media-related companies. I always see him when I go to the Valley, because he serves on Charlton's board of directors, but my sharpest memory of this colourful character goes back to the Mexico World Cup of 1986.

The BBC hired a small private plane to carry the commentary teams from one venue to another, so huge were the distances with games on consecutive days. Michael came out to watch a couple of matches, having recently been promoted. As we walked out from a tiny departure lounge on to a dusty runway to board the plane, he said to me, 'The time has come for the BBC to stop thinking primarily about ratings, and concentrate on its quality of programmes.'

He said something very similar when he gave his first interview this morning as chairman. 'Good ratings for good programmes' was his early battle cry. You almost feel he could combine the chairman's role with that of director general, such is his reputation as a programme person. However, the choice of the new DG is something he will turn his attention to forthwith. Let's hope we get somebody with a similar outlook and personality.

SATURDAY, APRIL 3RD

What is it about Manchester United and Villa Park? What is it about Ginger McCain and Aintree? Both thrived in their respective second homes on a day when BBC Sport attracted audiences of up to ten million.

Knowing Manchester United's record in FA Cup semi-finals, nobody should be surprised at their victory over Arsenal. Since Leeds and Billy Bremner beat them in a second replay at Bolton in 1970, United have played in 11 semi-finals and won them all. Three of those have been against Arsenal at Villa Park, where United have also beaten Aston Villa in the third round twice in the last three seasons. No wonder they steered clear of the suggestion that today's match should have been played at Cardiff.

They won without Van Nistelrooy, while Arsenal lost with only a late cameo appearance for Henry. The holders started well enough, but after Robert Pires had missed a great heading chance, and Edu had hit the bar, they lacked their usual fluency and looked heavy-legged in the second half.

So Manchester United rescued their season, and put a rather large question mark over Arsenal's ambition. Chelsea are coming up in the Champions League on Tuesday; three days later it's Liverpool in the league at Highbury; and 48 hours after that, Arsenal go to Newcastle. What was I saying just now about 1970? Even though Leeds went through to the FA Cup final, fixture congestion squeezed the life out of Don Revie's side. They lost to Chelsea in the replay, went out of the European Cup to Celtic in the semi-final, and finished runners-up to Everton in the League. Surely Arsenal can't also end up empty handed?

Which is something Ginger McCain will never be – and certainly not at Aintree. The veteran trainer won his fourth Grand National today, Amberleigh House following in the footsteps of Red Rum, who won it three times for Ginger in the seventies.

The six horses my family and I backed between us came absolutely nowhere, but when I got back to The Hollybush from Birmingham they told me I had won the pub sweep. Later I found the little slip in my wallet with Amberleigh House printed on it. For all but Arsenal supporters, not a bad day at all.

SUNDAY, APRIL 4TH

Millwall in the FA Cup final. Can you believe it? Whatever anybody says about them not playing a single Premiership team on the way to Cardiff, you couldn't argue with the strength of mind and indomitable spirit that saw them through their Old Trafford encounter with Sunderland today. Deprived of Paul Ifill and captain Kevin Muscat with first-half injuries, Dennis Wise's team earnt their player-manager a fifth FA Cup final appearance with a magnificent exhibition of stubborn defending in the second half.

On Friday night at our Birmingham hotel I was saying to Ian Wright that Tim Cahill is the best player I have seen outside the Premiership this season. He reminds me of Terry McDermott in Liverpool's conquering side of the late seventies and early eighties – great runs from deep to get beyond the ball and join the strikers. Cahill is effective in both penalty areas, has the energy to get between the two, and knows how to finish. His winning goal today was a fitting reflection on the season he has had.

The fact that Millwall will play Manchester United in the FA Cup final in seven weeks' time will not sink in until tomorrow. But when it has, I will tell you a little story about my childhood.

MONDAY, APRIL 5TH

Fifty-one years ago, Millwall drew Manchester United at home in the third round of the FA Cup. The Rev. William Motson, then the superintendent minister of the Deptford Methodist Mission, was among the crowd of 35,652 at the old Den. He could have walked there from his pulpit. His seven-year-old son had to stay at home and listen to the match on the radio. Having been taken to my first league game only a few months earlier, my father thought the large crowd would be too much of an ordeal for me.

The minutes were ticking away when United's Stan Pearson scored the only goal of the game. The young Motson was never destined to witness Millwall's cup exploits of the fifties – when they knocked out the redoubtable Newcastle United four years later, I was in my first year at boarding school.

But there was a consolation prize. Four months after that cup victory in 1953, Matt Busby's United returned to The Den for a friendly. It was played on a Saturday night in May – just hours after Blackpool had beaten Bolton 4–3 in the celebrated 'Matthews Cup final'. My father and I watched that in awe on a nine-inch black and white screen at the home of a family called Pepper in Deptford, just round the corner from the church. As I said, the Millwall ground was ten minutes away, and I can still remember walking under those eerie bridges towards Cold Blow Lane with Ken Wolstenholme's commentary on Blackpool's winning goal ringing in my ears.

The Millwall and Manchester United players would have been watching too, and in the evening they did their best to match the excitement at Wembley by playing out a 4–4 draw. All I can recall about the game is that there were two penalties, one from Millwall's dead-ball specialist Alex Jardine and one from United's future captain Roger Byrne, the England full-back who perished at Munich.

What a lucky boy I was. Just 24 hours earlier, Dad had taken me to Highbury to see Arsenal clinch the first-division championship on goal average with a 3–2 victory over Burnley. So, in the space of 24 hours a seven-year-old had seen the League Championship decided; Stanley Matthews win his elusive FA Cup-winner's medal at the age of 38; and an eight-goal thriller at Millwall. The Reverend Motson reminded his son he could not always guarantee 20 goals in such a short space of time. But then again, we could never have imagined that one day Millwall would play in Europe.

TUESDAY, APRIL 6TH

One man who did was Peter Mead, a leading figure in the advertising industry due to his long association with the agency Abbott, Mead and Vickers. As a young lad, Peter was indoctrinated into the Millwall culture by his father, and has served as a director for many years. Mead was in his usual seat in Langan's Brasserie today when I had the pleasure of entertaining Chelsea fan and former minister of sport Tony Banks, and feverish interviewer and future politician (my words) Garth Crooks.

Garth and I were reciprocating Tony's hospitality at the Houses of Parliament early in the season, and from the moment we sat down he could not hide his excitement about tonight's Champions League second-leg tie between Arsenal and Chelsea at Highbury.

Banks' memories as a fervent supporter go back to Chelsea's sole championship success in 1955 – their Golden Jubilee year. He still holds get togethers for the surviving members of that team, having formed a private committee outside the club to look after them.

Talking of surviving, I had dinner last night with Charles Dunstone, the founder and major owner of Carphone Warehouse. We meet four times a year along with Peter Erskine, the chief executive officer of O2 – sponsors of Arsenal and England's rugby World Cup winners – and Jim Currie, my lifelong friend and former flatmate who also once worked in the telephone industry.

In twelve days' time, Dunstone will be dropped off by a plane on a landing strip at the 89th latitude, and forced to walk the last 90 miles to the North Pole. He is attempting this feat to support two charities – The Prince's Trust and Hope HIV – and knowing the determination that

has taken him to the top of his field, I have no doubt that he will succeed.
I am proud to be a minor sponsor.

WEDNESDAY, APRIL 7TH

Tony Banks had been distinctly nervous before Chelsea's Champions League quarter-final at Highbury last night, but this morning he will be sharing the euphoria of Chelsea fans everywhere. Their 2–1 victory over Arsenal was their first over the Gunners in 18 games, and earnt them a semi-final against Monaco, who sprang an even bigger surprise by knocking out Real Madrid after being three goals down on aggregate. What with Millwall reaching the Cup final two days earlier, we were reminded again of the glorious unpredictability of our national game. Or, as Shaun Custis put it far more succinctly in *The Sun*: 'Football has gone mad.'

The other pertinent quote came from Arsenal manager Arsene Wenger: 'We have hit a wall,' he said, and we now know we weren't imagining things when Manchester United got the upper hand against his team in the last ten minutes of the league game at Highbury. Two thirds of the treble have disappeared since.

As for Claudio Ranieri, at this rate we shall be voting him Manager of the *Year*, not just Manager of the *Month* as of now. And could Chelsea sack him if they won the European Cup? I had plenty of time to reflect on that today, because I handed over my office and library to Peter Lupson, who is now well down the road with researching his book examining the contribution of Christian gentlemen to the origin and development of association football in this country. Peter is head of English at an independent Christian school in Hoylake, Cheshire, teaching Ian Rush's children among others. He combed my club histories for evidence of church backgrounds, and seemed pleased with what he found.

At any rate, he more or less wore out my photocopier.

THURSDAY, APRIL 8TH

Yes, football definitely has gone mad. As if events at Highbury and Monte Carlo were not bizarre enough on Tuesday, last night's Champions League match in La Coruna bordered on the unbelievable.

How could AC Milan, the defending champions holding a 4–1 lead from the first leg of their quarter-final, succumb to Deportivo of Spain in such unaccountable fashion? Let it be said straight away that Deportivo played some dazzling football. Three-nil up in the first half, they resisted the temptation to stop there and qualify on away goals; instead they continued to embarrass the Milan defence and scored again to go through on a 5–4 aggregate.

So now we have a semi-final line-up of Chelsea v Monaco, and Porto v Deportivo. What a good job I didn't tear up my betting slip when I backed La Coruna for the Champions League a few weeks ago.

The fact that the BBC does not have the contract means I have been watching this week's drama on our rival channels, but at least it has given me the chance to try another way of repairing my troublesome back. Referral pain is an expression I never want to hear again. Dean Austin has recommended me to Dr Antoni Jakubowski, a Harley Street chiropractor with a towering reputation for treating injured sportsmen. Antoni firmly believes he has identified the problem at the base of my spine, and he is equally firm in the way he treats it – a sharp twist as I lie on my side and I am out of the clinic in a matter of minutes.

I await the results with guarded optimism. But there doesn't look to be a quick fix for England's Gareth Southgate, who has sustained a medial ligament injury and has been ruled out for the rest of the season. What did I say a few days ago about enforced changes before major championships?

FRIDAY, APRIL 9TH

Easter, rather like Christmas, offers no holiday time for footballers, or those of us who cover the game. I have decided not to take in a Good Friday game, as I will be travelling north on Saturday and Monday, but it gives me a day to submit two of those interminable lists we get asked for from time to time when a major championship looms.

Four Four Two magazine want my all-time team of players who have appeared in the finals of the European Championship, based on the seven tournaments I have attended. I have come up with the following:

Schmeichel (Denmark 1992)

Kaltz (West Germany 1980) Nesta (Italy 2000)
Beckenbauer (West Germany 1976) Nedved (Czech Rep 1996, 2000)

Schuster (West Germany 1980) Tigana (France 1984)
Platini (France 1984) Gascoigne (England 1996)

Gullit (Holland 1988) Van Basten (Holland 1988)

Then the *Observer Sport Monthly* wanted my best ten goals over the same period. So here we go again. These, by the way, are in no particular order after the first two:

Marco Van Basten (Holland v Soviet Union 1988)
Paul Gascoigne (England v Scotland 1996)
Michel Platini (France v Portugal 1984)
John Jensen (Denmark v Germany 1992)
Ronnie Whelan (Republic of Ireland v Russia 1988)
Davor Suker (Croatia v Denmark 1996)
Alan Shearer (England v Germany 2000)
Karel Poborsky (Czech Republic v Portugal 1996)
Marco Tardelli (Italy v England 1980)
Alfonso (Spain v Yugoslavia 2000)

It wasn't always the sheer quality of the goal, sometimes the significance of the moment came into play. But with things like this one's first thoughts are usually the best, and I am happy to stand by my selections despite the friendly fire that will surely come my way.

SATURDAY, APRIL IOTH

Well, those three years went quickly didn't they? It only seems like yesterday that Garth Crooks and I, having covered Derby County v Ipswich on the last *Match of the Day* programme before the BBC lost the contract, drove after the match to Coventry to join their 'relegation wake' after the Sky Blues had lost their Premiership status.

A year later, Derby and Ipswich were themselves relegated, but Coventry's earlier loss of status means that this year, their third outside the Premiership, is their first without the 'parachute payment' which insulates demoted clubs for the first two years they are in the Nationwide League.

Driving up to Coventry today, partly to renew my acquaintance with friends at Highfield Road and partly to keep tabs on Millwall now they are in the FA Cup final, I wondered where the three years had gone – both for them and for the BBC, which welcomes back *Match of the Day* next season.

Chairman Mike McGinnity and chief executive Graham Hover gave me the harsh facts about relegation – followed by the collapse of the ITV Digital deal. Coventry came out of the Premiership with an annual wage bill of £16.8 million. At the end of this season, it will be reduced to about £3.5 million. In the meantime, they have managed, with the support of the local authority and various sponsors, to relocate to a new stadium – it will be ready the season after next – and develop a new academy facility.

McGinnity spoke for a number of his fellow Football League chairmen when he said that the gravy train for players at this level had ground to a halt. Rather than earning salaries of £12,000 (or more in some cases) a week, they now had to accept a basic wage of more like £2,500 per week, making up their money with bonuses for appearances and incentives – in other words, performance-related pay. That reality check is now accepted by most clubs in the three divisions of the Football League. With any luck, the Sky TV money not withstanding, it will soon percolate through to the Premiership.

As one of their chairmen said to me recently, 'When they write the history of football in the nineties, they will conclude that satellite television gave us enough money to shoot ourselves in the foot.' Then again, it was hardly television's fault. Alan Sugar, the former chairman of Tottenham, tells of an early meeting of the Premier League where he suggested putting a considerable sum – say £200 million – in the bank for a rainy day. The rainy day is just about here now, but nobody ever put the money in the bank. They gave nearly all of it to the players and their agents.

SUNDAY, APRIL 11TH

B eing a creature of habit, and the butt of many jokes as a result, I do not embrace change easily. But the events of Easter Sunday meant I had to.

The traditional Sunday run has been replaced by a session on the exercise bike. Antoni Jakubowski says no running while he is treating my lower back problem. So be it. Rather than run round the local estate, I now walk up to the garden shed.

The first phone call of the day was a wake-up call in itself. Scheduled to cover Aston Villa v Chelsea for Radio Five Live tomorrow, I was told to re-route to Spurs against Manchester City. The Saturday results had put a new complexion on the relegation battle, and Kevin Keegan – suffering from a back complaint not unlike mine – was confined to home while his City side flirted with the bottom three. It was only when I put aside my Villa Park preparation and looked at the White Hart Lane assignment that I realised City had won only two of their last 21 Premiership games. One of those, curiously, was the 4–1 spanking of United in the Manchester derby. At the other end of the table, sanity was restored with Arsenal drawing 0–0 at Newcastle and remaining unbeaten in the league. Any thoughts of the Gunners blowing the championship after their two cup disappointments are surely laid to rest now.

Elsewhere, life went on outside football. Mrs Motson went house hunting, while I attended evensong at St Mary's Parish Church at Redbourn. The Vicar, Duncan Swan, is a Chelsea fan, but with five services today, he was too busy to join in the endless radio phone-ins about Ranieri's future.

Euro 2004 injury note: After Gareth Southgate's injury, Ashley Cole was today carried off at Newcastle. How horribly right will my forecast prove to be?

MONDAY, APRIL 12TH

Tord Grip, Eriksson's assistant, saw fit to attend the Tottenham v Manchester City match at White Hart Lane today, keeping an eye, no doubt, on David James, Shaun Wright-Phillips and Jermain Defoe. I got there early for my Five Live stint, hoping to squeeze a sliver of information about the hunt for a new Tottenham manager, ready for a discussion slot at 1pm. I also wanted to clarify Kevin Keegan's latest medical bulletin – he has missed the last four matches with his back trouble.

David Pleat looked as tense as I have ever seen him. Tottenham were on 37 points, four more than City but still only six clear of the bottom three. Having produced seven goals here in that crazy FA Cup tie two months ago, the clubs scratched out a nervy 1–1 draw which did nothing to alleviate concern in either camp. A section of the Spurs crowd called for Pleat's dismissal. No chance of that this season. Chairman Daniel Levy told me he was appalled by their behaviour and Pleat said: 'My brief this season was simply to keep the club in the Premiership. Then we can restructure.'

But with who in charge? Levy told me discussions were on-going still, which confirmed my view that Spurs' original choice had dropped out – maybe for family reasons – and they were still talking to potential candidates. 'Where people get it wrong,' said a still perspiring Pleat more than an hour after the game, 'is that they think nobody will come to work here while I am director of football. You would be surprised how many managers would love to stick to coaching the first team and leave all the other transfer and scouting responsibilities to somebody else. The way it's going, we might just appoint a 100 to 1 outsider.'

The Manchester City camp made the Spurs directors look sanguine. With Blackburn, Leicester and Leeds still to play the second match of their Easter programme, they had no way of knowing whether today's result was a point gained or two points lost. Arthur Cox, taking charge of the team in Keegan's absence, said the manager's back operation had been more serious than reported. 'The specialist said he only sees two of those a year. But you know Kevin. He's coming back to work later this week.'

TUESDAY, APRIL 13TH

Keegan had obviously listened to the match on Radio Five Live, because I came out of Dean Austin's gym this morning to find three telephone messages from Arthur Cox. From his tone of voice, it was difficult to know where he was coming from. 'I'm told you had reason to dispute my sartorial appearance yesterday,' droned Arthur in his flat Midlands accent. 'Please call me when you get this message.' When I tried, Arthur, like me, was on voice mail. I knew what he meant, though. Sitting close to the dug-outs in the radio box, I had said Cox was wearing a long, sombre black overcoat – hopefully not a funereal omen for City!

In the prickly times in which we live – and I have some past experience of this – the remark could have been construed as insensitive. The word funereal is not the best when used out of context. I left Arthur a message saying the remark had been made in good humour and if anybody had taken offence I was sorry. As it turned out, I was becoming more paranoid than the managers! 'Just thought I'd let you know we shared the joke,' came back Arthur's reply. 'Kevin and my missus thought it was very funny.'

On the subject of comedy, I took Anne, Fred and his girlfriend Beth to Oxford tonight to see Ricky Gervais open his stage show at the New Theatre. They are all big fans. I preferred the solitude of the Morse Bar (named after the fictional inspector) in the Randolph Hotel. When they returned, we drove down to the Dormy House ready for the last significant meeting of the jump season at Cheltenham.

WEDNESDAY, APRIL 14TH

Friends made through football, almost invariably, are work contacts as well. Friends made through racing are just friends, and there is no other agenda. Sometimes I feel it is all the better for that.

Mel Davies, the founder and director of Faucets, the bathroom and shower experts, is well known on racecourses across the country for his generous sponsorship of different aspects of the sport. He also owns a considerable string of horses himself. It was through talking about Tottenham in his hospitality suite at Cheltenham a few years ago that I first got to know Mel, and today he kindly loaned his private box to our family while he and his co-sponsors, Mira Showers, entertained over 200 guests elsewhere on the course. They got together 20 years ago to sponsor what is now a £50,000 grade two steeplechase, the feature race on the first day of this two-day meeting.

This year the Faucets for Showers Silver Trophy Handicap Chase, to give the race its full name, was won by Tony McCoy on Seebald, owned by Robbie Fowler and Steve McManaman's 'Macca and Growler' partnership. The football connection did not end there. Mel told me he has just fitted out new showers at Stamford Bridge and at Chelsea's training ground. He mentioned what a charming man Claudio Ranieri was when they met to discuss Chelsea's requirements. Whether Ranieri will be around to enjoy a shower much longer remains to he seen.

THURSDAY, APRIL 15TH

L urid allegations about David Beckham's private life are dominating the
tabloid press, and Sven Goran Eriksson, who has some experience in
that field, must be getting twitchy about the state of his squad just two
months before the start of Euro 2004.

Eriksson spent tonight talking to a group of England supporters at
Soho Square about the possible consequences of any hooligan behaviour in
Portugal. UEFA have said England could get kicked out if things get out of
hand off the pitch. But when it comes to those who might have been on it,
Eriksson has already lost Gareth Southgate and now Chris Kirkland, the
potential No 3 goalkeeper, who has been ruled out for the season. One or
two more to follow, I fear.

I was following the horses again today. Cheltenham Business Club and
their guests were lunching in the National Hunt Room, where they asked
me to make a short speech and 'run through the card'. This is a task
traditionally given to jockeys or trainers at corporate events before racing
starts, so I was not too displeased with picking two winners and one
second out of the seven races. It makes you feel slightly uncomfortable
when people are spending money following your random selections!

From Cheltenham I drove the family to Bournemouth where my old
Sunday club, Roving Reporters, were assembling for their annual weekend
tour. This year's turn-out of 40 members – including veterans like myself
who hung up their boots years ago – is the biggest ever, and we have taken
over an entire hotel. Next year the club itself will reach the 40 mark –
chairman Roger Jones and I were among the four founder members in
1965.

FRIDAY, APRIL 16TH

M y first port of call when I come to Bournemouth is Alpha
Menswear, and today was no different. Fred and I were only in
Ray's shop for about 45 minutes, but we probably broke a record for trying
on shirts and trousers, and the bill very nearly broke my credit limit.

From there we moved on to the Bournemouth International Centre
where BBC Radio Solent have a small, self-operated studio. I was invited
to be an early afternoon guest on the Richard Cartridge show, a nice,

easy paced mixture of music (Ray Charles tempo) and conversation. Well, self-operated if you have any technical know-how at all. In my case, they decided not to take the risk, and Laurence Herdman, whose real job is commentating on Portsmouth matches home and away, kindly drove over from Southampton to make sure I got on the air.

The rest of the afternoon was spent in Bar Med – a favourite haunt of Roving Reporters. A lot of the younger members arrived at lunch time and joined up there with some of us veterans. John Watts, who played with me in the sixties, has a keen ear for football on radio and television, and he had us in stitches with his Stan Collymore and Steve Claridge impressions. Tonight John, Roger Jones and former treasurer Clive Townsend came round to our flat to watch Arsenal play Leeds. All four of us managed to fall asleep at some point during the game, but that was no reflection on Thierry Henry's breathtaking performance. More to do with the wine we had with dinner.

However, we were wide awake when he scored his four goals and took his Arsenal total to the 150 mark. It was his second successive hat-trick at Highbury – the last Arsenal player to do that was Doug Lishman in 1951.

SATURDAY, APRIL 17TH

The same four-man team went to Fratton Park for the lunch time kick-off between Portsmouth and Manchester United. The others caught up on some more sleep while I did the driving. The first person I met in the Pompey guest room was George Best, who is a great friend of their chairman Milan Mandaric. The morning papers were again full of the David Beckham saga, and I mentioned diplomatically to George that he knew a bit about life in the tabloids. 'Yes, it's the first time I've been relegated to page seven,' he replied. Best's premature retirement at the age of 26 came in my first season with *Match of the Day*, so there is no record of my commentating on one of his goals. But I still feel slightly in awe in his presence.

It is only when I come out of the commentary box to watch a match in the stand that I am reminded of how people's livelihoods are wrapped up in the fortunes of their club. I sat behind Portsmouth's chief executive Peter Storrie, who I knew well from his days at West Ham, and he must have kicked every ball in Pompey's 1–0 win. 'A massive result,' said Harry Redknapp, and it probably has assured Portsmouth's survival in the

Premiership. Later this afternoon, defeats for Leicester and Manchester City made their day even better. We heard the other results on the way back to Bournemouth, so there was plenty of ribbing for the Tottenham supporters from the Arsenal clan in our group. Spurs are now only one point better off than Portsmouth.

SUNDAY, APRIL 18TH

'Beckham confesses' screamed the *News of the World* headline this morning as the papers brought more text messages to light. One of them suggested Posh would be pushing for a trial separation. Whatever you choose to believe, the Beckhams are bigger copy now than ever before.

David would have been advised to stick to the *Sunday Times*. In that paper's 2004 'Rich List' he was classified as Britain's wealthiest young sportsman with an estimated fortune of £65 million – combined with Victoria that is. Their lawyers, one way or another, will get very rich too.

I went along to Lymington in the New Forest to see Roving Reporters play the second match of their tour. The club records state that I played in these matches some 20 years ago, but my performances are best forgotten. This year's tour had its sad side because Peter King – father of tour organiser Gary – passed away a few weeks ago. He was well known at Tottenham as a long-time member of their Centenary Club, and Peter was a warm-hearted companion of mine on the Bournemouth trips for many years. The weekend seemed to slip by very quickly and I realised I had not been home since Tuesday. The Euro 2004 videos are piling up and the eight weeks to the start of the tournament will also soon start to slide by.

Having seen Alexei Smertin play splendidly for Portsmouth yesterday, I made a mental note to ask Peter Storrie whether he would give me some background on the Russians. They play Spain in my first commentary match and I don't want to miss an opportunity to get some first-hand information.

MONDAY, APRIL 19TH

Three heroes of the modern generation look flawed and crestfallen for widely different reasons this morning. Diego Maradona, David

Beckham and Kevin Keegan must be wondering whether there was always going to be a flip side to fame and fortune. Maradona, arguably the greatest footballer of his time and maybe the best ever, is in a Buenos Aires clinic with a serious heart condition. They say it has nothing to do with his long battle against cocaine addiction, but at 43 he looks a broken man. Hopefully Maradona will survive, and maybe the Beckham marriage will too. Kevin Keegan's predicament is rather different, hounded by the press this morning only a few days after returning to work after a back operation.

Saturday's defeat at home to Southampton has left Manchester City a precarious two points above the danger line, or in Sky Sports terminology, 'the drop zone'. Estimated to be £50 million in debt – partly due to Keegan's bold signings – they face financial meltdown if they are relegated. What a switchback ride Keegan's managerial career has been. The inspiration behind revivals at Newcastle, Fulham, England (briefly) and City – three promotions behind him – he seems fated not to finish successfully the jobs he has so successfully kick-started.

What Keegan is facing in the north, David Pleat is coming up against in the south. Tottenham are four points better off than City, but with their history they are being classed as a crisis club. But if Spurs were to inflict Arsenal's first Premiership defeat of the season at White Hart Lane next Sunday, their supporters might forgive an awful lot. On the other hand, the Gunners could clinch the title on the territory of their greatest rivals, just as they did in 1971 – the year of their first double.

I booked my ticket today.

TUESDAY, APRIL 20TH

The pro-Ranieri lobby, which has grown in the national press to almost embarrassing proportions, collapsed in about 12 minutes tonight. The tinkering ceased to be a laugh and became Chelsea's downfall in the first leg of their Champions League semi-final in Monaco. How else can you justify holding a comfortable position at 1–1, and bringing on Juan Sebastien Veron, massively short of match practice, for Jesper Gronkjaer at half-time? And after Claude Makelele had unforgiveably over-reacted to a tap on the head which brought a red card and reduced Monaco to ten men, Chelsea slumped to a 3–1 defeat which reminded everybody that Ranieri has been in charge for four seasons at Stamford Bridge and, unless his team stage a remarkable recovery in the second leg in two weeks' time, has failed to win a trophy.

It would be churlish to suggest that Roman Abramovich and Peter Kenyon are laughing up their sleeves – who wouldn't want to reach the Champions League final? – but maybe the real truth lies somewhere between their ambition and Ranieri's limitations. Nobody would want to question his courtesy, his good humour and his integrity, but maybe the affection he was granted by all and sundry on the outside camouflaged the reality at Stamford Bridge.

Talk to the Chelsea faithful and you would get a sharp dichotomy of opinion, not just tonight, but over the whole season. Talk to those behind the scenes at the club, and you would not receive the unsolicited approval that Ranieri has been awarded from his peers and the press. No, I am not being wise after the event. Chelsea could turn things round in two weeks' time, but I am unconvinced. When you have the wherewithal to buy the best players, you need to pick your best team – and stick to it.

WEDNESDAY, APRIL 21ST

Graham Taylor phoned today checking a number with me, and I congratulated him on completing the London Marathon last Sunday in just over five hours. 'You'll never guess what happened at four-and-a-half hours,' chuckled Graham. 'I got cramp.' At this point we both dissolved into laughter. My sides were shaking and from the sound of it, so were his. Anybody listening would have thought we had taken leave of our senses.

To understand the joke, you would need to go back to the late seventies, when I put together a feature for the BBC *Sportsnight* programme on two young managers destined, we believed, for a big future.

In the first episode, Taylor was at Lincoln and Alan Durban at Shrewsbury. When we caught up with them again two years later, Graham had moved on to Watford and Durban was at Stoke. They played each other in a cup tie at Vicarage Road which went to extra time. Both agreed to allow our camera on to the pitch while they gave their players a pep talk at the end of 90 minutes.

'You've got what?' screamed Taylor to his star striker Luther Blissett. 'You've got cramp? You don't get cramp at this club.'

No sooner had Graham crossed the finishing line last Sunday, basking deservedly in the glow of relief, than his mobile phone was piling up the messages. Luther Blissett and former Watford colleague John Ward were the first to ring. 'You got what, Graham? You got cramp? You don't get cramp if you're a real athlete!' Taylor saw the funny side of it. Football people don't forget – even 25 years on. Cramp or not, he raised a tidy sum for his favourite charity and put me to shame as well. We did the Great North Run together three years ago, but I never contemplated attempting the Marathon.

THURSDAY, APRIL 22ND

Two football people who have become friends over the years were on *Breakfast Time* news for very different reasons this morning. Delia Smith, with whom I have shared some good times with BBC Books, was celebrating Norwich City's return to the Premiership. Their promotion was confirmed without actually playing, because Crystal Palace's victory over Sunderland means the Canaries are certain now to finish in the top two. Delia's delight was Ron Atkinson's despair. He was heard making racist and derogatory remarks about Chelsea's Marcel Desailly when he thought his microphone had been turned off in the ITV commentary box after Tuesday's Champions League semi-final.

Atkinson's graphic expressions had attracted almost a cult following since his partnership with Clive Tyldesley had settled down. On this occasion however, those listening overseas picked up on words he would immediately regret using. His resignation followed.

One or two papers were quick to point out that a few years ago I made a clumsy comment relating to black players in a radio interview. No insulting words were used, but I was still grateful for the support of Garth Crooks, Ian Wright, Mark Bright and Mitchell Thomas when a huge row broke out. For Ron Atkinson there is no way back, but for Delia Smith and Norwich, there certainly is. She once said to me that the trick was to get into the Premiership for one season, collect the money and use it wisely to secure the future of the club. Charlton and West Brom did things that way, now it is Norwich City's turn.

FRIDAY, APRIL 23RD

Angus Loughran was the first person I saw when I got to Sandown Park. No big surprise there; you could turn up at any major sporting event anywhere in the world, and there is a very good chance you would bump into Angus – 'Statto' to those who first noticed him on *Fantasy Football*.

Since then, he has gone on to bigger things, notably the betting arm of the BBC's racing coverage. He has given me some useful tips in the past, although I didn't need his help in picking the winner of the first race today. I don't usually expect credit for backing champion jockey Tony McCoy, but when he brought Mondial Jack home at 10 to 1, it got the afternoon off to a profitable start.

The least said about my subsequent bets the better. The fancied Intersky Falcon failed to make the first three, although Terry McDermott, one of the owners, told me later that the horse has had breathing problems. I am expecting a few of those myself on Sunday morning when I take to the streets again in the Flitwick 10k in Bedfordshire. Today was partly spent exercising my mind as to how feasible it will be to do the run, present the prizes to the winners, and then get to White Hart Lane in time for the gigantic North London derby.

It promises to be quite a weekend. And not just in the Premiership. This is the time of the season when tensions run high, nerves are in shreds and commentators probably get more sleep than players or managers.

SATURDAY, APRIL 24TH

So, professional footballers are a pampered, protected species, who have the most money, the best job and no worries. Is that really the case? Not if you'd met Andy Roberts in the circumstances that I did today. I was doing some FA Cup final swotting in the dressing room corridor at The Den, before watching Millwall play Reading, when Roberts walked up trying hard to mask a bitter disappointment. He had just been told that the knee injury he received in an Easter Monday fixture against West Bromwich Albion would keep him out for the rest of the season. In any other year, it would have probably been a minor inconvenience. But first-division Millwall are a month away from playing Manchester United in the FA Cup final – surely a once-in-a-lifetime experience for most of their squad.

Andy Roberts has just had his 30th birthday, and although he hasn't been a regular just recently, the injuries to other Millwall players – including right-back and captain Kevin Muscat – meant he was destined to play some part in Cardiff. For a professional who started as a Millwall trainee, then moved on to ply his trade with Crystal Palace and Wimbledon, Cup finals don't come round very often.

This one seems already to have knocked aside Millwall's promotion hopes. Their prospect of reaching the play-offs virtually disappeared with today's home defeat to a Shaun Goater goal, and Dennis Wise's team are now without a win in six matches since beating Sunderland in the semi-final. Danny Dichio won't be playing in the final either. He faces a suspension after a recent sending-off. For the likes of Dichio, Roberts and Muscat, the chance may not come again.

SUNDAY, APRIL 25TH

' Seventy-one, do it again,' chanted the Arsenal fans at White Hart Lane, and their unbeaten favourites duly secured the Premiership title on Tottenham territory in a 2–2 draw.

Sitting in the stand, I was reminded of the game which I believe marked the start of the two North London rivals going in different directions. It was worth reminding some of the younger supporters that in spite of the first Arsenal double, Spurs won more trophies than the Gunners in the seventies, and early eighties. When Arsenal came to White Hart Lane in the old first division on January 4th 1987, George Graham was developing a new young team in his first season as manager, while David Pleat was pointing Tottenham towards a treble in his first, one-year stint at the club. On the day Arsenal won 2–1, and I was accused by many Spurs supporters, as well as a viewer called Brian Clough, of being heavily biased in favour of Graham's team. Immodestly, I felt I had spotted a terrific team in the making.

Arsenal went on to knock out Tottenham in the semi-final of the League Cup – they also beat Liverpool in the final – while Spurs finished third in the table, one point and place above the Gunners, and lost in the FA Cup final to Coventry. George Graham went on to win two league championships, an FA Cup and League Cup double in 1993, and a European trophy. Spurs in the same period managed one FA Cup under Terry Venables, and in the ensuing period of Arsene Wenger's phenomenal success at Highbury, Tottenham can point to just one League Cup triumph – ironically under the aforementioned George Graham!

In the 17 years that have elapsed since that 'one-sided' commentary, I have seen Spurs change their manager eight times and Arsenal twice. Needless to say, the changeover in players has matched the turbulent times at Tottenham, while their neighbours have bought and sold to stunning effect. So if today's 2–2 draw, which Spurs salvaged thanks to a last-minute penalty, brought their supporters a modicum of comfort, the bragging rights in north London remained solidly at Highbury. And Arsenal are now four matches away from going through the Premiership season unbeaten. Football history is that close.

MONDAY, APRIL 26TH

Prophet of doom I may have been, but that potential England injury list is growing by the day. Jonathan Woodgate and Darius Vassell have been ruled out for the season; Kieron Dyer, Jermaine Jenas and Ledley King are still out injured. Add Gareth Southgate and Chris Kirkland, and seven possible members of Eriksson's squad are struggling. The centre-back situation is worrying. Sol Campbell has been nursing a nagging groin, and if Woodgate, Southgate and King don't make it, and Wes Brown is deemed to have come back too late, it looks as though John Terry alone may be still standing.

I spent the whole day on promotional work for *Motson's National Obsession*, the football trivia book due to be published next week. It was an opportunity to appear on chat shows with Steve Wright, Simon Mayo and Danny Kelly, prior to a launch party at Chelsea Village, but the schedule was tinged with sadness. Adam Ward, who did nearly all the work on the book, was properly credited and warmly remembered, but the tragedy of his premature death in a road accident was never far from our thoughts – especially when his parents, his brother and his partner with their two young sons attended the party.

Sanctuary Publishing and their enthusiastic team are talking up possible sales of nearly 100,000, which I find blindingly optimistic. It's a long time since I was so closely involved in a book – now, a bit like the proverbial buses, two have come along at once.

TUESDAY, APRIL 27TH

M ichael Parkinson made this morning's news with his transfer to ITV. I nearly said defection, but that would not be quite fair. It appears the BBC were unable to offer Parky his normal ten o'clock slot for the next Saturday night series – something to do with the return of a football programme called Match of the Day.

When I started in television, the two shows were inseparable. The audience figure for one underpinned the other – ten million regularly tuned in for the highlights of two matches (we didn't even show the goals from the other games in those days) before Parkinson and his guests took over at eleven o'clock. Now he is going, I guess our programme must be one of the longest surviving on BBC1. Even in those years when ITV 'pinched' league football from the BBC (1988–1992, 2001–2004) the Match of the Day brand was maintained with the FA Cup and England games.

The soothsayers and opinion formers in the press turned their attention from Ron Atkinson, with whom I had a telephone conversation today, to the impact of Parkinson's switch. Would he find the commercial breaks an irritation to his style, as some columnists felt they were for Des Lynam? – a view I do not share. Whatever the outcome for Parky – and the impact of any chat show will surely always depend on the quality of his guests – he will not be remembered only as a television animal. His trenchant contributions to the pages of Telegraph Sport have already seen to that.

WEDNESDAY, APRIL 28TH

S o Sepp Blatter, head honcho of FIFA, thinks we should do away with drawn games altogether, and resort to a penalty shoot-out at the end of 90 minutes. The idea was widely publicised and roundly ridiculed today. Let me say straight away that as far as league games are concerned, the proposal is utter nonsense. Teams that have worked hard to earn a point because they are evenly matched could hardly be subjected to a lottery that would leave one of them empty handed. But where I do think Blatter has hit on a germ of truth is in the case of major tournaments. Having discarded the golden goal, which settled the last two European Championships and was also used in the World Cup, the authorities are running the risk of subjecting us to those sterile extra 30 minutes when neither side is prepared to take a risk in extra time and just settle for penalties anyway.

When friends of mine look back fondly on Italia '90, for example, they do so because of England's exploits that almost took them to the final, and of course Gazza's tears. They forget the tedium some of us went through at the other matches, when Argentina notably, and certain other countries as well, made no attempt to settle the match in the closing minutes of normal time and precious little effort to raise a gallop in the extra period. Fittingly, Maradona's cynical team paid the ultimate price in the final, when they were beaten by a dubious penalty five minutes from the end of normal time.

THURSDAY, APRIL 29TH

I watched Germany lose 5–1 again today. But not to England this time. It was Romania who embarrassed Rudi Völler's team; despite failing to qualify for Euro 2004 themselves, they led the Germans by four goals to nil at half-time. It made me wonder exactly what has happened to German football since Franz Beckenbauer's team strode imperiously to the European Championship and the World Cup in the early seventies. Off the back of that all-conquering side, which included Gerd Muller, Rainer Bonhof, Paul Breitner and so on, emerged the next generation of Andreas Brehme, Jürgen Klinsmann, Lothar Matthaus and Völler himself. Following another World Cup in 1990, there came the European Championship again here in England in 1996. Not such a brilliant generation of German players perhaps, but still with an inbred will to win based on classic German organisation. The likes of Bierhoff, Ziege, Sammer and Möller were good enough to take their country to their ninth final in twelve major tournaments.

No European country could match that record since international football started. But the cracks were appearing when the Germans lost to Croatia in the quarter-final of the 1998 World Cup in Lyon – and their performance in Euro 2000 was frankly an embarrassment when they failed to win a game. As for the 2002 World Cup, when Germany stumbled into the final in Yokohama, you have to analyse who they beat on the way. Once they had qualified at the expense of Cameroon and Saudi Arabia, Völler's team scratched out 1–0 victories over Paraguay, the United States and South Korea.

The clue lies in the failure of German club sides to make much of an impact in European competition. The days when Bayern Munich stormed to three consecutive European Cups are well gone; Völler's team were seriously under strength in Romania last night, but they need a miracle if they are going to make an impact in Euro 2004.

FRIDAY, APRIL 30TH

Sven Goran Eriksson and Tord Grip have been talking up Switzerland and Croatia today. Good psychology when our Euro 2004 opponents are in winning action in midweek friendlies, although the respect afforded by the England coach and his assistant may not be misplaced. The danger of concentrating too hard on England's opening game against France lies in the fact that the result there may not matter as much as what happens when Beckham and company come up against their next two opponents.

England face Switzerland on June 17th in Coimbra and bearing in mind the damage done to us in the past by attacking midfield players (Figo in 2000, Rivaldo and Ronaldinho in 2002) they would be well advised to tail Hakan Yakin of Stuttgart very carefully. Eriksson witnessed his performance behind the Swiss front two, Stephane Chapuisat and Alexander Frei, in a 2–1 friendly victory over Slovenia.

Croatia, meantime, defeated Macedonia 1–0 in Skopje. Tord Grip would have remembered how England dropped two points to the Macedonians at Southampton in our qualifying group, but he would have been more concerned by the fact that Croatia won without their dashing centre-forward Dado Prso of Monaco.

Spooling through tapes of these and other nations as I prepare for commentaries ahead in Portugal, I cannot help feeling Eriksson and England are facing a mighty task. This could be one of the best championships of modern times, and that's without mentioning Holland and Spain, who the bookmakers have priced at 9 to 1 and 8 to 1 respectively. A little of the hard-earnt Motson money is going on them.

SATURDAY, MAY 1ST

After all the superlatives lavished on them this week, it was hard to find something new to say about Arsenal when I went to Highbury to cover the match against Birmingham City for Five Live. The morning papers had splashed out on David Beckham's future, and Tony Gubba had discussed with Arsene Wenger on *Football Focus* the possibility of him coming to Arsenal. I followed up with a live interview with vice-chairman David Dein, who simply said: 'Would we like him? Wouldn't any club? Could we afford him? Probably not.'

The presence of a gigantic crane over my left shoulder made the point for him. Arsenal are committed to a £400 million stadium just across the railway track, and the signings of Jose Antonio Reyes and (this week) Robin Van Persie have swallowed up most of the available transfer budget for this year.

The game itself fell dreadfully flat. Birmingham were solid and stubborn, Arsenal clearly subdued. There was hardly a shot on goal, and I said afterwards to Karren Brady, Birmingham's chief executive, that had their top scorer Mikael Forssell not been injured, they might have spoilt Arsenal's unbeaten Premiership record.

On the way out I bumped into Liam Brady, Arsenal's head of youth development and academy director. He has a crop of promising young British players coming through the system, and if certain senior squad members move on at the end of the season, boys like David Bentley, Justin Hoyte, Ryan Smith and Ryan Garry may get further chances in the first team. And that may give us something new to say about Arsenal. There are only two Englishmen in the first team today; in future there may have to be more if the books are to be balanced. And I don't think one of them will be David Beckham.

The early finish to the Arsenal match meant that Mrs Motson and I could enjoy the rare privilege of a Saturday night out. A couple who were neighbours of ours for 16 years in St Albans, Don and Dorothy Downes, were celebrating their 80th and 70th birthdays respectively – although neither looks a day over 60. Their two sons, Graham and Michael, had organised a surprise party at the Sopwell House Hotel, but before we joined a gathering of about 150 neighbours and friends, Anne and I had to endure the televised action from Pride Park.

Fred and his girlfriend Beth had made their usual pilgrimage to Derby, knowing this was the day their favourite team could either ensure their place in Division One, or face the unpalatable prospect of a second relegation in three seasons. Just before we left the house, Derby's Marco Reich struck their second goal against Millwall from a free-kick, and thanks to Walsall's defeat earlier in the afternoon at Crystal Palace, George Burley's team were safe. It was only when we were coming home from the party that I realised I had probably done my last commentary for Radio Five Live for some time. Just my luck that there wasn't a goal to go out on. How often do Arsenal fail to score at Highbury?

SUNDAY, MAY 2ND

Careful financial management is something Arsenal have always observed, and if their biggest test is still to come, they need look no further than Leeds United to see how not to do it. The famous Yorkshire club were relegated today – a 4–1 defeat at Bolton only confirming what has been on the cards for a long time – but in hindsight how could their spectacular collapse, from European Champions League semi-finalists to potential obscurity in three years, have been avoided?

It is a simplistic argument to say they signed their own death warrant by selling so many good players. Lee Bowyer and Robbie Fowler have hardly pulled up trees with their new clubs; Robbie Keane was out of the side when he was sold; Rio Ferdinand went for a considerable profit. The two departures which cost Leeds most dearly were Jonathan Woodgate – when financial meltdown had started – and Harry Kewell, whose transfer fee from Liverpool appears to have profited the player and his agent more than the club.

While all this was going on, Leeds were managed by two highly experienced men, Terry Venables and Peter Reid, and then by one of their most popular servants, Eddie Gray. None of them appeared able to treat the cancer that had set in, but it was interesting to hear former manager David O'Leary, whose Aston Villa side briefly held fourth position in the league today, saying that the players left on the staff should have been capable of achieving a mid-table position.

It was also a sad weekend for the supporters of Wolves and Leicester. They too will go back to the newly named Coca-Cola League, trying to follow the example of Charlton and West Brom, who managed their affairs sufficiently well to come straight back. As for Leeds, who must now auction off even more players just to stay in business, there is a stark comparison in prospect with the likes of Queens Park Rangers, Sheffield Wednesday, Nottingham Forest, Ipswich Town and Derby County. All five are still recovering from the cost of relegation and not one of them – unless Ipswich reach and win the play-offs – has managed to regain Premiership status.

What makes it more difficult is that relegated clubs lose the cushion of the parachute payment after two seasons out of the big league. Barnsley would be able to tell you a thing or two about that. They spent the 1997–98 season in the Premier League, and now languish in 13th position in Division Two. And the man charged with bringing Barnsley back into the limelight? Recently appointed chairman Peter Ridsdale, the man who presided over the rise and fall of Leeds United.

Football. Don't you just love it?

MONDAY, MAY 3RD

I read in a newspaper somewhere recently that Sir Alex Ferguson had given himself a day off. When he was asked how he spent it, he said he had watched six matches on his video machine, and the only time he had broken off was to eat the food his wife Cathy brought into the room.

Today I know how he felt. That pile of tapes featuring teams taking part in Euro 2004 has been playing on my mind for weeks. By midnight tonight, eyes bleary and concentration wavering, I finally turned off the video recorder when Robbie Keane slotted in the winning goal against the Czech Republic. I allowed myself a tea break to watch the climax of the Nationwide Conference play-off semi-finals. Sadly, two of my favourite clubs, Barnet and Hereford, lost on penalties to Shrewsbury and Aldershot respectively. No disrespect to those two clubs, who will meet for the right to return to the Football League with Chester, but the fact that Hereford finished 21 points ahead of Aldershot again calls the validity of the play-offs into question. It's an argument that has been going on since the system started. My only somewhat tame suggestion is that the team finishing third (or in the best position outside automatic promotion) should go straight through to the final, and let those below them play for the right to meet them.

Now that the Conference is being reorganised, and now third-division teams who have come down have in many cases found a swift route back, surely it is not too soon to increase the promotion and relegation to three up and three down? Mind you, knowing how long it took them to go from one promotion place to two, I am not holding my breath.

TUESDAY, MAY 4TH

M otson's *National Obsession* went into the bookshops this week, and my job today was to launch a publicity drive in London. *The Times* have been kind enough to publish three extracts in consecutive weeks, and their deputy football editor Catherine Riley met me this morning to conduct a short interview to go with the last instalment.

By coincidence, I have also been made the subject of a *Sunday Times* magazine feature called 'Time and Place' – a nostalgic reflection on the house I lived in as a child in Lewisham, south-east London. As a result of this, photographers from both the daily and Sunday paper turned up at the Great Eastern Hotel next to Liverpool Street Station – something of an unusual double – but both of them, and the cheerful, heavily pregnant Catherine, knew exactly what they wanted and gave me plenty of time to get to Waterstone's in Leadenhall Market for a lunch-time signing session.

I don't know about other authors, but my fear was that nobody would turn up. Fortunately, in spite of the driving rain that nearly brought London traffic to a standstill, the store had given *Obsession* a nice display, and around 60 devoted football fans queued up to get their copy signed.

It was much the same later in the day at the Virgin Megastore in Oxford Street. What struck me about both shops was the heavy but discreet security. It certainly wasn't there because of me and my book, but it was a reminder that the stock had to be carefully protected at all times.

I found myself signing copies not just for casual shoppers, but also for the sons of Roger Daltrey and of the late Bob Marley, at the request of the publishers. Sanctuary are big in music as well as literature. A number of people compared the book's size and appearance to *Schott's Original Miscellany*, which proved so successful last year. I only hope we can get somewhere near it in terms of sales.

WEDNESDAY, MAY 5TH

As I have mentioned, BBC producer Paul Wright has been charged with compiling a documentary to mark the 40th anniversary of *Match of the Day*. Today it was my turn to face the camera with a few memories, anecdotes and personal thoughts on television's longest-running football programme.

It had been in the schedules for seven years before I joined in 1971, but had progressed hugely even in that short time. From a one-match format to highlights of two major games each Saturday; from BBC2, where it started with a tiny audience, to BBC1, where an average of ten million watched in my first season; from black-and-white coverage to colour. David Coleman and Kenneth Wolstenholme were the backbone of the programme in those early years. Barry Davies had joined two years before me, Jimmy Hill two years afterwards. The Lynam and Lineker years were to follow.

It hasn't always been plain sailing. ITV tried their 'snatch of the day' in 1978, and forced the BBC to alternate on Saturday nights and Sunday afternoons; ten years later, they took over the rights of League football altogether, and from 1988 to 1992 the BBC majored on England matches and the FA Cup.

The same thing happened in 2001, and thankfully the 40th celebrations will be fittingly set alongside the return of *Match of the Day* to Saturday nights next season.

By far the biggest change in those years has been the growth of live football. When I started, only the FA Cup final was shown live – indeed it was the first live commentary I had ever done when I made my Wembley debut in 1977 – now you can watch two or three live matches a day if you haven't got anything else to do.

THURSDAY, MAY 6TH

Fifty years ago today, Roger Bannister ran the first sub-four-minute mile. I must have heard the good doctor on four or five radio and television programmes this morning, but the coverage I enjoyed most was in *Telegraph Sport*.

Bannister and Sebastian Coe shared their thoughts about what it took, in their respective eras, to achieve and hold the World Record. A detailed account of how the time has come down over the last half-century, so that the rarely run distance has now been covered nearly 20 seconds faster still, showed how 'the mile' has remained a holy grail for so many talented athletes.

The piece I enjoyed most, for obvious reasons, came from Sir Paul Fox, who was editor of BBC *Sportsview* when Bannister ran into history. The programme, introduced by Peter Dimmock, was only being screened for the third time, and the best they could manage was to send a film camera to the Iffley Road track at short notice. The re-run of the race could only be shown the following day, but on the night they rushed Bannister back from Oxford to appear live on the programme. It tells you something about the period when Fox recalled that Roger insisted on going home and changing into a suit and tie before appearing on the programme.

In many ways, that was the start of television sports coverage as we now know it. Not just showing the event, but interviewing the star performer and reacting to breaking news. *Sportsview* got a regular weekly slot out of the sub-four-minute mile; subsequently, the BBC launched *Grandstand*, *Match of the Day* and *Sportsnight*. The standards we try to match today were set by those pioneers.

The legacy of BBC Sport came up again when I had lunch today with *Telegraph Sport*'s columnist Robert Philip. He is kind enough to want to feature my 25th FA Cup final commentary in two weeks' time, but we had a chuckle over the fact that I am still only halfway towards Sir Peter O'Sullevan's towering record of 50 Grand Nationals.

Don't think I'll make that half-century somehow.

Most of the conversation, when the BBC football team assembled for our Euro 2004 press day, concerned the elimination from Europe of Chelsea and Newcastle at the semi-final stage. There was plenty of time to talk about that this morning, as Lineker, Hansen, Ian Wright etc. sat around waiting for individual photographs to be taken at a studio in north-west London. The fact that two French clubs, Monaco and Marseille, have reached their respective finals made us wonder whether this was a prelude to France successfully defending their title this summer.

The group photograph we had taken was the signal for the team to behave like schoolboys. Peter Schmeichel knocked one of the footballs we were given out of my hand, making me stumble and nearly knock Hazel Irvine over.

When the others broke for lunch, I went to a studio to record a commentary for the video presentation, which will be shown to the press when Eriksson announces his England squad in two weeks' time. The FA had covered themselves by getting me to record 34 names, with caps, ages and goals; Jonathan Woodgate and Gareth Southgate were included, despite their injuries, but one absentee was Shaun Wright-Phillips – much to Ian's disappointment.

This afternoon some 35 writers from newspapers and magazines came to conduct interviews with the presenters, commentators and reporters who will be covering Euro 2004 for the BBC. The most asked question? 'Who will win?' The most popular answer? 'France'. I begged to differ, putting my money on a Holland v Italy final.

A delegation from the National Football Museum came to our house this morning to formally receive the sheepskin coat I am discarding after seven years of service and donating to the museum at Preston. Mark Bushell, the curator, and his two colleagues Hannah Broadbelt and Richard Cuthbert were on something of a mission in the South. They were collecting an old pair of boots that George Best had kept from his Manchester United days, and also going to White Hart Lane to officially induct Bill Nicholson into the managers' 'Hall of Fame'.

I watched Chelsea secure second place in the Premiership at Manchester United's expense – a unique position in their history and a nice postscript for Claudio Ranieri, who is surely about to be replaced. Later, as divisions two and three wound up their seasons, a late Cheltenham goal against Huddersfield cost me dear. Torquay, to the great credit of Leroy Rosenior, pipped the Yorkshire side for third place, otherwise I would have landed a nice treble, having picked Huddersfield, Bristol City and West Brom all to finish in the first three of their respective divisions.

Tonight I presented the cups and medals at the Barnet Sunday League dinner and dance. Time doesn't allow me to attend many of their functions in my capacity as president, but having played in the inaugural season in 1966–67, I am delighted to maintain the association.

SUNDAY, MAY 9TH

The last day of the Nationwide League. Next season, Division One will be renamed the Football League Coca-Cola Championship or 'The Championship' for short, and Fred is mighty relieved that his team Derby County will be in it. When we arranged months ago to go to their last game in Milton Keynes today, there was a fear that Derby would be facing relegation. Not so after last Saturday, and Wimbledon, their opponents today, can relax as well – they have already been relegated.

Fred and our old friend from Derby, Joe Redmond, had tickets with the away supporters. I sat next to the Mayor of Milton Keynes, Councillor John Monk. His Liberal Democrats, along with the two other main parties, are wholly in favour of Wimbledon's plan to relocate to a new stadium at Denbigh, in the south of the city. But Peter Winkelman, still brimming with enthusiasm for the project, told me the court case coming up this week, in which the Inland Revenue are using Wimbledon as a test case to challenge the right of players to be preferential creditors when a club goes into administration, was still an obstacle.

On the pitch, a Wimbledon side with an average age of little more than 19 were too much of an obstacle for Derby, who they beat 1–0. The whole occasion had an end-of-season feel about it, with both clubs needing the breathing space this summer to regroup after a turbulent season.

There were two lingering glimpses of the old Wimbledon. Dean Holdsworth made his farewell appearance as a late substitute, and Robbie

Earle sat in front of me alongside the veteran scout Ron Suart. It seemed a long way away from Plough Lane, and the original 'Crazy Gang', but one thing is certain – the blame for the demise of Wimbledon does not lie with those trying to kick-start League football in Milton Keynes.

MONDAY, MAY 10TH

I never intended to publish two books in one year – it just happened that way. Today I set out on a three-day, whistle-stop tour of the North to promote *Motson's National Obsession*. Sanctuary Publishing's newly appointed marketing manager Diana Bell had things organised down to the last detail. It was a good job she had, because our schedule was mighty tight.

The first stop was Glasgow, where we visited bookshops near the airport and in East Kilbride, but the highlight of day one came in the evening, when Ottakar's in Buchanan Street organised a trivia quiz for customers, with yours truly as question master. There were eight teams of five, and one of them had us chuckling right at the start by calling themselves 'Barry Davies' Fan Club'. Needless to say, I made sure they finished second (only joking) but although the tenor of the quiz was light-hearted, I was most impressed by the high standard of the answers.

Most of those taking part were Celtic supporters, although there was one Rotherham United fan operating as a one-man team, and they seemed to know their English football as thoroughly as they trotted out their Scottish facts and figures. Ottakar's gave the book a generous display at the front of the shop, but I wondered whether there was enough Scottish content to command the attention of those north of the border.

TUESDAY, MAY 11TH

From Glasgow we caught the train to Newcastle, and jumped in a taxi to Sunderland. The Wearside branch of Ottakar's was our next port of call, and plenty of Black Cat supporters were there to meet us. Sunderland may have been beaten in the semi-final of the FA Cup, but they had just finished third in the first division and were preparing for a play-off semi-final against Crystal Palace. Hardly had I sat down in the shop to start the signing session, than a copy of the *Wearside Roar* – a 56-page magazine for Sunderland supporters – was thrust into my hand.

Again, the shop had gone out of its way to promote the book and quite a few customers asked me to sign their copies with personal dedications. The allotted hour absolutely flew by.

Waterstone's in Newcastle were even more ambitious. They had alerted three local newspapers as well as the regional BBC news programme, which goes out at 6.30pm in the North East. They turned the tables nicely by setting a quiz for me on camera, and I managed to stammer out five correct answers on North East football.

But nobody gets a book plugged absolutely for free – at least not on a news programme. The ongoing row regarding Bobby Robson's remark about Newcastle's supporters last Sunday – an aside made after an interview when the camera had been switched off – was still simmering two days later and I was one of many whose opinion was sought. I would never knock the Newcastle fans or Robson – their passion for the game is paramount and deep down he is one of them – but I can understand his, and their, frustration. Some of the younger Newcastle players have failed to deliver, and their season looks like ending in meltdown.

WEDNESDAY, MAY 12TH

Ray Adler walked into Sportspages in Manchester and introduced himself as the man from page 139. He was being modest. But he was right about the page number, where his story is told under the heading 'Fantastic Fan'. His collection of Manchester United memorabilia is unrivalled – even my old BBC colleague John Rowlinson (who, like Mr Adler, has every United home programme since the war) cannot match Ray's magnificent display of tickets, photographs, dinner menus and brochures. His collection is valued at £1.2 million, but don't get any ideas about burgling his house – the most valuable items are kept in a bank vault.

Sportspages – the sister shop to the one in London's Charing Cross Road – specialises in football videos as well as books. I picked off the shelf the full telerecording of the England v Hungary match in 1953 – something to add to my own collection.

Just across the road at Waterstone's, I met another affable queue of football fans, and by now most of them were talking enthusiastically about the return of *Match of the Day* next season while getting their *Obsession* book signed. Then Faber and Faber's account manager in the North West, Judith Stead, drove Diana and me to Bolton where we visited Sweeton's, a delightful, quaint bookshop run by Stella Morris and her sister Isabel. Here there were some 40 copies which had been reserved by people who were at work when we called, all of them asking for a personal dedication. The news came through that the book had sold 1,000 copies in its first two weeks in the shops, so we set off for Liverpool in good heart.

Our last stop was Waterstone's in Bold Street, where we were given the warmest of Scouse welcomes by shop managers Doreen Roper and Anna Johnson. The *Liverpool Daily Post* photographer got me out into the pedestrian precinct for a shot with some local lads kicking a football. The nearest I have ever come to playing on Merseyside.

THURSDAY, MAY 13TH

The first time I had my picture taken with the FA Cup was 15 years ago. It was on the pitch at Plough Lane during a Wimbledon press day when the original, unique Dons were holders of the famous trophy. Although the photograph has pride of place next to the television in my office, I wasn't going to complain about having it updated. The invitation to FA headquarters in Soho Square came via the *Daily Telegraph*, who needed a picture to go with Robert Philip's article about my 25th FA Cup final.

With the end of the Premiership season only two days away, the Barclaycard voting panel held their last meeting to decide on the Manager and Player of the Year. We voted unanimously for Arsene Wenger and Thierry Henry, although Sky's Richard Keys registered a solitary vote for Sam Allardyce, and it was agreed there should be a special award for retiring referee Paul Durkin.

The busy day continued with a drive to White Hart Lane, where former manager Keith Burkinshaw was to be inducted into the Tottenham Hall of Fame, following Bill Nicholson earlier this year. Again there was a big turnout of players from that era. Glenn Hoddle, Pat Jennings, Garth Crooks and Steve Perryman were among the stalwarts who came to support the man with whom they won two FA Cups and the UEFA Cup in the early eighties.

But the star of the evening was Ricky Villa, who was flown over especially for the event and enjoyed reliving his FA Cup-winning goal as much as the 350 supporters who packed the restaurant.

I interviewed them all on the stage, and Keith himself had no compunction about reviving his famous quote when he left in 1984. 'There used to be a football club here,' he said then, when the new power brokers at Spurs, Irving Scholar and Paul Bobroff, moved in with a wide range of business ideas to support the launching of Tottenham as a PLC. Now, 20 years later, with Spurs languishing in the bottom half of the Premiership without a trophy in sight, Burkinshaw was unrepentant and still singing from the same hymn sheet.

'Get back to being a football club,' he answered when I asked him the one message he would impart to the modern Tottenham owners. The audience roared their approval, and the queue for autographs of the eighties' heroes stretched nearly twice round the room.

It was an emotional night, with videos of the finals backed up by footage from *Top of the Pops*, with Chas and Dave belting out 'Ossie's Dream' and 'Tottenham, Tottenham'. But as Fred and I drove away from the ground, there was sadness too. A club with Tottenham's great tradition were left to languish in the achievements of two decades ago, while their north London neighbours were on the verge of making football history. It was great to see Ricky Villa again, but how long is it going to take for Spurs to revive those glory days?

FRIDAY, MAY 14TH

Iain MacGregor, Sanctuary's managing editor, phoned me on my way to the hairdresser this morning to say that *Obsession* was in the top ten non-fiction hardback charts in the *Independent*. He was thrilled because Sanctuary had never had a book in the top ten before, and felt it was the direct result of the promotional tour this week. Later, Fred found our book in third place in the 'sports and pastimes' section on the Amazon website. When I got to The Hollybush tonight, my companion Robert Murphy said he had been to three bookshops in Luton and they had completely sold out. All very pleasing, and a great compliment again to the research and dedication of the late Adam Ward. How I wish he was here to collect the plaudits and share the champagne.

There was none of that at Selhurst Park tonight, because the semi-final play-off between Crystal Palace and Sunderland has only reached half-time. Iain Dowie's Palace snatched a 3–2 lead late in an absorbing game, but it left me with mixed feelings. Dowie was a popular and amusing neighbour of ours in Harpenden for several years; Sunderland boss Mick McCarthy will be part of our BBC commentary team at Euro 2004. One of them will be manager of a club £20 million richer by then; the other will be preparing for another season in the first division.

Tomorrow the Premiership clubs play their last match of the season, but for the first time in 12 years all the major issues have already been settled. It should be a day for congratulations, celebrations, recriminations and laps of honour. But curiously, more clubs than not have serious issues to address off the field.

SATURDAY, MAY 15TH

Today belonged to Arsenal. In fact, the *season* belonged to Arsenal. Their monumental achievement in going through the entire 38-match campaign unbeaten will surely never be matched – not in my lifetime anyway.

The scenes at Highbury, after the Gunners had come from behind to beat relegated Leicester, will live in the memory for a long time. Rather different, one assumes, from the way Preston North End – the old 'invincibles' – must have celebrated when they completed a top-division programme without defeat in 1889!

I was at Villa Park touching up my Cup final homework on Manchester United, and the way they started against Aston Villa made a mockery of the 15 point gap between them and Arsenal. They were two up in no time and ran out easy winners. For Villa, it was a big disappointment to miss out on a UEFA Cup place on goal difference. The point Newcastle won in a 1–1 draw at Anfield meant that Villa finished sixth – still a big improvement on their 16th place a year ago. David O'Leary, having supervised that improvement, said he needed six new players for next season. Chairman Doug Ellis, with whom I shared a drink afterwards, told me he would now shelve plans to increase the capacity at Villa Park from today's 42,600 to more than 50,000 for at least a year.

All of which again highlights the narrow margin between success and failure. One position in the financially led Premiership makes a difference of some £700,000, but the prize money is just part of it. Success brings more money for television appearances, and Europe is the real goldmine.

So while the flags flew proudly above Highbury, brows were furrowed elsewhere as to how the rest can keep up. And along the way, there are going to be victims – even before next season gets under way.

SUNDAY, MAY 16TH

Let's start with Claudio Ranieri, who almost certainly said farewell to Chelsea when he saluted the fans after yesterday's match against Leeds. His dismissal has been on the cards for months, despite the fact that he led the club to their second-best finish in 99 years of League football. That, and a Champions League semi-final, is not good enough for Mr Abramovich.

Money is also talking at Liverpool, where manager Gérard Houllier is clearly rattled by the turmoil of a week in which two very different financial tycoons flexed their muscles in a bid to buy into the club. Long-time Liverpool fan and local property developer Steve Morgan offered a reported £73 million to underwrite a new share issue, but made it clear he was dissatisfied with Houllier's record and the players he has signed. Houllier hit back in an emotive interview, defending his team's achievement in qualifying for the Champions League.

Chairman David Moores and his board continued their discussions with the Prime Minister of Thailand, Thaksin Shinawatra, who had himself come up with a £60 million offer for a stake in the club.

Liverpool clinching fourth place meant the consolation of the UEFA Cup for Newcastle, where Bobby Robson retained his dignity if not the unequivocal support of his chairman Freddy Shepherd, who came on Garry Richardson's *Sportsweek* programme this morning and repeated himself on two occasions: 'Bobby Robson has one year left on his contract.'

If that suggested dissent behind the scenes, you didn't need to skim the surface to find a chairman-manager conflict at Portsmouth. Harry Redknapp and Milan Mandaric were at odds over who wanted to sack Harry's assistant Jim Smith. Pompey's 5–1 victory over Middlesbrough in the last match papered over the cracks, but for how long? Surely 13th place was beyond their dreams.

A 5–1 win on the final day too for Manchester City, but a mere consolation for supporters who saw their team win only four of their last

27 league games. Kevin Keegan said things would be better next season, which he also declared would be his last but one as a manager.

Everton were the team on the end of that hiding, which left them one place above the relegation zone. 'Sack the board!' chanted their supporters, and manager David Moyes faced the prospect of trying to improve his team with little or no money.

Tottenham, like Everton, were not so long ago regarded as members of the 'big five'. They crept into 14th place this season by winning their last match at relegated Wolves. But there was still no word on a new manager for a club failing to meet even modest expectations.

So where were the relative successes in the Premiership? Which clubs will enjoy a summer of quiet satisfaction as well as feverish activity to improve the side? Look no further than positions seven to ten. Charlton, Bolton, Fulham and Birmingham all produced not only their highest Premiership finish, but their best performance in the top division that most of their supporters could remember. Had Charlton not been coerced into selling their best player, Scott Parker, in the January transfer window, they may well have qualified for Europe. As it was, they collected £7.6 million in prize money and reached their highest position (seventh) since Jimmy Seed's team of the fifties finished fifth in the old Division One 51 years ago.

It was a similar story at Fulham. They lost Louis Saha to Manchester United halfway through the season, but marked Chris Coleman's first full season in charge by finishing ninth, one place above their previous best in the top flight 44 years ago.

The team that Fulham beat yesterday, Bolton Wanderers, came sixth that year. This season's eighth position is their best in the senior division since then – a big mark for Sam Allardyce's overseas transfer policy.

Steve Bruce at Birmingham has been just as crafty in the market, but more at home than abroad. City finished in tenth spot – the first time they have figured in the top half of the big league since 1973, when Trevor Francis was a teenage sensation.

But the real winners in this turbulent season were the fans. Most Premiership matches were sold out weeks ahead, and the see-saw fix of daily football news provided a backcloth for furious excitement on the pitch and a captivating soap opera off it.

Sadly in some ways, we won't get the chance to recharge our batteries. Football will continue to fill our pages, and our thoughts, all through the summer.

MONDAY, MAY 17TH

The start of Cup final week. A few years ago that would have meant numerous newspaper features; a big build-up on television even five days ahead, and nervous energy starting to drain the commentator – even that far away. Today, it hardly occurred to me. Robert Philip's article in *Telegraph Sport* was smoothly appropriate and the call came from Five Live to join in their extensive coverage from the pitch at Cardiff on Saturday morning. But other things took precedence. Like Sven Goran Eriksson revealing his hand with the 23 names who will represent England in Portugal this summer. Looking back seven weeks, I wasn't too far away with my selections – injuries to Woodgate and Southgate have brought in Jamie Carragher and Ledley King, otherwise I was more or less there.

Having recorded the names and details of the squad for the press conference, I had no need to be there, and was able to join a convivial lunch with Sir Peter O'Sullevan, my old BBC colleague John Rowlinson, and host Mike Dillon of Ladbrokes, at the Wolseley restaurant in Piccadilly. Talk about putting things into perspective. Sir Peter, having broadcast his 50th Grand National commentary at the age of 79, is currently preoccupied writing a book entitled *Peter O'Sullevan's Heroes*. The subject is obviously racing and not football, but where we share a common bond is that neither of us is computer trained. I am still using my portable typewriter, but Peter is writing his in longhand.

TUESDAY, MAY 18TH

Yesterday's lunch was a bit of fun, but today's was more about business. Garth Crooks and I, in our capacity as England reporter and commentator respectively, entertained Colin Gibson, the FA's communications director, and head of media relations Adrian Bevington, ahead of Euro 2004. Once these tournaments start, the schedule is so hectic that nobody has time for leisurely discussion. It was important that we cemented our understanding as to what access we would be allowed to the England camp both on match days and in between.

Gibson has had vast newspaper experience as a senior football correspondent and sports editor. He knows the territory inside out from a reporter's point of view, and that can only be beneficial in building up a trust between those on our side of the fence and Eriksson's squad. The enormous media demands mean that Bevington has a schedule that would do credit to a major airline. Every day from this coming Sunday, when the squad assemble, to the end of the tournament, whenever that might be for England, is meticulously planned.

That is not to say it is predictable. Once a story breaks, the best-laid plans have to be adapted and the head of media relations is never off his mobile phone. One of Bevington's predecessors got so stressed during a World Cup some years ago that he locked himself in his hotel room!

I was hoping the days of eating two heavy meals were behind me, but this evening our 'football committee' at The Hollybush met to settle our seasonal wagers. There are seven of us involved, and each man lays out £50 at the start of the season along with his forecast as to who will occupy the top four and bottom three positions in the Premiership. There is a monthly prize to which everybody contributes a further £10, and halfway through the season, if one or more of your selections are looking wayward, you can make a maximum of two changes – at a cost of an extra £60!

What all this adds up to is a 'pot' of £650 that is divided between the winner (£400), the runner-up (£150) and the third-best forecaster (£100). Bob Sims, who works out the points according to the bookmakers' prices at the beginning of the season, then adds on bonus points if you get the team in exactly the right position, took great delight in reading the results in reverse order.

Fred and I (known in the group as Motty Minor and Motty Major) knew we were in with a shout, but you can imagine the reaction of the others when we walked off with the top two prizes. Both of us had correctly forecast that Arsenal, Chelsea and Manchester United would occupy the top three places in that order; I had put Wolves and Leeds in my bottom three and Fred scored with Leicester.

Dave Carr then treated us all to a slap-up meal in the pub restaurant. Ricky George came along as a guest and agreed to join next season's bet. I'm already thinking of nominating Chelsea as champions in 2004/5. It is their centenary year and I reckon their second title (the first was in 1955) is written in the stars.

Even though they haven't appointed a manager yet!

WEDNESDAY, MAY 19TH

Things became a little clearer on the managerial front today. Frank Arnesen from PSV Eindhoven was appointed as Tottenham's sporting director, surely to be followed by a Dutch coach.

And the tabloids lifted the lid on the goings-on at Liverpool. As the Thailand bid for part-ownership in the club started to fade, so did Gérard Houllier's chances of keeping his job. Nobody on the inside of Anfield was saying anything, but had the manager been fireproof they would surely have come out and denied the rumours. Talking of which, the names of Martin O'Neill and Kenny Dalglish have both been linked with Liverpool in recent speculation.

A year ago tonight O'Neill's Celtic lost to Porto in the UEFA Cup final. This season the finalists were Marseille, conquerors of Liverpool and Newcastle, and newly crowned Spanish champions Valencia. Barry Davies has traditionally commentated on the European final, which the BBC covers at the end of the season, so I had the best seat in our lounge as Fabien Barthez got sent off for an eccentric challenge, and Valencia comfortably took care of Marseille.

The UEFA Cup is a poor relation of the Champions League, and the plan to transform it into a group competition next season strikes me as a backward step. Having said that, had Liverpool or Newcastle beaten Marseille, Gérard Houllier and Bobby Robson might have been celebrating tonight rather than worrying about the future.

THURSDAY, MAY 20TH

I have to be honest. I had never heard of Curtis Weston until this morning. Thanks to Deano Standing, the energetic Millwall press officer, his name was coloured in on my Cup final chart by lunch time.

The potential story is almost too good to happen. Weston is a 17-year-old who made his Millwall debut as a midfield substitute in the last league match of the season against Bradford. Now, depending on the fitness of player-manager Dennis Wise, he could become the youngest FA Cup finalist for two decades. I had to check the records to make sure of that. Paul Allen took the title in 1980 from Howard Kendall, who had also made a Cup final appearance at the age of 17 when he played for Preston against West Ham 16 years earlier. But both of them were close to their 18th birthday. Weston was only 17 in January, and the story gets better. Talk about local boy making good – he was born in Greenwich, just down the road from The Den.

Millwall have taken 17 players to Cardiff, and by Saturday afternoon all this could be rendered obsolete. If Wise is fit and Weston is an unused substitute – or even left off the bench – my homework won't matter a jot. Then again, it could be the best story of a Cup final that, with less than 48 hours to go, hasn't yet captured the public imagination.

Somehow, the uncertainty sums up the appeal of the FA Cup. You never know what could happen. The commentator's job is to try to be prepared for it.

FRIDAY, MAY 21ST

This is getting decidedly scary. The day before the Cup final and I am feeling too relaxed. All those wobbly nerves of a few years ago seem to have disappeared. What a pity we can't turn the clock back. I would never suggest that the Cup final doesn't have the prestige of years gone by, but maybe the whole scene is different. Just why the first test at Lord's against New Zealand is happening on the same weekend defeats me. Either the cricket people have got it wrong, or football has become too preoccupied with itself.

Certainly times have changed since my first final in 1977 when the only other live game on television was England v Scotland. Now we have had live play-off semi-finals on Sky on Monday, Tuesday and Thursday, with the UEFA Cup final in between.

But all those reservations went on hold when Gordon Riddick, a former professional with 500 games under his belt and now a BBC liaison man, picked me up for the journey to Cardiff. We collected Garth Crooks at Reading Services on the M4 and suddenly the chat was all about the final and, yes, the odd butterfly did flutter in the stomach.

The BBC base outside Cardiff is the Celtic Manor hotel, a comfortable retreat based in a golfing complex. Tradition has it that the main body of presenters, producers and performers have a private dinner together on the Friday night. I sat next to Peter Schmeichel, who wanted to know whether I had the definitive Manchester United team. Having played in three FA Cup finals for them himself, he's asking me? I told him I had spoken to Sir Alex Ferguson earlier and kept him guessing. Schmeichel has become a popular and humorous member of the BBC team. He and Lineker, Hansen, Lawrenson and Crooks all went to bed early. Must be their professional football training.

SATURDAY, MAY 22ND

Peter Salmon, the BBC Director of Sport, kindly sent an expensive bottle of Champagne to the BBC compound to mark my 25th Cup final commentary. Before each and every one of them, I have told myself the Cup final is just another match. Pointless. It just isn't. For a start, you know the scrutiny of the BBC audience – estimated today at seven million – will be intense. Any mistake is magnified, any slip of the tongue seized upon. Brushing up on the history of the FA Cup is one thing – today 17-year-old Curtis Weston of Millwall did become the youngest ever finalist – but what you cannot prepare for is the unusual or unlikely occurence on the day that demands explanation over the pictures.

It happened twice today. Dennis Wise, no respecter of FA protocol, decided his five-year-old son Henry should be the Millwall mascot. Nothing wrong with that, except that the player-manager then pushed two of his injured players – Kevin Muscat and Tony Warner – to the front of the team as they lined up in the tunnel. Press officer Deano Standing warned me of this when I went down to the tunnel as the teams arrived. But what I wasn't prepared for, after Manchester United had won a low-key final 3–0, was their team all donning shirts with the number '36' and the name 'Davis' on the back before they went up to collect their medals.

Twenty-one-year-old Jimmy Davis was killed in a car accident on the eve of the season, just as he was joining Watford from United on loan. It was a thoughtful and moving gesture by Roy Keane and his team and it required the right words. I am not sure whether I found them, but the incident was another reminder that live commentary is spontaneous and unscripted. You don't expect your critics to make allowances for that, but you know that's the knife edge that comes with the territory. Another Cup final over, and I'm still surviving.

Garth Crooks, who played in two FA Cup finals and got the first pitch interview yesterday, asked me on the way home last night how long it takes me to wind down from the Cup final commentary. He was pouring me a decent glass of red wine at the time, and maybe therein lies the answer, but it depends entirely on how the game has gone in the commentary box. I had many happy years at Wembley with Trevor Brooking, but for some reason I have enjoyed the final in Cardiff's Millennium Stadium a great deal more. As a commentator, you are closer to the pitch and I find the atmosphere a lot friendlier than it was at the old Wembley. A point Mark Lawrenson made when he sat next to me yesterday.

Mark's waspish sense of humour has helped me to relax at the microphone ever since he accidentally spilt a bottle of water over my notes during the Euro 2000 final in Rotterdam. Without trivialising the occasion we managed a few laughs during yesterday's game, and by lunch time today I was back to normal – if a tiny bit surprised at how the papers had panned the final. It certainly wasn't one to remember, but I won't forget the enthusiasm of the Millwall supporters before, during and after the game; nor the sparkling skills of 19-year-old Cristiano Ronaldo; nor trying to get Garth back to his car when we realised he had left it on the other side of the service station to the homebound carriageway.

Time to refocus. It is less than three weeks until my first match in Euro 2004.

Gérard Houllier was officially sacked this morning. At the Anfield press conference, chief executive Rick Parry said the time had come for a change; Houllier himself, sitting alongside him, made it clear he had wanted to keep the job.

So what went wrong at Liverpool between 2001, when they won three cups and finished third in the league, and 2004, when there was no sign of a trophy in the cabinet?

For a start, the treble they won three years ago was not quite what it may have seemed. In the League Cup, Liverpool beat Crystal Palace in the semi-final and Nationwide League Birmingham City on penalties in the final. In the FA Cup, Tranmere Rovers and Wycombe Wanderers were their last two opponents before they beat Arsenal at Cardiff in a match that even some Liverpool fans admitted they should have lost.

This in no way belittles Houllier's achievement, especially as Liverpool beat Roma, Porto and Barcelona on their way to winning the UEFA Cup. And bear in mind too, it was only last season that they won the League Cup again, beating Manchester United in the final. All I am saying is that the triple cup success was not necessarily a prelude to the Premiership title, not when the likes of Arsenal and Manchester United had more variety in their game.

And that brings me to my major theory. Three years ago, Liverpool had inventive midfield players like Gary McAllister, Patrik Berger and Jari Litmanen in their squad. When those three left for one reason or another, I don't believe they were ever replaced by the same kind of player. Houllier's life-threatening illness could not have helped either. But the last word on his Anfield career should go wholly in his favour. A more intelligent football man it would be hard to meet.

TUESDAY, MAY 25TH

Another manager for whom I have a long-held respect has lost his job in this period of Premiership turmoil. David Pleat's departure from Tottenham ends a six-year spell at White Hart Lane as director of football.

In a management career of 20 years before that, Pleat was briefly in charge at Tottenham for one of their most successful seasons in recent times. In 1986–87, they reached the FA Cup final, the League Cup semi-final, and finished third in the League – a position they have not bettered since.

Pleat has also had three spells as acting manager, including the eight months since Glenn Hoddle was sacked last September. The plan seemed to be to bring in a new, young coach under Pleat, but now his director's job has gone to the Dane, Frank Arnesen, there is no job for him at all.

Piecing together what the Spurs board have been up to for the last few months is not easy – little information has emanated from White Hart Lane – but it seems to me they were pinning their hopes on the Italian Giovanni Trapattoni, until his wife's illness cooled his desire for the job.

There were a few Spurs supporters round the table when I attended a farewell lunch today at The Connaught Hotel for Colin Miles, Ladbroke

Racing's financial director who is going to work for the Hong Kong Jockey Club. I told them I thought that the managerial merry-go-round would settle down in the next two weeks. Rafael Benitez appears the favourite for Liverpool; Porto's Jose Mourinho seems set to succeed Claudio Ranieri at Chelsea; and Kevin Blackwell has finally been appointed at Leeds after they apparently flirted with Iain Dowie.

WEDNESDAY, MAY 26TH

Alastair Campbell kept his promise. Mr and Mrs Motson have been invited to Chequers for dinner with the Prime Minister and his wife. Plus a few others, of course. The call from Downing Street was made by Jo Gibbons, now a member of the Tony Blair team, but known to me through her involvement with her friend Verity Fifer in the abortive 2006 World Cup bid. Through no fault of theirs, it failed miserably.

And so too, at first, did my response to her invitation. The first date she offered, in July, coincides with our family holiday. No point in flying back from Vancouver two days early, even for the Prime Minister! Jo was as good as her word and phoned back a few hours later. 'Can you make October 9th?' she asked. Thinking I could easily swap my *Match of the Day* assignment, or else make sure it was in London, I was frustrated again; that is the day England play Wales in a World Cup qualifier, live on the BBC. Probably the biggest match of the autumn. Third time lucky, we hope. Jo says there will be another dinner at Chequers in November. At least it gives me time to buy a new suit.

Tonight Porto brushed aside Monaco in the Champions League final. Mourinho cut short his personal celebrations and was soon seen on his mobile phone. To Chelsea, or to his agent, no doubt.

THURSDAY, MAY 27TH

This morning Jonathan Pearce and I solemnly (or perhaps not too solemnly) laid down our one-hour commentary on the Animal Games.

Wipe that smile off your face at once. This is a one-hour, prime-time BBC1 programme due to be transmitted just days before the Olympics open in Athens in August. Elephants, centipedes, skunks and cheetahs, together with all manner of other contenders from the animal kingdom, take each other on in the 100 metres, the long jump, shooting and weightlifting. To make sure it is a fair competition, the smaller insects have been scaled up to the same size as their bigger counterparts.

Confused? Not as much as we were. Even when we had finished – and the job took the best part of four hours – Jonathan and I were still not sure which animals were real or computer generated. 'One of the more unusual things we have done, don't you think?' smiled Pearcey over a pint round the corner from the studio. I didn't like to remind him that not only are the real Olympics just days away when this programme is broadcast, but so is the return of *Match of the Day*, at which point we shall both assume the role of serious football commentator. But after this, with a sense of humour for sure.

FRIDAY, MAY 28TH

Awards come tumbling on top of each other at this time of year, so why not another one? Today I had the pleasure of awarding Mr Stephen F Kelly the top prize in the 'John Motson Football Book of the Season' competition. There was no official ceremony. In fact, there was nobody other than me in the room. More to the point, I have never met Mr Kelly and, in the short term, am not likely to.

However, a lady called Sharon Benjamin at Robson Books, who I have never met either, kindly sent me a review copy of *Mr Shankly's Photograph: a Journey from the Kop to the Cavern*.

Kelly, a former political journalist who has written several books on and around Liverpool football, says in his preface that the book started out as a non-fictional account of life in the city between 1960 and 2000. It finished as the charming story of one boy's love for Shankly – whom he first meets in a garden in Huddersfield – and for the Merseyside culture of the time. The Beatles et al.

The *Sunday Times* reviewer said: 'This is *Fever Pitch* for the new decade – but better.' I could not improve on that. I had friends myself in Liverpool in the sixties – rather like Gérard Houllier, I was a visiting fan on The Kop on more than one occasion – and the book stirred a few memories for me too. Perhaps that is why the runner-up in my self-styled competition also came from that era. *George Best and 21 Others*, by Colin Shindler, focuses on the 1964

FA Youth Cup semi-final between Manchester United and Manchester City, charting what happened to all the young hopefuls afterwards.

Should I ever meet Mr Kelly or Mr Shindler I'd like to feel we may have something in common. I had better get a prize ready just in case.

SATURDAY, MAY 29TH

I only saw Crystal Palace play once this season. That was at the end of November, when they won 1–0 at Stoke under the temporary charge of Kit Symons. At the time Palace were struggling in the bottom half of Division One, and despite a winning goal that night from Andy Johnson, relegation was not out of the question.

Enter Iain Dowie, who had moved his family lock, stock and barrel to the North West when he took his first managerial post at Oldham. I was at Loftus Road this time last year when Queens Park Rangers put Dowie's team out of the play-offs in the semi-finals. Earlier this season, having been forced to sell most of his best players, he somehow kept Oldham afloat and out of possible liquidation. The call to Selhurst Park came three days before Christmas, with Palace 19th in the division. Chairman Simon Jordan had spent an estimated £32 million, but seven managers had come and gone, leaving the club three points behind Walsall, who would later be relegated.

Dowie introduced unusual training schedules, mostly drawn up at seven o'clock in the morning when he arrived for work with the cleaning lady. He was always unorthodox, even as a player, but the 'madness' of his methods bore fruit worth £25 million before a crowd of 72,523 at the Millennium Stadium. It was a bigger attendance than for the FA Cup final – and this year the prize was bigger too.

Quite simply, Crystal Palace, having finished sixth in the league, beat West Ham 1–0 to earn the lucrative Premiership promotion. It was one of the best stories of the season – unless you are a West Ham supporter.

SUNDAY, MAY 30TH

I met two of those today: one called Mike as I sat outside our local at lunch time – still wearing his claret and blue shirt from the day before

– and another called Steve in the evening, when I presented the cups and medals at the Roving Reporters' end-of-season party. Both were distraught. Defeat always hurts supporters – sometimes, I think, more than players – but this was particularly hard to take. The Hammers fans were incapable of forgetting the missed chances, the disallowed goals, the late penalty appeal dismissed by Graham Poll, and their manager's substitutions.

Alan Pardew would have had his own reasons for taking off Bobby Zamora, Marlon Harewood and David Connolly. On the day, his strikers just weren't doing it for him. My mind went back to a cup of tea with Pardew soon after he took over from stand-in boss Trevor Brooking last autumn. 'I've got 18 months to get this club into the Premiership, otherwise I could be out of a job,' he said bluntly. It's at times like this that I'm pleased to be a commentator, and not somebody whose living and stress level is dictated by events within football you sometimes cannot control.

Anne, Fred and I spent a happy afternoon with the Dudley family. The last time I had eaten with Simon and Sally was in a windy car park at Kempton Park at Christmas, when they kindly provided a picnic before racing. Today we drank champagne and Pimm's on the lawn behind their country house, before going inside for the best roast beef I have tasted in ages.

Iain Dowie would have been enjoying his Sunday lunch with his family, too. But for Alan Pardew and West Ham, the sweet taste of promotion is at least another year away.

MONDAY, MAY 31ST

'Slow torture,' Steve Claridge called it on Five Live. And Chelsea finally put Claudio Ranieri out of his misery by announcing his dismissal in a terse statement this afternoon. Everybody knew it was coming, and the Italian is expected to walk away with a compensation cheque of around £6 million. It will only be a matter of hours before Jose Mourinho is appointed in Ranieri's place. The turnover of players at Stamford Bridge – with the new man wanting to bring in several of his own – may break all records this summer.

Lower down the league, where they talk in thousands rather than millions, Huddersfield Town brought the domestic season to a close by beating Mansfield on penalties in the third-division play-off. So tight are these nail-biting games that you almost expect a penalty kick to settle a season. It did so yesterday, when Leon Knight's cool delivery near the end of normal time earnt Brighton a place in Division One next season at the expense of Bristol City.

Both successful clubs figured on my travels round the grounds as I completed the 92. The togetherness of everybody at Huddersfield I mentioned at the time, while Brighton's campaign for a new stadium at Falmer will be given fresh impetus now.

On the international front, with Euro 2004 now only 12 days away, Sven Goran Eriksson prepared what he called his strongest team for tomorrow's match against Japan. He surprised a few people by playing Frank Lampard in the 'holding' midfield role in the final training session, and leaving out Nicky Butt. But his main concern must be that none of his 23 players get injured in the two matches this week. As I was saying, it keeps happening just before big tournaments.

TUESDAY, JUNE 1ST

As it turned out, the injuries were minor ones. David Beckham went off to nurse a tender ankle that has been bothering him for some time and Gary Neville was replaced after a kick on the thigh. What was more worrying for Sven was the way England faded after a promising start, and the debate about the personnel in his midfield 'diamond' intensified. Most of us would prefer to see the in-form Frank Lampard released from his 'holding' role, with that responsibility given to Nicky Butt or — and this is my preference — Owen Hargreaves. This would release Lampard to play his natural game further forward — he scored 15 goals for Chelsea this last season — but the same central role also suits Steven Gerrard better than having to veer out left to give the shape balance.

So what is the answer? With David Beckham certain to play to the right, the time may have come to examine the role of Paul Scholes. He hasn't scored an international goal for exactly three years, so would it be better to play him just off Michael Owen and leave out Wayne Rooney, or would Eriksson consider something he said he never would and leave Scholes out altogether?

There was a worry defensively too. Alex Santos, Japan's Brazilian-born left-winger, made life uncomfortable for England in the second half when they could quite easily have lost the game. Then again, warm-up friendlies are habitually misleading and Eriksson said he saw enough to know England are on the right lines for Portugal. But this was the team with which he hopes to start against France, and he now has just one more match to bed it down conclusively.

WEDNESDAY, JUNE 2ND

How quickly things change in football. I had just bought a copy of the *Evening Standard* outside a London hotel and glanced at the back-page headline – 'Revealed: Ranieri in Tottenham Talks' – when two of horse racing's finest, Tony McCoy and Richard Dunwoody, came out of the front door to tell me it wasn't true. McCoy had picked up an award at a Royal Variety Club lunch, where Ranieri too had been honoured. And in his acceptance speech the sacked Chelsea coach told the audience he had indeed talked to Tottenham, but he had decided to return to Spain and coach Valencia, one of his former clubs.

Just across London, Chelsea confirmed the appointment of Jose Mourinho on a three-year contract, but he didn't stop in the capital for long. Off he went to Manchester, to meet and greet the Chelsea players in the England squad – with full FA approval. Meanwhile, the tearful resignation of Rafael Benitez, which opened up the Valencia post for Ranieri, means he is certain to take over at Liverpool – something Michael Owen had suggested might happen when he joined the BBC team on FA Cup final day. Liverpool chief executive Rick Parry made no secret of the fact that senior players like Owen and Gerrard were consulted about the appointment. So it's two in and two out where foreign coaches in the Premiership are concerned. Where does that leave our aspiring young English managers, I wonder?

THURSDAY, JUNE 3RD

Not taking over as manager of Tottenham, that's for sure. Jacques Santini made it three overseas appointments in a matter of days when the current French national coach was unveiled as the new team boss at White Hart Lane, working under the new sporting director Frank Arnesen. The news came as something of a surprise to Spurs supporters, the media and apparently the French Federation, who had dragged their heels over offering Santini an extension to his contract beyond Euro 2004. So the coach who will guide the fortunes of Henry, Vieira and Pires against England in ten days' time will next season be pitting his wits against them and Arsene Wenger in North London.

The trend continued with the news that Carlos Queiroz, dismissed after a poor season by Real Madrid standards, is returning to Manchester United as No 2 to Sir Alex Ferguson. Did I detect in his quotes that he expects the main man at Old Trafford to step down sooner rather than later? The inference was that Queiroz would be in a strong position to take over from Ferguson. How long can the man with the pacemaker keep up the pace?

The affection for imported talent started with players, and that continues to be the case. I mentioned the other day that promising young Englishmen like Arsenal's David Bentley would be hoping for more chances in the Premiership next season. Well, he will get them, but not with Arsenal. They have loaned him for the season to promoted Norwich City, a move that at first sight seems to suit all parties. As does the departure of Juan Sebastian Veron from Chelsea – surely the first of many – meaning that Inter Milan will be hoping to get something more out of a man who must qualify as the most expensive misfit to have figured in the Premiership.

FRIDAY, JUNE 4TH

We're all allowed a bit of hero worship whatever our age, and last night I felt I was in the presence of greatness. Peter Shilton may be 54 now, but that did not stop him throwing himself around a greasy goalmouth with all the enthusiasm and energy that he exuded as a 21-year-old when he won the first of his 125 England caps. The occasion was the Reuters Penalty Challenge held at the Broadgate Centre, a tight arena tucked neatly into the City of London. Twenty banks and finance houses had qualified for the finals, each fielding a team of five who took one penalty each in a series of group matches.

At this stage of the evening, Shilton was coaching the goalkeepers while I did the commentary, but when we reached the quarter-final stage the 'goalie', as Gary Lineker used to call him when they roomed together, took up his familiar position between the posts. I am still not certain whether his massive presence overawed some of the kickers, or whether they were inspired by the opportunity to beat him. Not many of them did, but the successful team, Morgan Stanley, certainly had no complaints about their prize: a three-day trip to Portugal to see England play France.

Which brings me back to the European Championship. The BBC's two assiduous sports assistants Alex Kunawicz and Chris Slegg today delivered their 363-page 'bible' with all the facts, figures and player information any commentator or reporter would require. So the secret's out. No, we don't originate all our own research, but we still have to absorb the information and tailor it to our individual needs. My first match is just over a week away and, believe me, there is still an awful lot to do.

SATURDAY, JUNE 5TH

My last commitment before leaving for Portugal next Tuesday was to open the 30th International Football Memorabilia and Programme Fair at London's New Connaught Rooms this morning. The indefatigable figure at the helm of this event is 74-year-old David Stacey, the editor and events organiser of the *Football Programme Directory*, a magazine that goes out to collectors every month. David and his team of helpers start work in the early hours of the morning, helping the various dealers to set out their stalls ready for a stream of up to 1500 customers and collectors who pay £2.50 for the privilege of inspecting, with the opportunity to buy, thousands of programmes, books, tickets, badges and cigarette cards on display in two huge rooms housing 25 stall-holders.

Visitors come from all over the country, from Scotland, Denmark and several other parts of the world. They range from enthusiastic ten-year-old schoolboys to those who have been collecting for years. Our old friend Ray Adler from Manchester was among those at the front of the queue.

Memorabilia is big business. One insurance agent who offers cover for the big collections estimated that in one year a total of £100 million changes hands for football and cricket items alone. I also liked the touch of history attached to the venue. Stuart Barnes, the deputy general manager of the New Connaught Rooms, reminded me they are built on the site of the old Freemasons' Tavern, where the Football Association was founded in October 1863. The programmes on sale today didn't quite go back that far, but one dealer had the small match card for the 1890 FA Cup final between Blackburn Rovers and Sheffield Wednesday. My own collection of finals goes back to 1920, so I had a lot in common with some of the enthusiasts I met today.

SUNDAY, JUNE 6TH

Do you believe in omens? Just for fun, it might be a good idea to pretend that today we do. England's 6–1 victory over Iceland yesterday means Eriksson's squad set off for Portugal in good heart, and brought reminders of a certain 6–1 victory 38 years ago.

On June 29th, 1966, Alf Ramsey's England team warmed up for the forthcoming World Cup by crushing Norway by that score in Oslo with a hat-trick from Jimmy Greaves. Exactly a month later, England were world champions.

Could their biggest victory in 38 matches under their Scandinavian coach be a prelude to England winning Euro 2004? Fanciful thinking perhaps, except that my misgivings about fitness of key players prior to major tournaments in the past seem to have been laid to rest this time. Apart from 'maintenance' to David Beckham's back – a phrase used by the medical staff when he went to hospital for an injection after playing the first half yesterday – there appear to be no late injury scares to trouble the squad. What a difference from two years ago, when Beckham and Owen went to Japan short of full fitness, and Gerrard and Gary Neville did not go at all.

And what a difference too when England reverted to 4–4–2 from the much discussed 'diamond' formation. The four-man midfield was the same in terms of personnel, but they all looked more comfortable with the traditional shape. Nobody more so than Paul Scholes, who put anybody suggesting he should be left out firmly in their place. So too Wayne Rooney. His two goals were a bonus, but playing a more withdrawn role behind Michael Owen clearly suits him and the team.

Here goes, then. Eriksson seems to have got the ship on course. Flags are flying out of car windows already. Let's hope that they still are a week today.

MONDAY, JUNE 7TH

After watching France beat Ukraine in their final warm-up match last night – very decent of Eurosport to show England's first opponents live a week before they meet – I stayed up late to watch the emotional and very moving scenes from the Normandy beaches, marking the 60th anniversary of the D-Day landings.

Talk about putting football into perspective. The sight of hundreds of veterans – most of them now in their eighties – paying their own tribute to the 800 colleagues who died during those two days in 1944 was a timely reminder that they, and thousands of others, sacrificed so much for our freedom. Not forgetting for one moment those who continue to do so in Iraq. Some of those still out there will, I am sure, find a way of following England's fortunes in Portugal. Troops of one sort supporting troops of another – but let's keep our priorities in order.

As for the departing commentator, a last haircut was the order of the day. When I arrived at Steve's salon after a farewell lunch with Ricky George – how sorry I am that he won't be a companion in Portugal as he was in Japan – I found myself at the back of a long queue. However, my favourite barber had a way of dealing with that.

'Would you mind waiting a few minutes? John is rushing to the airport to cover the European Championships,' he said to his next customer.

There was a bit of journalistic licence here, since I am not actually going until tomorrow, but the gentleman (called Les) accepted the situation gracefully, allowing me first turn in the chair. As luck would have it, I had brought a couple of copies of *Motson's National Obsession* with me – Les and Steve seemed happy to accept a signed copy each.

Later, Fred and I enjoyed a last drink at The Hollybush with the new manager, Gary, and a few of the regulars. They all wished me well, but I am only going to watch football, after all.

TUESDAY, JUNE 8TH

England's first game may be five days away, but my opening encounter of Euro 2004 involved a couple of two-year-olds, together with their mum and dad. The venue was the children's room in the British Airways Terrace Lounge on the fourth floor of Gatwick Airport – and after a dodgy opening, I recovered to win an important victory.

Before leaving home for the airport, I had received a video cassette of Russia's last warm-up match in Austria, but there was no commentary on it. It was only on the way to Gatwick that I managed to elicit from the BBC International Unit the names and numbers of the Russian players.

Not knowing whether my hotel in Faro – our first stop for the Spain v Russia match – would have a video-playing service, I decided to err on the side of caution and asked the lady on the British Airways desk whether there was a video player I could use.

'There is one,' she said helpfully, 'but it's mainly for kids. You'll have to fight your way through the children.' What she didn't tell me was that behind the strike force of two-year-olds watching *Race for Your Life, Charlie Brown*, stood a pair of solid centre-backs in the shape of a menacing mother and a formidable father.

'You've no right to come in here and try to take over,' they said. 'This room is strictly for children.' Pleading that I had British Airways permission cut no ice either, until a helpful lady on the desk stepped in as referee and calmed the situation down.

In the end mother gave way, even though father continued to fume behind his newspaper. Charlie Brown was ejected from the video player, and Austria v Russia slotted in. By the time our flight was called I had brushed up my identification while the kids played happily with their toys.

Come to think of it, the parents probably thought I was more like a two-year-old, trying to get my own way like that. But I'm in Euro 2004 mode now, and as Trevor Brooking said when I persuaded a Japanese lady to re-open her café so we could watch Ireland play during the last World Cup – I can be quite persistent when it matters.

WEDNESDAY, JUNE 9TH

You are only as good as the organisation behind you, and it still amazes me, even going into my 16th major tournament, how the BBC juggernaut roars into life and manages to negotiate a clear run for its contributors – or 'performing seals' as somebody irreverently once called us.

Today we went to the stadium at Faro to get our media accreditation – that's a badge round your neck with a photograph, without which you won't get further than the road outside the ground – which meant we were admitted to Holland's training session tonight. The Dutch are staying just down the road from us, and so with next Tuesday's live match against Germany in mind, it was useful to run the eye over their 23 players and make sure of my identification. Training can be boring to watch, but I normally manage to commandeer a reporter from the country concerned – in this case Marc van den Heuvel from a Dutch football magazine – to help me 'spot' the players I don't recognise.

Just to show you are never far from home, the first thing my producer Mark Demuth and I learnt from our two Portuguese 'fixers' – Nuno Gomes and Rui Fernandes – was that they had both taken a three-year course in Film and TV Studies with Broadcasting Media at the University of Derby. Fred would be proud to learn that they numbered their visits to Pride Park among the highlights of their time in England.

THURSDAY, JUNE 10TH

This morning my 'spotter' at the German training session was Thomas Strunz, who played in their Euro '96 winning team and now works in television. Again, I was able to come away feeling rather more confident about putting names to faces.

Our family friend Joe Redmond has a villa at Dunas Douramas – just a few hundred yards away from the German hotel and training ground. Mark, Nuno and I shared a couple of beers with Joe and his son Jack and arranged to meet them for dinner tonight.

Having laid the foundations for my first commentary, and knowing Spain and Russia will be training in the stadium at Faro tomorrow night, I am starting to think about the England v France match that falls in between. The games come thick and fast once tournaments like this start, so I try to do as much advance preparation as possible. I have made out my own 'squad lists' for 13 of the 16 countries, denoting the player's age, position, club, caps won and goals scored. For the moment, I have not turned my attention to Bulgaria, Greece or Latvia, on the basis that these three teams are unlikely to come my way.

However, every so often you need a break from the endless succession of names and pronunciations, so I managed 45 minutes in the hotel gym this afternoon. It made me realise what an advantage it is to be supervised by a personal trainer – working on my own without Dean Austin was a real struggle.

Later on, Joe arrived with Bob Murphy – another friend from home who has a property down here – and took Mark and me out for a very decent dinner. I'm getting to like the Algarve a bit too much – soon it will be a distant memory when we travel north to Lisbon and Porto for the main body of the championship.

FRIDAY, JUNE 11TH

What was I saying about injuries always afflicting England in the build-up to a major championship? Just when the whole squad looked like reporting fit, John Terry picked up a hamstring injury and is now certain to miss Sunday's opening match against France. There is clearly a curse over the centre-back position. With Rio Ferdinand banned, Jonathan Woodgate, Gareth Southgate and now Terry injured, Eriksson is down to his fifth-choice partner for Sol Campbell. Ledley King, who scored in February's friendly here in Portugal, looks likely to edge out Jamie Carragher.

Even though my first match is here in Faro tomorrow, I put a fair amount of work in towards Sunday's game as well. Two matches in two days leaves little time to wind down and start preparing again from scratch.

As it happened, the line-ups for the Spain v Russia encounter became pretty clear when we watched both teams train in the stadium tonight. English-speaking colleagues from the two countries were more than helpful, even though a Russian radio reporter seemed to be more concerned about persuading me to visit St Petersburg!

Mick McCarthy, whose Ireland team played competitive matches against both nations two years ago, joined up with us tonight. He worked with the BBC during Euro 2000 and will be my co-commentator tomorrow. Although he is still clearly frustrated by the outcome of Sunderland's season – third in the table, beaten narrowly in the play-offs and coming within a whisker of the FA Cup final – McCarthy remains an engaging character and kept us entertained until after midnight with stories from his days with the Ireland team. And yes, Roy Keane did get a mention!

SATURDAY, JUNE 12TH

At last the waiting is over. The 368 players selected by 16 countries for the 12th European Championships have completed their preparations and are ready for action. So, hopefully, are the commentators.

One man who is off to a great start is my former companion in the commentary box, Trevor Brooking. From now on it will be *Sir* Trevor – a fitting reward for his work in football and at Sport England. The new title will add some gravitas to the challenging position he now occupies at Soho Square.

We went to the stadium early to catch the opening match between Portugal and Greece, and it was a good job we did. There were horrendous technical problems to sort out and our engineer Jeremy Mosler – an expert in all things to do with the complicated business of television sound and vision – had been at the ground since lunch time wrestling with more teething troubles than usual. It was only a few minutes prior to kick-off that Jeremy confirmed the circuits were through to London, and once Gary Lineker had cued us in from Porto, where our live studio team had just finished their coverage of the opening game, away we went.

For an hour, Portsmouth's Alexei Smertin marshalled his Russian troops to deny the Spanish Armada of Raul and Morientes. Then Spain's coach Inaki Saez made what must be one of the cutest substitutions in the history of the European Championship. Juan Carlos Valeron replaced Morientes and scored just 36 seconds after coming on. Good job I had memorised his shirt number, because calling the first goalscorer incorrectly would have been an unthinkable start for me.

Mick McCarthy played a fine game alongside me. He made the point that there was less pressure in the commentary box than on the touchline, where he had been when Ireland met tonight's teams two years ago. I've never been on the touchline, but when things are as fraught technically as they were tonight, I think there is quite enough stress in television for me.

SUNDAY, JUNE 13TH

With Mark Demuth at the wheel and Mick McCarthy in the front passenger seat, we made the three-hour car journey from the Algarve to Lisbon. We were sorry to leave Club Aldiana, the hotel complex that has been our base just outside Albufera for the past five nights, and the hustle and bustle of Lisbon soon hit us when we met up with the main BBC team and found our competitors from ITV were sharing the same hotel.

Iain MacGregor from Sanctuary Publishing dropped in for a beer at lunch time – *Motson's National Obsession* has now sold somewhere in the region of 40,000 copies. There must have been around that number of England fans in the new Estadio da Luz when the teams came out for tonight's game.

For 90 minutes, Eriksson's team did all that could have been expected of them against the defending champions – apart from David Beckham failing to beat his old team mate Fabien Barthez from the penalty spot. It was to prove a costly miss. In a mirror image of the 1999 Champions League final, when Manchester United snatched victory from the jaws of defeat, France and Zinedine Zidane left England numbed with two goals in stoppage time.

The inquests at our hotel went on well into the night. Peter Reid, Sam Allardyce, Steve Bruce, Graham Taylor, Bobby Robson and Gareth Southgate all had a view.

My take on the game? I agreed with my England co-commentator Joe Royle that David James could have done better with the free-kick and was reckless in conceding the penalty. It was only Sven Goran Eriksson's second competitive defeat in charge of England. And the first one was also down to an unexpected error of judgement by a senior goalkeeper when Ronaldinho foxed Seaman in Japan two years ago.

Where are you now Peter Shilton?

MONDAY, JUNE 14TH

Another three-hour car journey this morning – this time from Lisbon to Porto, where the scenery is in marked contrast to Lisbon. The BBC hotel is located in Espinho, a charming seaside town where the pace of life seems almost languid. We picked up the English papers on the way and on the whole they were kind to Eriksson, although a lot of the match reports would have been hastily rewritten when France did a somersault in stoppage time.

UEFA, who celebrate their 50th birthday this week, have placed all the referees and their assistants in the Solverde hotel. Such is their fear of anybody trying to influence them, we are not supposed to speak to them, even in friendly conversation, although the English referee Mike Riley and his assistants Phil Sharp and Glenn Turner were quite happy to pass the time of day when I bumped into them in reception. This means that the main restaurant is exclusively for the use of the referees, but we don't mind about that. The BBC have their own private room that doubles up as our regional office with a big screen, a fridge, and a regular diet of room service.

Fred flew out today to join us for the Holland v Germany game, as did Gary Lineker's wife Michelle and their four boys. There wasn't much Coca Cola left in the fridge after that.

ITV were live with both matches today. For the second day running, the afternoon game ended in a goalless draw. Yesterday it was Switzerland and Croatia, today Italy and Denmark. It disappoints me that when teams have gone through hell and high water to qualify, they start so negatively in the finals. Tonight was much better though. Sweden put their foot down hard on the accelerator and blasted five goals past Bulgaria. Hopefully this will signal a more open approach to the whole tournament.

TUESDAY, JUNE 15TH

Any commentator will tell you that the quality of his work depends partly – perhaps even largely – on the position he is given in the stadium.

With so many countries covering Euro 2004, UEFA section off a large area in the main stand for television, press and radio, serviced by monitor sets and a huge media centre where the newspaper reporters and photographers assemble before and after the game. Our position at the Estadio da Luz on Sunday was perfect – right opposite the halfway line, at exactly the right height, and with no obstructions blocking our view of the pitch.

Not so in Porto's Dragao stadium for tonight's Germany v Holland game. The venue director here had seated the commentators right at the back of a very steep stand. Mark Lawrenson and I could not see the near touchline without standing up, and the players on the far side of the pitch looked like midgets.

When Germany took the lead after half an hour, my experience got me out of a tricky corner. In Bratislava during the qualifiers, David Beckham scored against Slovakia with a free-kick that went straight in – although at first sight many people thought Michael Owen had got a touch. Tonight the same thing happened. Torsten Frings took a free-kick for Germany and it flew through a crowd of players and went in off the far post. From our distant viewpoint it was impossible to see if anybody got a touch and the replay we were shown by Portuguese television was inconclusive. I gambled and gave the goal to Frings.

Although the Dutch equalised later, it was a poor performance by the team I have backed to win the Championship. But the Germans surprised us – they have uncovered some new talent in Philip Lahm, Bastian Schweinsteiger and Kevin Kuranyi.

WEDNESDAY, JUNE 16TH

There are no days off for commentators at a major tournament. This morning I managed to get half an hour on the running machine in the hotel gym, but I was totally outclassed on the adjacent machine by Michelle Lineker. She ran faster, further and burnt up more calories. At least Dean Austin will be pleased I have made some concession to fitness.

After that it was back to work. Mark Demuth had organised a VHS tape of Switzerland v Croatia, the two countries England will meet next. Although the game itself was uneventful, it was ideal for brushing up my identification of players on both sides.

It has been great to have Fred here, especially as our girls organised a day pass which enabled him to sit with us at the commentary position last night. Michelle took Fred back to the airport with the four little Linekers today, and he went home clutching two bottles of the finest port, which Mark Lawrenson had purloined from one of the sponsors at the game.

After Fred had gone, Mark, Mick McCarthy and I travelled by car to the Bessa stadium – home of Boavista – to see Greece play Spain. I was not working as such, but the fact that the Greeks won their opening match means they could conceivably play England in a quarter-final. You are constantly covering all the options in the early stages of a championship.

Greece maintained their reputation as tournament party-poopers by holding Spain to a draw. I watched the start of the evening game in a tent in the television compound surrounded by Portuguese technicians willing their team to beat Russia and stay alive in the group. That they did. However, before I could think of joining any local celebrations, there was the little matter of England v Switzerland. Instead, I ate a cheeseburger with Gordon Strachan and went to bed.

THURSDAY, JUNE 17TH

Coimbra is about two hours' drive from Espinho. We had a lunch time rendezvous at a convenient hotel restaurant with Joe Redmond, his brother and two friends. Thereby hangs a tale.

I had managed to purchase two tickets to the England v Switzerland game for Joe. When we left him after lunch he went on his way to the stadium by taxi while Joe Royle, Mark, Jeremy and I jumped into a BBC car. No sooner had I reached the commentary position than my mobile rang. 'John?' gasped a clearly distraught Joe. 'I've had my tickets stolen, somebody's snatched them from my pocket.'

Memories of the pickpocket incident in Macedonia came flooding back, but this was one petty thief who we were determined would not beat us. There was not time to trace the numbers of the tickets, so we had to find replacements. Our England producer Stephen Booth, working with Garth Crooks on the interview beat, came up with two spares in a matter of minutes, and an embarrassed Joe did manage to see the game.

Wayne Rooney continued his mercurial rise to fame by scoring two goals, the first of which put him in the record books yet again as the youngest goalscorer in European Championship Finals history, and England coasted to a 3–0 win without playing as well as they did against France. I thought Sol Campbell was awesome again, but David Beckham and Michael Owen still haven't caught fire.

Tonight's 2–2 draw between Croatia and France means a draw against Croatia next Monday would almost certainly put England through to the quarter-finals. From now on every England match will be live on the BBC. But how many will there be?

FRIDAY, JUNE 18TH

The *Mail on Sunday* property section rang to ask if they could run a story on the Motsons moving house. We have had our offer on a house in a nearby village accepted, so this might help us to sell ours.

Speaking of newspapers, I hear that *The Times* are running a readers' poll called 'Big Bother' in which one television presenter, pundit or commentator is 'evicted' every few days. Of the ten original candidates, eight still survive. So far I have escaped, although I am at the bottom of the list as a 16-1 outsider to be there at the finish.

Bearing in mind the BBC audience for England v Croatia next Monday is likely to be around 20 million, I shan't last longer than that. Ninety minutes live and unscripted on a night like that means at least one slip of the tongue.

Gordon Strachan has joined our team and is proving a witty and restless character – both on and off the screen. He sees his television role as a perfect interlude between coaching jobs, although I am certain it won't be long before he is back in the game.

This has been my quietest day so far, so I took the chance to have an early look at the Croatians on the video machine. It was most reassuring to see that they have improved their shirt numbers since they finished third in the 1998 World Cup. They were indecipherable then, and I remember covering Croatia v Romania after all the Romanian players had dyed their hair yellow. I can't recall another match when none of the players was instantly recognisable – unless it was Mexico v Ecuador in Japan.

Tonight Mark Demuth and I sat among 30,000 Swedish supporters in the Dragao Stadium in Porto as they hauled their way back to a 1–1 draw against Italy. Barry Davies was the BBC commentator on the other side of the ground and I could guess what he was saying about the Italian mentality.

After a sparkling first half, in which Zambrotta caused havoc down the left and Cassano scored from a cross from Panucci, they reverted to type and tried to close the game by substituting three attackers with three defensively minded midfield players.

It was a Swedish substitute, Mattias Jonson, who clinched the game. Italy were forced to defend deeper and, five minutes from the end, Zlatan Ibrahimovic scored with an overhead kick, leaving Trapattoni beating his fist against the dug-out in frustration, just as he had in Korea two years ago. I love the Italian people, but I just wish their football team would shed their cloak of negativity.

On the home front, Mark Bright, who is fielding the views of those at home on our interactive programme, told me that many viewers are still pessimistic about England's chances. A lot of callers have called for David Beckham, Michael Owen and David James to be dropped.

SATURDAY, JUNE 19TH

There are football matches, good football matches, and great football matches. I have been privileged, after tonight, to have been the BBC commentator on three of the best in the history of the European Championship.

Twenty years ago, in Marseille, I saw Michel Platini score in the last minute of extra time to settle a semi-final between France and Portugal.

The goal came from a great run and cross by Jean Tigana who was in the television compound tonight as a pundit.

Then in Bruges during Euro 2000, I witnessed a crazy, compelling game between Spain and Yugoslavia at the end of the group phase. Spain scored twice in the last few minutes to win 4–3, but it wasn't until after the final whistle that Yugoslavia realised that they too had qualified.

Tonight I fell upon another classic. Holland were two up in 20 minutes against the Czech Republic, who came back to win 3–2 with a goal by Vladimir Smicer two minutes from the end.

But these bare facts do not go even halfway to doing justice to a game in which there were 35 shots, countless saves from goalkeepers Van der Sar and Peter Cech, dazzling wing play by Arjen Robben and Andy Van der Meyde (until the Dutch coach took them both off) and a vintage midfield battle between the indefatigable Edgar Davids and the masterful Pavel Nedved.

The emotions at the end were something to behold. Nedved shed tears of joy; the Dutch were utterly shell-shocked. We were the real winners – the neutral spectators in the delightful little stadium in Aveiro.

Was it the best of the three? Hard to call, but it was right up there, even though I still believe the most memorable game of all in my 16 major tournaments was Italy's 3–2 victory over Brazil in the 1982 World Cup. Tonight was very special though. It put a marker down for the rest of the tournament as far as our BBC team were concerned, and although it was full of tactical nuances, it showed once again how gloriously unpredictable football can be.

And just to think, I started the day intending to write about getting my laundry done!

SUNDAY, JUNE 20TH

There was no time to go for a walk along the beach and luxuriate in the memory of last night's theatre. Today we set off on our way to Lisbon for England's crunch match with Croatia tomorrow night.

So well collated are England's media arrangements these days, that a five-minute 'window' for me with Sven Goran Eriksson had been allocated alongside his other commitments by Adrian Bevington – a promise made at our lunch in May.

Sven knows the form with broadcasters. He has worked as a co-commentator himself for Swedish television and understands that any insight he gives me is strictly off the record until the match starts. Eriksson confirmed the England team would be unchanged and said that he was 99 per cent certain they would keep the 4–4–2 shape. I also checked his record at Benfica when he was a coach here in Lisbon – three championships in five years and two European finals – 'I think you would say quite successful,' he said with a smile. He also mentioned that he and the players had watched the Holland v Czech Republic match on BBC1 last night.

We are expecting a huge audience tomorrow, hopefully to rival the 19 million ITV got for England v France. Does that make me nervous? Not really. My first international tournament was the 1974 World Cup, and if I can't do the job after 30 years then it's a bit late to start worrying now. Somebody worked out that I did my 100th England game three years ago, and competitions like these bring the memories flooding back.

I had to wait for my first sight of England in the finals of a major championship. They missed out in the World Cups of 1974 and 1978, and the 1976 European Finals, but I was there in 1980 when ugly hooliganism reared its head in Italy and the police sprayed the fans with tear gas as England played Belgium.

Two years later, in my first World Cup as the England commentator, Bryan Robson scored in 27 seconds against France in Bilbao. We never made the European Finals in 1984, but four years later I described Marco van Basten's hat-trick against England in Düsseldorf, and two years further on there were the penalties against the Germans in Turin – Gazza's tears and all that.

Gascoigne figured again in Euro '96, scoring that impudent goal against Scotland at Wembley, and in the next tournament four years later I was calling Alan Shearer's header that beat Germany in Charleroi. Little more than a year later, my most cherished England memory – the 5–1 triumph in Munich courtesy of a Michael Owen hat-trick. Sven sometimes even mimics my line: 'It's getting better and better and better.'

Well, let's hope I'm saying something like that tomorrow night. I've never seen England in the final of a major championship, and I may not have too many more opportunities.

MONDAY, JUNE 21ST

This morning, I heard that *The Times* proudly announced my eviction from the 'Big Bother' competition. Privately, I was absolutely delighted to get all this nonsense out of the way. There was quite enough for me to think about in preparing a commentary that could be heard by half the nation.

At lunch time I enjoyed a short interlude with some civilised England supporters in the restaurant at our hotel. Jim White in *Telegraph Sport* wrote a piece today about how successfully the hooligans have been kept away from the England matches out here, and my experience justifies everything he said.

If only the Government and the FA had got the police to instigate a 'banned list' 25 years ago. My first taste of the beer-bellied, tattooed hordes was at the European Finals of 1980 in Italy, and if the Government had shown any foresight then, rather than allowing them to travel, misbehave, and return home without punishment, we could perhaps have avoided so much wanton damage in so many European cities.

When we arrived at the stadium, there must have been 40,000 England fans there. And what a treat they had in store. I can't remember covering a more eventful England game in the European Championships, and tonight's 4–2 victory over Croatia is just a prelude to what I am sure will be a gripping quarter-final against Portugal on Thursday.

TUESDAY, JUNE 22ND

The audience figures came through this morning and we broke the 20-million barrier. Predictions are that we could even reach 23 or 24 million for the quarter-final between England and Portugal on Thursday evening. Wayne Rooney, with four goals in two games, was splashed across every paper here and at home. A nation has a new hero.

Mark Demuth and I gave ourselves the best part of the day off and drove to the seaside town of Carcavelos to meet John and Mary Mortimore and their daughter Alison. Like Sven Goran Eriksson, John had two spells as coach at Benfica and is something of a living legend in and around Lisbon. He was constantly recognised by the locals as we made our way to a nice fish restaurant on the beach. I also found out that Mary and I have something in common – both our fathers were Methodist preachers and we went to neighbouring Methodist boarding schools in the fifties.

When we got back to Lisbon we heard news of the tragic death in the early hours of this morning of England fan Stephen Smith, allegedly stabbed by a Ukrainian pickpocket near Lisbon's Rossio Square.

Football takes second place to the awful and premature end of a 28-year-old life. The peculiar outcome of Group C, where the 2–2 draw between Denmark and Sweden was the only result that could eliminate Italy after they beat Bulgaria, came way down the news bulletins. FA Chief Executive Mark Palios went on Portuguese television to express his condolences to the young man's family, and must be hoping that there is no misguided attempt at revenge by Englishmen.

WEDNESDAY, JUNE 23RD

With England's quarter-final against Portugal coming up tomorrow, it was time to make my first visit to the team hotel to speak in person to Sven Goran Eriksson. Our previous conversation, before the Croatia match, had been on the telephone.

After recording an interview with Garth Crooks for transmission before the match tomorrow, Eriksson gave me ten minutes to myself, in which he confirmed that the team and formation would be the same. He said he had reminded his players that Ronaldo, Deco and Figo could all do damage if they were allowed to run with the ball – especially in a one-on-one situation – so he wanted to see plenty of cover and support, but no specific man-to-man marking.

I asked if he had already selected his penalty takers in case the match went to a shoot-out. 'Not yet,' he replied. 'We shall practise penalties this afternoon and I hope eight or nine players will want to take one. Then I will decide which five to nominate after extra time, depending who is on the pitch and looks positive.'

Before leaving to watch the Germany v Czech Republic match, I had a chance conversation with 43-year-old Marco Tavares, an air traffic controller at Faro airport on the Algarve. He speaks perfect English with a detectable American accent. Marco is in Lisbon as an instructor on a course for trainee recruits, but while he has been 'on secondment' there has been high drama at his normal place of work. A Russian airline overshot the runway at Faro and had to abort take-off. None of the 87 passengers was injured. Marco explained that every airport runway has a gravel 'safety zone' beyond it. Good thing too. Life is so fragile, as poor Stephen Smith found out yesterday.

THURSDAY, JUNE 24TH

I am not naturally superstitious, but on a day like this everybody gets a bit twitchy. Peter Reid and Ian Wright, for instance, elected to follow the same routine as for the Croatia match three days earlier. Walking the same route, looking out of the same windows, even insisting on buying yours truly a coke at the same bar.

I didn't see any black cats or walk under any ladders, but the aforementioned Joe Redmond put my nerves on edge by getting hopelessly lost in Lisbon and arriving two hours late with his brother for lunch. There are two Tivoli hotels in the city – trust Joe to drive to the wrong one!

That minor drama helped take my mind off the game, until a contact of mine in the England camp rang to say Ledley King was on a flight home because his partner was about to give birth prematurely. The baby was born later in the day, but it meant that King would not be taking part against Portugal.

When I reached the BBC compound on the edge of the stadium the mood seemed bright and optimistic. The make-up girls were busy ironing shirts for Lineker, Hansen, Wright and Reid. In weather like this, the studio team travel to the stadium in T-shirt and shorts and change into their smart gear just before they start rehearsals. Even I have given up my old custom of wearing a shirt and tie for England games. Years ago when I started it was meant to be a mark of respect. Nowadays there is carte blanche as to how broadcasters and reporters turn up. One overseas commentator was working in his bare feet, and in the media centre you had to look hard even for a smart shirt and a decent pair of trousers.

The players set an example in getting off the team coach in their regulation outfits and for once the time up to kick-off seemed to fly past. Joe Royle rejoined me after flying back from a court case in Manchester and gave me the customary handshake a couple of minutes before we went on the air. Did I say I wasn't superstitious?

Within two minutes I was shouting the place down as Michael Owen put England ahead. He had done so, of course, in the quarter-final against

Brazil two years ago, so I spent the next few minutes telling myself to keep the lid on any excessive optimism. The old commentators' creed: 'Don't get too carried away, you never know what will happen next'.

And something *did* happen. The injury to Wayne Rooney with less than half an hour gone did, in hindsight, unhinge all that England had achieved and made a mockery of all the might-have-beens. It was in that moment that the dependency on an 18-year-old whose career has scarcely started exposed England's lack of a 'Plan B'.

Now the dangers of defending too deep, which had contributed to England's late downfall against France and had been evident at times against Croatia, provided Portugal with the invitation to come forward. Luis Felipe Scolari, Eriksson's old adversary from Brazil, breathed new life into his Portuguese side with attacking substitutes. And two of them, Helder Postiga of Tottenham and the veteran Rui Costa, put England behind.

In between, there was the moment which will remain with every England fan as long as they play international football. In a moment of déjà vu, going back to the 1998 World Cup when Sol Campbell's header could have been the winning goal against Argentina had it not been disallowed, the same thing happened to the same player.

Just as they did in St Etienne six years ago, Campbell and his team mates ran celebrating to the side of the pitch, only to turn round and see, in what must have seemed to them like *Groundhog Day*, the ball back in play following a Portuguese free-kick.

When he blew the whistle seconds later to signal extra time, Swiss referee Urs Meier gestured with both hands, suggesting he had disallowed the goal for a push by John Terry. Not one of five replay angles confirmed his view. The Zurich grocer had tipped the scales against England, and although Frank Lampard belligerently eclipsed Rui Costa's goal to keep England alive in extra time, we knew then it was the dreaded penalty shoot-out.

In the commentary position, my mind went back to Turin 1990. Down in the presentation studio, Gary Lineker's did too, but for very different reasons. He actually took one against the Germans and scored.

When Beckham slipped on the sandy penalty spot (surely a good referee would have had the penalties taken at the other end?), his skied shot was a reminder of poor Chris Waddle 14 years ago. Owen, Lampard, Terry, Hargreaves and Ashley Cole all did their job; this time it was Darius

Vassell who had to swallow hard – just as Waddle, Stuart Pearce, Gareth Southgate and David Batty did before him.

So when the dust settles, the inquests will begin. I'm not usually affected deeply by England disappointments – I have seen quite enough over the years – but tonight I couldn't summon up any enthusiasm for drowning my sorrows. I drank one whisky and went to bed – my earliest night of the trip.

FRIDAY, JUNE 25TH

The first thing to be said is that no way was it David James' fault. Our much maligned goalkeeper stood no chance with the two Portuguese goals nor with the penalties – having to endure the final ignominy of the winning kick being placed right in the corner by his opposite number, Ricardo.

Nor do I attach much blame to our defence. Gary Neville, Sol Campbell and the outstanding Ashley Cole all had good tournaments. The disappointments came further forward. Frank Lampard avoided burn-out by providing willing legs and three goals, but more was expected of Paul Scholes, Steven Gerrard and David Beckham.

Particularly Beckham. Two or three years ago, when the England ship was floundering, the captain would take the wheel and steer the team on to a safer course. Remember Greece at Old Trafford? And not just because of the free-kick either.

This was, by comparison, a subdued superstar. Sensible, certainly, in the way he stayed wide on the right so that England kept their shape. Unselfish, even, in the number of times he dropped back to help Gary Neville. But it was not the Beckham of old, and I don't think many of us will ever get close enough to him to know how much of that was down to fitness or fanciful disclosures about his private life.

Which brings us, finally and fittingly, to the strikers. With Michael Owen firing only spasmodically, the revelation called Rooney took on the rest of Europe as though he was playing street football. Unfazed, uninhibited, unbridled, it all seemed set for the ultimate *Boy's Own* story.

And that is where it kicks you in the teeth. Wayne's world was widening so fast a wall was going to get in the way somewhere. From his point of view, we hope it's a minor setback and not one that is going to stop him reaching his breathtaking potential. After George Best, Paul Gascoigne and Alan Hudson, it would be nice to see a spellbinding talent fulfilled.

For now, England are out. Eriksson, I'm sure, will be encouraged to stay on. But he is no longer a 'lucky manager'.

SATURDAY, JUNE 26TH

As Ruud Gullit said to me while he was working for the BBC at Euro '96, 'Every game boils down to one small detail.' I was reminded of that again this morning when the English newspapers arrived. The football correspondents had had 24 hours to consider their verdict on Thursday night's defeat and England's tournament overall.

Had the penalty shootout gone England's way, they would have been cast in the role of heroes for an unlikely comeback in extra time. Come to that, had Wayne Rooney not been injured, or had Sol Campbell's last-minute goal counted, we would have surely won the match in normal time, in which case the nation would have been sticking its chest out rather than contemplating its navel. Instead, there are now serious issues to be addressed before the World Cup qualifiers start in September. Why has David Beckham's form and influence dipped so sharply? Does Eriksson do enough coaching with the accent on the positive? Why have we not blooded a new young goalkeeper? And do we really think we can make do and mend on the left side of midfield?

The man who I think can come up with some answers, other than the coach himself, is Sir Trevor Brooking. His role as director of football development aside, I believe that Trevor will have studied England's performance from a more privileged perspective than most. He will doubtless express some views that will not be aired publicly.

Nobody with any sound judgement would suggest Eriksson should go – not unless England make a mess of the World Cup qualifiers, which with his record is highly unlikely. There is no obvious successor on the horizon, which could explain why the FA went to such lengths to keep him when Chelsea came calling.

The brief now for the FA – especially for Mark Palios who will lean on Trevor for advice – is to find a new coach, preferably an Englishman, to succeed Eriksson after 2006. Nobody would seriously expect him to stay after the World Cup in Germany.

But let's lay the England inquest to one side and remind ourselves that we still have a Championship to enjoy. Tonight, Mark Bright and I suffered in stifling heat in Faro as Holland locked horns with Sweden. I could be cruel and say we witnessed a largely tedious game, but if we were uncomfortable with a temperature of 31 degrees in the shade, goodness knows what it was like for the players on the pitch.

Extra time brought the game to life. Sweden hit the post and the bar, but overall the Dutch, maddeningly frustrating though they are, just about had the edge. But there had to be doubts about their mentality when it came to the penalty shoot-out. Holland had exited the last three European Championships by this method. Their record in this department was worse than England's! After the Dutch had squeezed home by five penalties to four, Radio Five's Mark Pougatch grabbed me as we made our way out of the stadium. 'You know what that means, don't you?' he said with a smile, I could sense his next column for *The Times* forming in his mind, 'England will win the next time we go to penalties.'

Fine Mark, as long as the five kickers are not Chris Waddle, Stuart Pearce, Gareth Southgate, David Batty and Darius Vassell.

SUNDAY, JUNE 27TH

After our three-hour stint at the microphone last night, it was a relief to wake up this morning and realise my next commentary was not until Wednesday. A three-day break after doing eight matches in 15 days is just what is required.

My Dutch broadcasting friend Eddy Poelmann, who I have known since my first World Cup in 1974, came over to lunch with Rob Fleur, a reporter with NOS Sports Radio. The afternoon sped by as we discussed news from the Dutch camp ahead of Wednesday's semi-final. I have always believed English and Dutch broadcasters have a lot in common. They approach the job in much the same way as we do, and rather like us, their access to the players has been strategically reduced down the years. Gone are the days when, thanks largely to Eddy, I found myself in Rudi Krol's bedroom interviewing Johann Cruyff.

Towards the end of the afternoon, I started to feel I had been dealt the best hand at Club Aldiana. The Germany holiday makers were clearly enjoying themselves, but in a polite and restrained way. We made a few friends and our minds turned to the 2006 World Cup in two years' time.

Even the drama of the false teeth rebounded in my favour. As I have mentioned, two of my front teeth are false and fitted onto a plastic plate, which I take out at night. To my horror this morning, I looked in the glass and the teeth were missing.

It turned out that a chambermaid had discovered them somewhere in the room and left them discreetly on the table next to the television. They always said I was a toothless broadcaster.

MONDAY, JUNE 28TH

One rule about writing a diary like this – and I promise I have stuck to it – is never to go back and change anything. For one thing, my editor wouldn't allow it, and secondly, it would be cheating to abuse the value of hindsight. What was said on the day stays there, for better or worse.

So I had no prior knowledge when I suggested on Saturday that Trevor Brooking would be a key figure in the post-Championship discussions at Soho Square. Now it appears that Mark Palios has asked him to compile a detailed report on England's escapade.

Having worked alongside Brooking for many years, I know the supposedly bland exterior to be a myth. When Trevor gets his teeth into something, like Sport England or the emergency management of West Ham United, he can be as decisive and as unyielding as the best of them.

Whether his report becomes public knowledge or not, it will be a no-holds-barred document. Whatever its content with regard to the players and their preparation and performance, I have no doubt it will refer in some way to Eriksson's back-up staff, both on the playing and administrative side. There is certainly no shortage of bodies, and the money the FA spent on hotel accommodation and travel, including the cost of financing the trip for the players' wives and girlfriends, would make an interesting comparison with, say, that spent by Greece or the Czech Republic.

However, I have no complaints about the co-operation I received. Gibson and Bevington kept their promises to the letter. I'm just sorry I'm not phoning them about the semi-final.

Today Mark Demuth, engineer Jeremy and I took our leave of Club Aldiana and drove back to Lisbon. Before leaving we met the general manager of the complex, Eric Schumann, and I told him I might well come back for a holiday next year.

TUESDAY, JUNE 29TH

We went to the beach today. But it was work, honestly. Every member of our studio and commentary teams has to select their favourite moment of the tournament and record the reason why in front of the camera. With appropriate footage, these will be shown in a montage at the start of our last programme on the night of the final.

My first choice would have been Vladimir Smicer's winning goal in the classic match of the tournament so far – the Czech Republic's laudable come-back against Holland, but Alan Hansen had got in first with that one. Sol Campbell's unforgettable header against Portugal was Garth Crooks' selection and word was that Peter Reid would plump for Wayne Rooney's impact.

So I fell back on 20-year-old Arjen Robben's winning penalty for Holland in the shoot-out against Sweden. It was the first penalty he had ever taken at top level; it meant Holland got the monkey off their back after four failures in shoot-outs; and there was a moment of humour too – Edwin van der Sar had saved the fifth Swedish penalty from Olof Mellberg, and Holland's Michael Reiziger had gone dancing down the pitch thinking it was all over. When he turned round, he found Robben walking past him to take what proved to be the last kick!

So where did the beach come into it? Well, so that we didn't all appear with the same backdrop, I persuaded our hard-working camera crew to come to Carcavelos, where we had such an enjoyable afternoon with the Mortimore family a week ago today. My 30 seconds to camera went without a hitch. The lunch afterwards lasted a bit longer.

On the way home, Nuno Gomes (our version) drove us to the national stadium where England trained while they were here. I had always wanted to see the scene of Celtic's famous European Cup triumph of 1967, and it was a pleasant surprise.

The ground is surrounded by a forest of trees, and is almost entirely in the open. With its renovated seating and 38,000 capacity it looks like a more elegant, up-market version of Brighton's Withdean Stadium. No club team plays there, but on the day of the Portuguese Cup final it is traditional for supporters to picnic in the surrounding forest.

We were shown round by 75-year-old Joao Miranda Batista who began work at the stadium in 1941, three years before it was completed. He had a fund of stories, including bearing witness to a row between Celtic and Inter Milan as to who should have which dressing room in the build-up to that European Cup final 37 years ago. Jock Stein and Helenio Herrera were playing mind games even then.

Tonight I had dinner with Gary Lineker, Ian Wright and Head of Football, Niall Sloane. Wrighty was reluctant to come at first (yes, really) but when I persuaded him he quickly moved into top gear and we had a cracking evening in a classy restaurant. Ian's energy and zest for life always continues to amaze me. What you see on the television is what you get in real life – a hyperactive bundle of fun with a huge heart.

Lineker was just Lineker. The coolest man on the planet. He even managed to pay the bill when nobody else was looking.

WEDNESDAY, JUNE 30TH

People often ask me how much the commentator watches the game on the pitch with the naked eye, and how much he refers to his monitor that shows him the picture the viewer is seeing at home. I can't speak for my colleagues, but I have always trusted my own vision for 95 per cent of the time, especially when the ball is in play. A quick glance down to the monitor when the director brings up a close-up is essential, as it is when talking over replays. But for the most part I prefer to see the whole field of play so that I can spot players running off the ball, assistant referees raising their flags, and which players are making their way forward for corners and free-kicks.

My preferred policy paid off in tonight's semi-final between Portugal and Holland. The host broadcasting consortium have been mainly using Portuguese directors to produce the pictures and tonight's coverage was, to say the least, well below the standard we would expect at home.

When Ronaldo put Portugal ahead and pulled off his shirt in celebration, it was quite clear from where I was sitting that Swedish referee Anders Frisk was running towards him and reaching for his yellow card – UEFA have instructed referees to caution players who remove their shirts. It was four or five minutes later when we actually got pictures to back up my words. The director then 'cut in' a shot of the booking that he had obviously found on another camera. I don't know which commentator he was listening to as a guide, but it certainly wasn't me.

Worse was to follow. Shortly after half-time with Portugal leading 1−0, they took a short corner on the left. 'Maniche!' I shouted as he hit a screamer into the far corner of the net for what was almost certainly the goal of the tournament. 'Astonishing, where did that come from?' I was jabbering as the scorer disappeared under a pile of jubilant Portuguese players. Amid all the din, my producer Phil Bigwood hissed into my ear, 'Motty, they missed it. Apologise to the viewers and explain this is not BBC coverage.'

Missing a goal is a match director's worst nightmare. The Portuguese producer had been unwise enough to try to replay an earlier incident just as they took the corner. He cut back to live pictures as Maniche's shot bulged the back of the net.

It has been a golden rule at the BBC for many years never to put in a replay when a team are about to take a corner. And it has been a golden rule of mine not to take my eye off the pitch when the ball is in play.

So when I get asked that question in future, I shall reply with a one-word answer: 'Maniche'.

J U L Y

THURSDAY, JULY 1ST

On Van Nistelrooy's and Kluivert's 28th birthdays, the Dutch team flew home. Kluivert did not get on the pitch in any of Holland's five matches because Dick Advocaat had already decided that the strikers could not play together. Bearing in mind how isolated Van Nistelrooy looked, and how the manager swapped his wingers around, I wonder if he regrets that now.

While the Dutch departed, like England victims of a Portuguese side that showed more ambition, the home nation celebrated. They didn't keep me awake though – I was shattered after last night's broadcast, which reminded me once again just how narrow the line is between an acceptable commentary and one that gets remembered for the wrong reasons.

With Sunday's final in mind, Jeremy, Mark Demuth and I drove back to Porto to watch the second semi-final between Greece and the Czech Republic. I had only seen them play once in the flesh and had never covered the Greeks in commentary.

And what a good thing I went. The Czech Republic started the semi-final as hot favourites, and my favourite player of the whole competition, Tomas Rosicky, hit the bar. But when they lost Pavel Nedved five minutes before half-time, the Czechs lost their master planner and found the Greeks impossible to break down. We then witnessed a moment of football history when Traianos Dellas headed the first (and probably last) 'silver goal' in a major championship. The Czechs hardly had time to kick off before Pierluigi Collina, taking charge of his last international, blew his whistle to end the game.

The devastated Czechs were by no means the only ones going home. Quite a few of our BBC team were at the end of a long and demanding stint, and I had a late-night snack with Steve Wilson who had just completed his second major tournament for BBC Television.

Steve was already thinking ahead to the return of *Match of the Day,* and he wasn't the only one. Sky picked their live Premiership games up to Christmas today and soon we shall know where we will be starting on August 14th. Let's get this final out of the way first, shall we?

FRIDAY, JULY 2ND

Before leaving the Solverde Hotel at Espinho for the second and last time, I managed two sessions on the running machine to bring my total for the month to four. 'Try to work out once a week just to keep ticking over,' Dean Austin had said.

I have already decided to bring Anne out to Portugal on holiday next year, so it was only 'au revoir' to the staff at the Solverde. Mark, Jeremy and I had a lovely lunch at the Cabana restaurant on the seafront at Espinho before leaving.

In the car on the way back to Lisbon, my mind was already turning to Sunday's final and to what I could say about Greece. A few mischievous lines crossed my mind, but references to Homer (hopefully not Markus Merk the referee), Achilles, Cyclops and defenders bearing gifts will be studiously avoided – unless the goalkeeper takes one eye off the ball of course!

Our two resident statisticians, Chris Slegg and Alex Kunawicz, dropped into the hotel bar for a drink so that I could thank them for the wealth of information they have put my way. Why on earth did it take so long for the BBC to appreciate the value of making those appointments?

For about 25 years the commentators were given a few biographical notes and left to get on with it. Chris and Alex have produced a twice-daily bulletin that would do justice to any newspaper. Wherever we have been in Portugal, the newsletter has been pushed underneath my bedroom door, bringing me up to date on the tournament as a whole, summarising stories in the papers back home, and previewing my next match with all the facts and figures I need.

It is all part of the outstanding teamwork that has made this trip such a smooth and memorable one for me. Now it's down to me to make some sense of Sunday's final.

SATURDAY, JULY 3RD

I definitely shouldn't have worn that shirt. Not the beach holiday number with all those sharks on it.

Mark Lawrenson, Garth Crooks and Ray Stubbs had every reason to poke fun at this commentator on *Football Focus*, comparing my outfit with a shirt Steve Bruce had worn – and been suitably chastised for – earlier in the tournament.

My rare appearance in the studio for the last *Focus* of the season, to join in a discussion about the tournament in general and England's participation in particular, coincided with Ray's last show in the chair from which he has compered *Focus* for the last five years. The biggest compliment I can pay him and his editor, Andrew Clement, is that when the BBC lost the Premiership highlights three years ago, *Football Focus* maintained its Saturday lunch time profile and reputation despite not having any league action. Producers and reporters just had to be more imaginative – and they were.

Ray is now taking on a bigger project. The BBC has decided to go 'interactive' on a Saturday afternoon, running a minute-by-minute scores service culminating in *Final Score* on BBC1 which attracts an audience of around 5 million – more than twice as many as *Focus*.

Mark, Garth and I were all asked by Stubbsy to select our team of the tournament, and mine read like this ...

Isaksson (Sweden)

Puyol (Spain) Dellas (Greece) Carvalho (Portugal) Cole (England)

Ronaldo (Portugal) Rosicky (Czech Rep) Maniche and Figo (Portugal)

Rooney (England) Baros (Czech Republic)

It says something when I can't find room for any Italian, German or Dutch players.

After the programme, over lunch, Andrew wanted our votes for 'Goal of the Tournament'. We had run the competition before Maniche's belter in the semi-final – a good job really because it was so poorly covered. In the end, the winner was Henrik Larsson's diving header against Bulgaria.

Tonight Des Lynam and our mutual agent Jane Morgan came to the hotel for a drink. Tomorrow is Des's last major sports broadcast on television, although I suspect it will not be the last we see or hear of him on the air.

SUNDAY, JULY 4TH

So here we are. 336 days after setting out for that friendly at Northampton, I have reached my season's destination – the final of the European Championship in Lisbon. Pity England aren't here, but in my heart of hearts I never thought they would be.

Of the 16 World Cup and European Championship tournaments I have covered since 1974, England have been present at eleven. They have reached the semi-finals twice; the quarter-finals (or last eight) four times; and on the other five occasions have gone out in the group stage or second round.

You can argue about near misses, bad luck or being beaten by the eventual winners as much as you like, but as I said on *Football Focus* yesterday, English players have been behind their continental and South American counterparts in touch, technique and tactics since Hungary proved that point in 1953.

Having said that, they were not markedly inferior to the other teams at Euro 2004. It has been a tournament of tarnished reputations, where the big players and established nations fell well below expectations.

Our BBC panel blamed part of it on the demands of the Champions League. Having said that, five of the Portuguese team in tonight's final went all the way in that competition with Porto.

Look at it the other way round. The success of Turkey and South Korea at the last World Cup, together with that of the finalists Greece here, suggest that hunger and desire may be back on the agenda. They turned up fresh and fully fit, whereas one or two other countries seemed to think turning up was all they had to do.

The BBC team 'turned up' for the final a good four hours before the kick-off. Alan Hansen and Gary Lineker passed the time watching the Wimbledon final between Federer and Roddick on a screen in the television compound.

I received a good-luck call from Ricky George, and managed to buy some of the elusive tournament programmes, which I knew I would get asked for when I got home.

'We'll get no sleep tonight if Portugal win,' was a comment I heard three or four times, but when the teams came out you would have thought it was Greece who were at home. Their supporters made enough noise to numb the senses, and it was clear when the game started that they were going to be every bit as obdurate as they had been against France and the Czech Republic.

Whether Portugal were still nervous after losing to the Greeks in the opening match I'm not sure, but their play was spasmodic and the game itself fitful and at times scrappy.

It did not make for a flowing commentary and for once Scolari on the Portuguese bench met his match. The German Otto Rehhagel became, at 65, the oldest man to lead a team to the European Championship, and the first coach to do so from a different country.

Had I been able to revise the team of the tournament I selected yesterday, I would have added Theo Zagorakis in midfield. He and Traianos Dellos played with a vigour and influence that seemed to pass them by when they were at Leicester and Sheffield United.

As Figo, Ronaldo and company melted away, it was the ultimate football odyssey. Greece travelled further than anybody expected, largely on the back of a rugged, resolute defence that conceded just four goals in six games.

It was a philosophy, of a football kind, designed by Rehhagel to suit the players he had at his disposal. Whether that qualified him to be mentioned in the same breath as Socrates is debatable, but with an ancient civilisation behind them and the modern Olympic Games in Athens just 40 days ahead, the Greek footballers made a slice of history all of their own.

MONDAY, JULY 5TH

We were like schoolboys breaking up at the end of term. A coach arrived at the hotel to take the presenters, pundits and commentator (I was the only one still there) to Lisbon airport for the midday flight to London.

The ITV team were travelling on the same flight, and all seemed well when the crew did their safety check and the captain told us we would be at Heathrow in two hours' time.

Then came one of those delays that make you fidget nervously, and soon an announcement from the flight deck that some of the baggage in the hold was unaccounted for.

Apparently a computer fault had caused the paperwork to go haywire, and an hour and a half later we were still on the tarmac. Ten passengers, including Sir Bobby Robson, were asked to go down the steps and identify the luggage they had checked in.

Deprived of food and drink in this period, everybody stayed amazingly calm. We were all short of sleep after our late-night party on a river boat, but as Lineker said to me after France '98 when our coach was delayed on the way to the airport, 'It's only half a day in your life, Motty. There's always another plane.'

Remembering that today made me think how stressed and irritable I used to get covering these major tournaments. As the baggage problem went away and we took to the air, I realised with quiet satisfaction that on this trip, to my knowledge anyway, I had not had a cross word with anybody or got steamed up over minor hitches.

A lot of that was down to having a calm companion in Mark Demuth, and to the receptive and polite attitude of the Portuguese people. Everywhere we went, in hotels, stadiums or streets, we were treated with patience and kindness.

It has been such a warm and welcoming environment that I have already decided to bring Anne on holiday here next year. Same three venues – Espinho, Lisbon and the Algarve – and the same three hotels if I can arrange it.

This year's holiday starts on Friday, when we fly to Alaska and cruise from Anchorage to Vancouver. That will certainly clear the mind of football for a while. No English papers and no mobile phones.

I finally got home at tea time, just in time for a surprise 'welcome back' party at The Hollybush, thoughtfully organised by the manager, Gary Stanley, who had packed the public bar for the big matches by bringing in a rear-projection screen. Needless to say, a lot of the regulars were still talking about Sol Campbell's header.

Somebody asked me how many more of these tournaments I am going to do. Germany in 2006, health permitting, is certainly on the agenda; after that, who knows? Lynam said he wanted to quit frontline sport before he was called an old fart, and I think I will know when the time has come to hand over my microphone on the big occasion to one of my younger colleagues.

In the meantime, there's something I have got to do when I come back in August. It's called *Match of the Day*.

PICTURE CREDITS

All photos courtesy of the author except:

SECTION 1
Page 1 (below) Charles Green;
Page 2 (above) Mark Kelleher, (below) Ivanhoe Photography;
Page 3 (above) Derby Evening Telegraph;
Page 6 (below) Chris Wood;
Page 7 (above) Ray Pickard, (below) Martin Ogden;
Page 8 Mirror Syndication.

SECTION 2
Page 1 Russell Cheyne;
Page 2 Getty Images (above) Jim Watson, (below) Matthew Peters;
Page 3 Getty Images (above) Martin Hayhow;
Page 3 Empics (below), (left) Mike Egerton, (right) Tony Marshall;
Page 4/5 John Cassidy;
Page 6 Getty Images (above) Paul Barker;
Page 7 Getty Images (above) Alex Livesey, (below) Jamie Mcdonald;
Page 8 Getty Images (above) Alex Livesey, (below) Aris Messinis/
AFP/ Getty.

MATCH OF THE DAY FOOTBALL YEARBOOK 2004/2005

Endorsed by John Motson

The *Match Of The Day Football Yearbook* is the premier authority on the beautiful game. Tens of thousands of individual statistics allow you to compare your club and its star players with the best in Europe and the rest of the UK. With more than 6,000 charts and 1,000 pictures, this book provides a level of detail that goes far beyond anything else on the market in a totally independent and credible way.

The *Match Of The Day Football Yearbook* is also a form guidebook, making it the perfect betting and fantasy-league companion – looking at the key players in the top divisions in breathtaking detail.

Football is a game of opinion, and this book will help you to speculate knowledgeably, defend your views and gain a deeper understanding of the English, Scottish and top European leagues.

Fully endorsed by BBC commentator John Motson, this yearbook is the only guide you will need to the coming season.

ISBN: 0 563 52135 X

MATCH OF THE DAY 40TH ANNIVERSARY

by Martyn Smith

Match of the Day is a national institution with a theme tune that has become shorthand for football. This year sees the 40th anniversary of the programme and this book pays homage to all the great players, matches, scores and records since 1964, celebrating both football itself as well as the classic *Match of the Day* line-ups.

We have Wilson in goal, Wolstenholme, Coleman, Hanson and Lawrenson in defence, Brooking, Lynam, Hill and Stubbs in midfield and Davies and Lineker upfront with Crooks, Gubba and Sinstadt on the team and commentary by John Motson.

This is the most comprehensive story of the show ever written and brings to life the BBC's footballing flagship along with all the characters and stories that it has featured during the past four decades.

ISBN: 0 563 52181 3